Unearthing Geomorphological Clues: A Comprehensive Exploration of Earth's Surface Features and the Hidden Narratives

TABLE OF CONTENTS

FIGURES AND TABLES

FIGURES

Chapter 1

Chapter 2

Chapter 3

TABLES

Chapter 2

Chapter 4

Chapter 5

Chapter 6

Chapter 7

ABSTRACT

A combination of archaeological and geomorphic techniques was used to study erosion hazard at Aboriginal shell midden sites in the Northern Rivers region of New South Wales, Australia. In the absence of artifactual material, biological and taphonomic analyses were undertaken to determine the likelihood a deposit was anthropogenic in origin. These analyses were also used to gain an understanding of site formation processes.

The relationship between, and relative influence of, anthropogenic and non-anthropogenic erosive factors at shell midden sites in different geomorphic settings was used to formulate three erosion hazard assessment methods. Each method was designed to address the needs of a different stakeholder group. The archaeological method includes analysis of the effects of bank erosion, cultivation, anthropogenic and biological excavation, wind and wave erosion. Erosive factors are compared between sites and geomorphic settings. The rapid assessment technique designed for use by Aboriginal Land Councils and local Indigenous communities includes an Erosion Hazard Pro Forma and uses relatively simple geomorphic analyses which can be performed in the field. A handbook containing straightforward, user-friendly instructions on how to complete the Erosion Hazard Pro Forma is also included, along with a scoring system used to quantify erosion hazard and rank the study sites. A GIS model generated using soil, land use, vegetation and elevation data is also used to quantify erosion hazard and rank the study sites.

Agreement between results obtained using the three assessment methods, based on the relative influence of erosive factors, confirms their usefulness as cultural heritage management tools. Study sites at Sleeper Island, Minnie Water, Woombah Site A, Woombah Site B, Plover Island and Wooli are ranked, in that order, from greatest to least erosion hazard. Major factors contributing to erosion at Sleeper Island include boat traffic, steep banks, low site elevation and vegetation coverage and a history of farming. At Minnie Water unconsolidated dunes in close proximity to ocean swell, low vegetation coverage and high exposure to prevailing winds all influence erosion. Human activity (historic cultivation and excavation) is the major factor causing erosion at the Woombah study sites. These processes have not only disturbed large portions of the midden complex, they have also had a negative influence on vegetation coverage and bank slope. Exposure to prevailing winds, coupled with its situation within a walking track, are the major causes of erosion and disturbance of the surface stone artifact scatter and *in situ* stone artifact deposit on Plover Island. Minimal disturbance at the Wooli Aboriginal shell midden deposit is due to its burial in a low energy environment, gentle bank slope, high vegetation coverage and minimal anthropogenic impact. Research findings indicate vegetation coverage and bank slope are the primary factors influencing erosion at estuarine sites. Elevation (above water level), exposure to prevailing winds and vegetation coverage were found to be the primary factors influencing erosion at coastal sites.

Two sets of conservation recommendations were formulated. The first set comprises general guidelines for management of sites based on their geomorphic setting. Secondly, specific guidelines for management and conservation of the study sites were formulated in accordance with the wishes of the Yaegl Local Aboriginal Land Council. Implementation of these recommendations will ensure effective cultural heritage management at these sites. Further application of the methodologies developed in this study would greatly increase the effectiveness of cultural heritage management at Aboriginal shell middens as well as other types of coastal archaeological sites.

1. INTRODUCTION

1.1 INTRODUCTION

The Clarence River estuary and surrounding coastline, northern New South Wales, Australia (Figures 1.1 and 1.2), is host to a number of Aboriginal shell midden deposits. These deposits are found in a variety of geomorphic environments including estuarine sites (riverbank/creekbank) and coastal sites (beach foredune, headland). The availability of study sites in a variety of geomorphic environments, coupled with the enthusiasm of the Yaegl Local Aboriginal Land Council (LALC) to participate in the study meant the study area was an ideal location to undertake research into geomorphic processes affecting the accumulation, degradation and preservation of Aboriginal shell midden sites.

The ancestral Yaegl community inhabited the land surrounding the mouth of the Clarence River and spoke the language Yaygirr (Muurbay Aboriginal Language and Culture Cooperative). At the time of European contact the Yaegl people had a well developed material culture, including sophisticated wooden canoes and permanent settlements comprising large bark huts (McSwan, 1978). By as early as 1929, however, only a couple of Yaygirr speakers remained, and the language was no longer spoken right through (Muurbay Aboriginal Language and Culture Cooperative). Given the rich ancestral history of the area and its Indigenous inhabitants, the current Yaegl Local Aboriginal Land Council are highly active in, and determined to, preserve all possible aspects of their cultural history. This research project makes a significant contribution to this aim.

Providing the Yaegl LALC with effective site-specific conservation management recommendations, as well as more general, environment-specific management guidelines for broader application, requires a comprehensive understanding of the processes causing accumulation, degradation and preservation of midden sites, referred to as site formation processes. Adopting a multidisciplinary approach involving the synthesis of analysis techniques used in the disciplines of Environmental Science and Archaeology was essential in the development of the 3 erosion hazard assessment techniques presented in this Book.

Study sites were proposed and approved by the Yaegl Local Aboriginal Land Council based on local knowledge and information contained in the state of New South Wales' Aboriginal Sites Register. Appropriate Government permits were obtained on the basis that there would be minimal disturbance of the sites through sampling. One of the strengths of the erosion hazard assessment methods developed in this study is that they are able to be performed with minimal sampling, and thus minimal disturbance, to Aboriginal shell midden sites.

Figure 1.1: Location of the study sites.

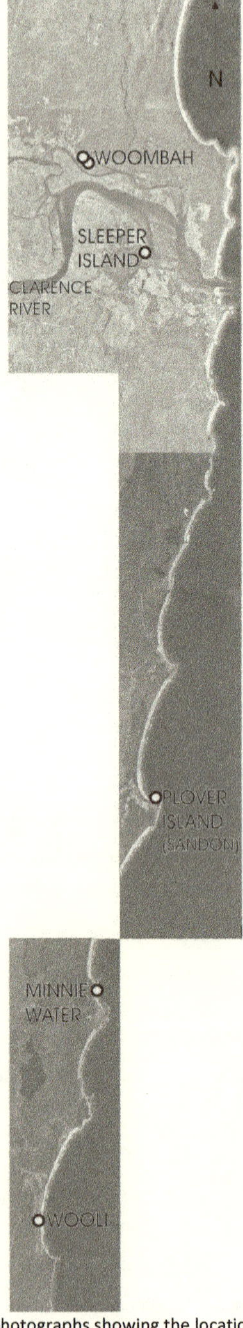

Figure 1.2: Aerial photographs showing the location of the study sites.

1.2 AIMS

The key aims of this project were:

- **To prepare accurate site descriptions for inclusion in the AHIMS (Aboriginal Heritage Information Management System) database.**
- **To document and interpret the taphonomy of shell and artifactual material present in the Aboriginal shell midden deposits.** Understanding environmental processes to which shells and artifacts may have been subjected can assist determination of the origin of a deposit and how it has formed.
- **To document and interpret the species composition of the deposits.** The study of species composition provides information regarding the environments in which the species lived, and also whether anthropogenic selection or size-sorting as a result of environmental processes has occurred.
- **To compare site formation processes between the study sites.** Identification of similar environmental impacts in similar geomorphic contexts is used to formulate environment-specific midden management and conservation guidelines. Identification of different environmental impacts in similar geomorphic contexts is used to formulate site-specific midden management and conservation guidelines.
- **To develop 3 erosion hazard assessment techniques which can be used by different stakeholder groups** – Environmental Scientists, Archaeologists and Aboriginal community groups/Local Aboriginal Land Councils. Development of a standardised, comprehensive management strategy facilitates greater ownership of cultural resources by local Aboriginal communities as well as more effective communication between stakeholder groups.

- **To develop site-specific and broader environment-specific management and conservation recommendations for Aboriginal shell midden sites.** The development of site-specific recommendations specifically satisfies the requirements of the Yaegl LALC. Environment-specific recommendations can be used by the Yaegl LALC as well as other Australian Indigenous Land Councils and also international indigenous communities.

1.3 OUTLINE

Chapter 2 reviews the geology and stratigraphy of the Clarence-Moreton Basin within a Quaternary geomorphic context and includes a preliminary discussion of coastal and estuary dynamics in the study area. The concept of the discipline of Geoarchaeology is also introduced, along with an explanation of how geoarchaeological techniques have been used by other researchers to study site formation processes. Previous archaeological studies undertaken in the study area are reviewed and the process of identification of research sites for the current study is outlined.

Chapter 3 introduces the study sites and provides information on their location, geomorphic context and a brief description of the archaeological material present. Research methodologies are presented in Chapter 4 prior to the presentation and discussion of results. This chapter includes a discussion of analysis and data collection techniques and presents information on techniques used to assess site formation processes and major geomorphic impacts at the study sites.

Chapters 5, 6 and 7 present a comprehensive analysis of site formation processes and major impacts causing site degradation through interpretation of sites' stratigraphy (Chapter 5), biological and taphonomic analyses of archaeological material (Chapter 6) and analysis of erosiove processes (Chapter 7). In Chapter 5 stratigraphic information is linked between sites in similar geomorphic environments and with previous local studies. This facilitates a sound understanding of the environmental context of the Aboriginal shell midden deposits. The results of biological and taphonomic analyses are presented and discussed in Chapter 6. Analyses include species composition, size range of shells and post-mortem modification of the condition of shells and artifacts. This information is used to determine the likely origin of the deposits and the likely agents of reworking if it has taken place. Analysis of erosive processes is presented in Chapter 7. This encompasses analyses of the past, present and potential impact of anthropogenic channel modifications to the Clarence River estuary, sea level change, flooding, tidal inundation and erosion. This information is then used to formulate 3 erosion hazard assessment techniques. The methodology of each technique is presented in Chapter 4. Outcomes and validity of the techniques are presented and discussed in Chapter 7.

Site-specific and environment-specific management and conservation guidelines, based on the outcomes of the erosion hazard assessment techniques, are presented in Chapter 8. Conclusions, broader applications of the methodologies developed in this study and areas for further research are presented in Chapter 9.

2. BACKGROUND AND CONCEPTUAL FRAMEWORK

An essential prerequisite of the study of archaeological site formation processes involves a review of local and regional geology and stratigraphy within a Quaternary geomorphic context. A review of the geology of the Clarence-Moreton Basin provides the necessary framework for a preliminary discussion of coastal and estuary dynamics in the study area, presented in section 2.1.5. The concept of the discipline of Geoarchaeology is introduced in section 2.2, along with an explanation of how geoarchaeological techniques have been used by other researchers to study site formation processes. A process-based approach to the study of Aboriginal shell midden accumulation, degradation and preservation is the key principle of this research project. Section 2.2.8 reviews previous archaeological studies undertaken in the study area and outlines the process of identification of research sites for the current study.

2.1 GEOLOGY AND STRATIGRAPHY

2.1.1 **Introduction**

The Clarence River estuary overlies the Clarence-Moreton Basin (Figure 2.1), a narrow extension of the Great Artesian Basin (Haworth and Ollier, 1992), with an area of ~40000 square kilometres (Day *et al.,* 1974). The Clarence-Moreton Basin is only open to the coast between Broom's Head and Schnapper Point and the bedrock here is present at shallow depths (Haworth and Ollier, 1992; Roberts and Boyd, 2004). The Clarence-Moreton Basin began to develop in the Late Triassic (Day *et al.,* 1974) and the basin sequence is entirely Mesozoic (McElroy, 1969). The basin forms part of the Tasman Geosyncline and unconformably overlies Palaeozoic rocks of the New England Fold Belt and Yarraman, D'Aguilar and Beenleigh Blocks, as well as rocks of the older Triassic Esk Trough and Ipswich and Tarong Basin sediments (Day *et al.,* 1974). The intermontane Clarence-Moreton Basin is part of a craton which stabilised in Late Triassic – Early Jurassic time, with the initiation of extensive quartzose sandstone sedimentation (Day *et al.,* 1974).

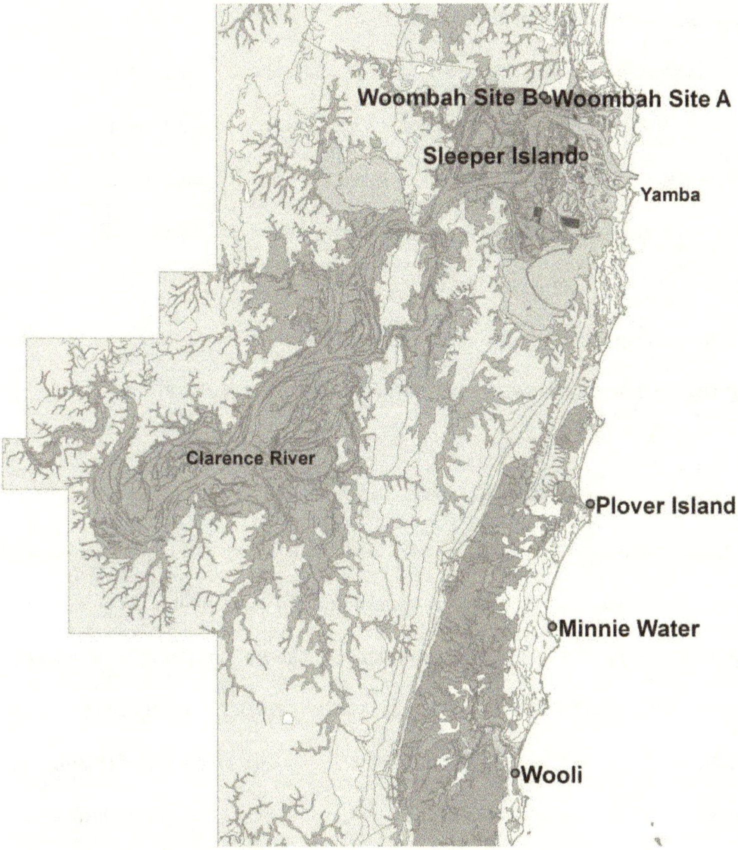

Figure 2.1: Regional geology of the study area.

KEY:

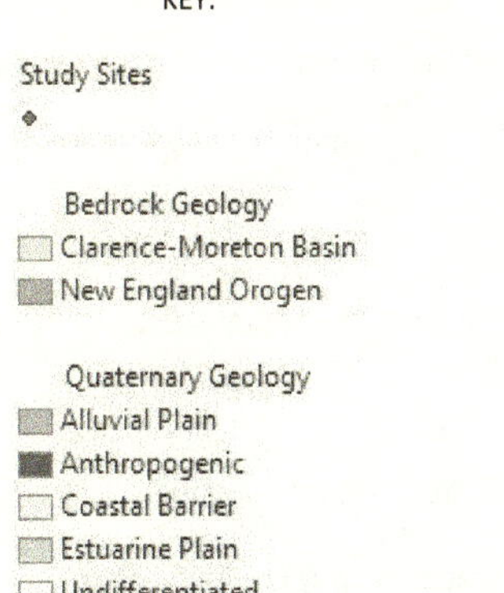

2.1.2 **Sedimentation and Major Stratigraphic Units**

The present erosional margin of sediments of the Bundamba Group (McElroy, 1962) defines the margins of the Clarence-Moreton Basin (Day *et al.,* 1974). Day *et al.* (1974) and Cranfield and Schwarzbock (1972) refer to this unit as the Woogaroo sub-Group. Rocks of the Bundamba Group form a near continuous outcrop containing arenaceous sediments with characteristic cross-bedded units (McElroy, 1962). Friable sandstone with considerable iron-staining is present in the northeast quarter of the outcrop (McElroy, 1962). The deposition of extensive quartzose sandstones (McElroy, 1969) forming this outcrop occurred in the Triassic – Jurassic (Day *et al.,* 1974).

The Marburg Formation is a less quartzose unit which conformably overlies the Bundamba Group (McElroy, 1969). Formation of this unit occurred no later than the Upper Triassic, as indicated by the presence of a labyrinthodont jaw (*Austropelor wadleyi*) (Whitehouse, 1952). The Marburg Formation is more labile (Day *et al.,* 1974) and contains a higher proportion of shale and silty sandstones than the underlying Bundamba Group (McElroy, 1962). It is predominantly composed of cross-bedded medium to coarse quartz sandstones with a variable proportion of clay matrix and rock fragments interbedded with grey shales and claystones (McElroy, 1962). Igneous intrusions are absent (McElroy, 1969).

McElroy (1962) divided the southern part of the Marburg Formation into two distinct formations; a basal conglomerate he referred to as the Layton's Range Conglomerate and an overlying siltstone-sandstone formation named the Mill Creek Sandstone. These units do not appear on Day *et al.*'s (1974) Upper Triassic – Lower Cretaceous stratigraphic sections.

Conformably overlying the Marburg Formation are the Walloon Coal Measures. McElroy (1962) describes this unit as predominantly consisting of grey claystones which are commonly carbonaceous, or contain thin coal seams and fine to medium grained soft grey lithic sandstones.

The sandstones are usually calcareous and concretionary ironstones are common. McElroy (1962) also notes the characteristics of the Walloon Coal Measures differ in the Nymboida-Kangaroo Creek area. Here quartz-lithic sandstone containing very little shale or claystone predominates in the sequence.

Planar cross-bedding is well developed in the quartzose Kangaroo Creek Sandstone which is largely made up of medium to coarse white and cream sandstone; iron stained matrix is common and this affords the sandstone some friability (McElroy, 1962; 1969). The Kangaroo Creek Sandstone has also been secondarily cemented by iron oxides, and there is evidence of the burrowing activity of the Banded Bee (*Anthrophora* sp.) (McElroy, 1962). In parts this unit lies unconformably on the Walloon Coal Measures, however it grades conformably upwards into the Grafton Formation (McElroy, 1962).

Lithic sandstones with an even, well-sorted texture dominate the Grafton Formation which contains a sequence of poorly outcropping soft sandstones, siltstones and claystones, at times interbedded with carbonaceous or coaly bands (McElroy, 1969). The Grafton Formation extends along the Clarence-Moreton Basin south of Grafton to north of Casino (McElroy, 1962). It is not overlain by other consolidated sediments and the outcrop is masked by extensive areas of Quaternary alluvium associated with the Clarence and Richmond Rivers (McElroy, 1962). Tertiary volcanic rock is present in the north of the basin and runs northwest through Lismore and Toowoomba (Haworth and Ollier, 1992).

2.1.3 **Uplift of Australia's Eastern Highlands**

Uplift of the Eastern Highlands, which border the Clarence-Moreton Basin to the west, has likely played a significant role in the development of the current drainage pattern of the Clarence River (Haworth and Ollier, 1992). In order to interpret the modern drainage pattern of the Clarence

River it is necessary to understand the origins of the river systems in this area and the effect tectonic uplift has had on these systems.

It is generally agreed that formation of the Eastern Highlands was initiated around 90 Ma ago (Ollier, 1978; Jones and Veevers, 1983; Wellman, 1987). The removal of the lower lithosphere underneath the highlands caused tectonic uplift due to crustal underplating and crustal heating (Wellman, 1987). This process took place at the time of rifting which formed the Tasman and Coral seas (Jones and Veevers, 1983). Early Cretaceous sediments are present on the summit and slopes of the highlands in Queensland and northern New South Wales, showing most uplift occurred in the region after this time (Wellman, 1987).

2.1.4 **Drainage Pattern of the Clarence River**

Dendritic drainage patterns are characteristic of terrain which has a uniform lithology and where faulting and jointing are insignificant (Whittow, 1984). Some characteristics of simple river systems are as follows:

- tributaries have a steeper gradient than the main stream but their junctions are at the same elevation (Playfair's Law).
- tributaries join the main stream at an acute angle pointing downstream.
- simple valleys increase in width and become flatter in the downstream direction.

The Clarence River has an anomalous drainage pattern (Haworth and Ollier, 1992). Its catchment is asymmetrical in shape and its trunk stream runs along a valley ~200 km long. The major feeders to the Clarence River originate on the New England Block and flow east across the Great Escarpment (Haworth and Ollier, 1992). The Continental Divide separates the Condamine River to the west, with a simple dendritic drainage pattern, from the Clarence River to the east, with a highly complex drainage pattern (Ollier, 1978). Ollier (1978) suggests the complex drainage pattern east of the Continental Divide was a result of folding and faulting during the Late Tertiary, as the eastern Australian coastline shifted west.

2.1.5 **Quaternary Sediments and Geomorphology**

McElroy (1962) briefly describes Quaternary sediments of the Clarence-Moreton Basin in his published work on basin stratigraphy. This description includes the presence of extensive Quaternary alluvium, consisting predominantly of silt and sand, associated with the lower course of the Clarence River. Thicknesses of Quaternary sediments were measured at Grafton no. 1 bore (104 ft) and Bungawalbyn Creek near the Richmond River junction (88 ft). He also observed the presence of carbonaceous sandrock in sea cliffs in the Redcliffe – Wooli areas, associated with leached and redeposited humic material.

Since this work, further geomorphic studies involving shoreline morphodynamics (Roy *et al.*, 1994; Carter and Woodroffe, 1994), offshore sediments and stratigraphy and Late Holocene shoreline alignment (Roberts and Boyd, 2004; Goodwin *et al.*, 2006) have been published. Various studies of estuarine dynamics (including Carter and Woodroffe, 1994; Eyre, 1998 and Roy *et al.*, 2001), local floodplain environments (Brierley *et al.*, 1995 and references therein) and general local geomorphology and soil landscapes (Morand, 2001) have increased our understanding of Quaternary sediments and geomorphology of the Clarence River, estuary and coast.

2.1.5.1 *Coastal sediments and geomorphology*

Southeast Australia is a wave- and oceanic current-dominated coast (Roy *et al.*, 1994; Roberts and Boyd, 2004). Sand is moved and deposited largely by waves and wave-induced currents, although ebb tide deltas do form at the mouths of larger rivers such as the Clarence (Roy *et al.*, 1994). In contrast to Swift and Thorne's (1991) accommodation-dominated settings, where basins supplied with sediment are large compared with sediment input, Roberts and Boyd (2004) class the NSW coast as low-accommodation. Geological inheritance plays an important role in the geomorphology of modern coasts (Roy *et al.*, 1994). It is therefore necessary to focus some attention on nearshore deposits in order to understand the origin of beach sediments and the history of the Clarence coast.

Underlying the inner- and mid-shelf sediments in the Yamba-Tweed Heads region are laterally continuous terraces of the offshore Yamba trough, an extension of the Clarence-Moreton Basin (Shaw *et al.*, 2001). The shelf physiography in this region is narrow and steep (Roberts and Boyd, 2004). Bedrock-compartmentalised beaches extend to submerged reefs at depths of <25-30 m and a lobate (10 × 20 km) subaqueous delta front extends seaward of the Clarence River (Roberts and Boyd, 2004). An extensive lobe of shoreface sand occurs north from Iluka Bluff and another northeast from the Shelly Beach Head – One Man Bluff area (Goodwin *et al.*, 2006).

Roberts and Boyd (2004) have identified the timing of the Pleistocene-Holocene post-glacial marine transgression in the offshore Clarence region at 12 780 +/- 150 BP. Estuarine deposits were formed during this time, but the relative thinness of offshore estuarine channel fill led Roberts and Boyd (2004) to suggest that valleys were not deeply incised seaward of the modern shoreline, and that much of the earlier estuarine deposits outside the channels has been removed by wave/current action.

Well sorted, fine- to medium-grained, angular to subangular quartz-rich shoreface sands with low carbonate and mud content fine seaward (Goodwin *et al.*, 2006). Inner shelf muddy sands and sandy muds are poorly sorted, fine- to medium-grained quartz-rich sediments with up to 30% mud content (Walsh and Roy, 1983). The source of these sediments is the Clarence River (Roberts and Boyd, 2004). Roberts and Boyd (2004) state these fine sediments are able to accumulate on the seafloor due to the weakened influence of the East Australia Current between Ballina and Yamba.

Goodwin *et al.* (2006), however, note some southward transport of outer-shelf sediments by the East Australia Current.

Shoreline alignment on the NSW north coast during the Late Holocene sea level stillstand has been dynamic. Episodes of shoreline recession and realignment have punctuated barrier progradation during this time (Goodwin *et al.*, 2006). The Iluka-Woody Bay sand barrier forms part of one of the most extensive Holocene strandplains on the NSW far north coast (Roy, 1982). Its morphology has been influenced by longshore gradients in sand transport and fluctuations in mean wave direction on centennial to millennial time scales (Goodwin *et al.*, 2006). The history of Late Holocene shoreline alignment can be seen in Figures 2.2 and 2.3. Migrating sediment not only changed the shape of the beaches between Woody Head and the main Clarence River entrance, it also changed the dynamics of the Clarence River, with the North Arm no longer reaching the ocean after ~1500 years BP.

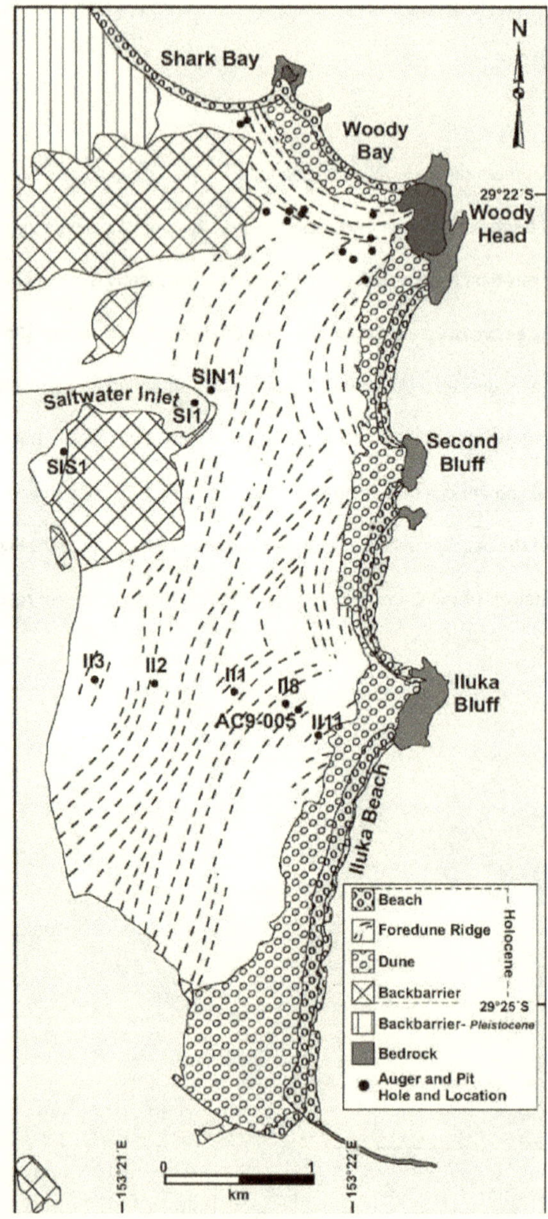

Figure 2.2: Pleistocene and Holocene geomorphology of the Iluka to Woody Bay sand barrier. Dashed lines indicate relic foredune ridges comprising the Holocene strandplain. Source: Goodwin *et al.,* 2006, p. 130.

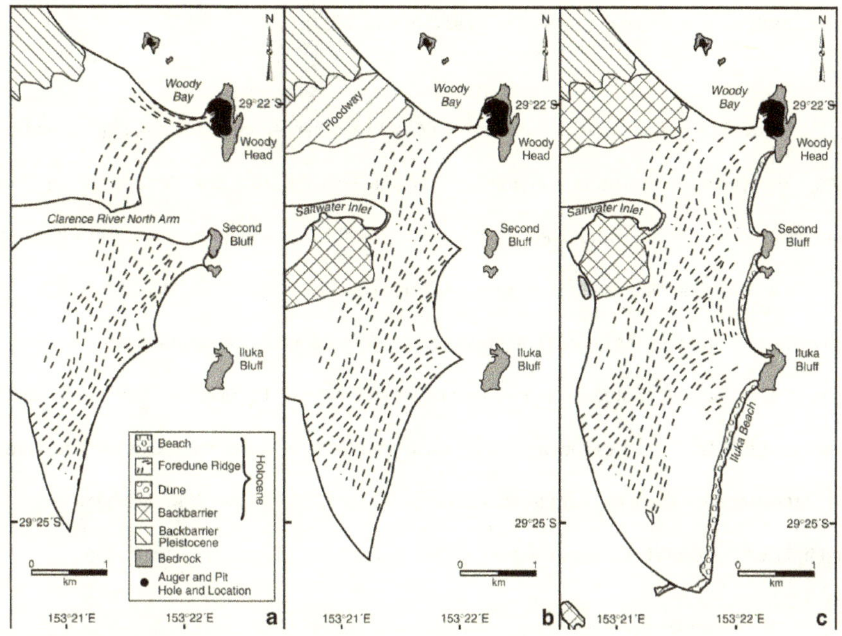

Figure 2.3: Configuration of the coastline and Clarence River entrances at (a) 1600 yr BP, (b) 1500 yr BP, and (c) 1000 BP. Dashed lines indicate relic foredune ridge crests, showing the successive position and shape of the shoreline. Source: Goodwin *et al.,* 2006, p. 136.

Large deposits of Quaternary sand occur along the coast in what Morand (2001) has termed the Bundjalung and Angourie Dunefields. Pleistocene dune systems are situated inland of Holocene beaches, foredunes and hind dunes; Quaternary deposits are composed of marine and aeolian quartz sands (Morand, 2001). The Bundjalung Dunefield occurs parallel to the coast. Dunes, sandsheets and beach ridges are common and swamps are present in poorly drained areas such as swales and deflation depressions. The rocky headlands of Snapper Point, Woody Head and Iluka Head are outliers of the Clarence-Moreton Basin (Morand, 2001). Deep Podozols (humus podzols) are common on Pleistocene dunes. Holocene beach sands contain rapidly drained Shelly or Arenic Rudozols (calcareous and siliceous sands) and associated dunes contain rapidly drained Arenic

Rudosols. Sandsheets within swamps commonly contain Organosols and Hydrosols, and Anthroposols occur within old sand mining areas (Morand, 2001).

Following is a description of the Clarence Coast beach/barrier landscape given by Morand (2001). The type location for this environment is Ten Mile Beach at Shark Bay. Beaches (swash zone) have a relief of <5 m with slopes at 1-3%. Barrier beaches, including Ten Mile, Evans Head and Iluka, are usually >5 km long and >50 m wide. Mainland beaches, including Red Hill, Yamba and Convent, are <1 km long, their configuration and extent determined by the surrounding headlands. Dunes form moderately to steeply inclined sand ridges with a relief of 5-15 m and slopes at 20-50%. An incipient foredune, at times with a small wave-cut scarp at its seaward edge, generally lies at the foot of these dunes. These incipient foredunes are generally 30-50 m wide, showing a hummocky, wind-induced microrelief. Dunes are aligned parallel to the coast and blowouts are common.

2.1.5.2 *Estuarine sediments and geomorphology*

Estuary morphodynamics are a function of inherited topography, including geological factors which control the size and shape of the estuary basin and nature of the sediment, and sea level changes (Carter and Woodroffe, 1994; Roy and Boyd, 1996; Roy *et al.,* 2001; Figure 2.3). During glacial periods estuaries became displaced onto the continental shelf and coastal sediments were eroded as rivers cut through previously submerged terrain (Roy and Boyd, 1996). During interglacial periods coastal valleys became drowned, subsequently forming estuaries which started to fill with marine, fluvial and terrestrial sediment (Roy *et al.,* 2001). Repeat glacial-interglacial cycles have left a complex sedimentary record in NSW estuaries (Roy and Boyd, 1996). The most recent phase of estuary sedimentation on the NSW coast began ~7-8 ka ago, during the Pleistocene-Holocene Post-glacial Marine Transgression (Roy *et al.,* 2001). The size and shape of existing valleys are the result of prior erosion and emplacement of coastal sand barriers, and this inherited pre-Holocene topography determines the accommodation space available for Holocene sedimentation (Roy *et al.*, 2001).

Along the northern NSW coast storm and swell waves and oceanic and meteorological currents affect the hydrodynamic regime of estuaries (Roy *et al.*, 2001). Waves are the dominant force controlling sediment movement so sand barriers at the mouths of bedrock valleys are common. Locally, variability in the size and orientation of embayments and headlands plays an important role in estuary mouth hydrodynamics (Roy *et al.*, 2001).

River dominance and evolution are linked by the concept of estuary maturity (Roy and Boyd, 1996). The level of maturity of an estuary affects sedimentation, water quality and biological productivity. Allowed sufficient time, an estuary will infill with sediment and become mature. Fluvial sedimentation and the expansion of alluvial plains over former estuary lagoon/lake basins causes sediment infilling leading to increased river dominance where fresh water is discharged directly to the sea through a mature alluvial plain (Roy and Boyd, 1996). As estuaries approach maturity salinity gradients become more pronounced, particularly in semi-mature barrier estuaries where their side arms (eg. cut-off embayments) exhibit more marine conditions than the main channel; saline bottom waters can become trapped and deoxygenated (Roy *et al.*, 2001). Discharges of acid groundwater from acid sulphate soils predominantly affect riverine channels. Biological productivity is at its peak during intermediate and semi-mature stages of estuary evolution, as the expansion of fluvial deltas allows for an increase in the diversity of biological habitats (Roy *et al.*, 2001).

The Clarence River estuary is a mesotidal mature barrier estuary which enters the high energy wave regime of the south west Pacific Ocean (Carter and Woodroffe, 1994; Roy *et al.*, 2001). It is composed of 2 fluvioestuarine basins separated by a bedrock barrier; the inner basin is protected by this barrier and lacks high energy Holocene coastal features, being divided into extensive low energy backwater swamps, the outer basin has a similar morphology to other south eastern Australian barrier-basins (Carter and Woodroffe, 1994). A coastal barrier of marine sands impounds the outer basin. These sands were driven shoreward during the Pleistocene-Holocene Post-glacial Marine Transgression (Carter and Woodroffe, 1994). Progradation of the Clarence River delta front has formed the cut-off embayments of Lake Wooloweyah, the Broadwater and Everlasting Swamp, which are at progressive stages of infilling (Roy *et al.,* 2001). The islands of the outer basin originated as estuarine sand shoals (Roy, 1984).

Barrier estuaries such as the Clarence, are wave-dominated (Carter and Woodroffe, 1994; Roy and Boyd, 1996; Roy *et al.,* 2001). Highly variable river flows (Eyre, 1998) coupled with their situation on a wave-dominated coastline (Roy and Boyd, 1996) means many south east Australian estuaries fall into this category. Wave-dominated estuaries occur behind sand barriers on exposed sections of the coast and thus their tidal inlets are constricted by wave-deposited beach sand (Roy *et al.,* 2001). Estuary mouth sands are typically composed of fine-grained shelly and coarse low-shell sand facies and only rarely exceed thicknesses of 15-20 m (Roy and Boyd, 1996). Dominant sediment transport mechanisms include local wind waves and wind-induced water movements however river discharge also has a strong influence leading to well developed flood tide deltas (Roy *et al.,* 2001). Ebb tide deltas can also form at the mouths of larger rivers such as the Clarence (Roy *et al.,* 1994). Delta growth during sea level stillstand conditions occurs at the inner edge of active entrance channels but this is a relatively minor contribution, as deposits are mostly, and more rapidly, emplaced towards the end of transgressive sea level conditions (Roy and Boyd, 1996).

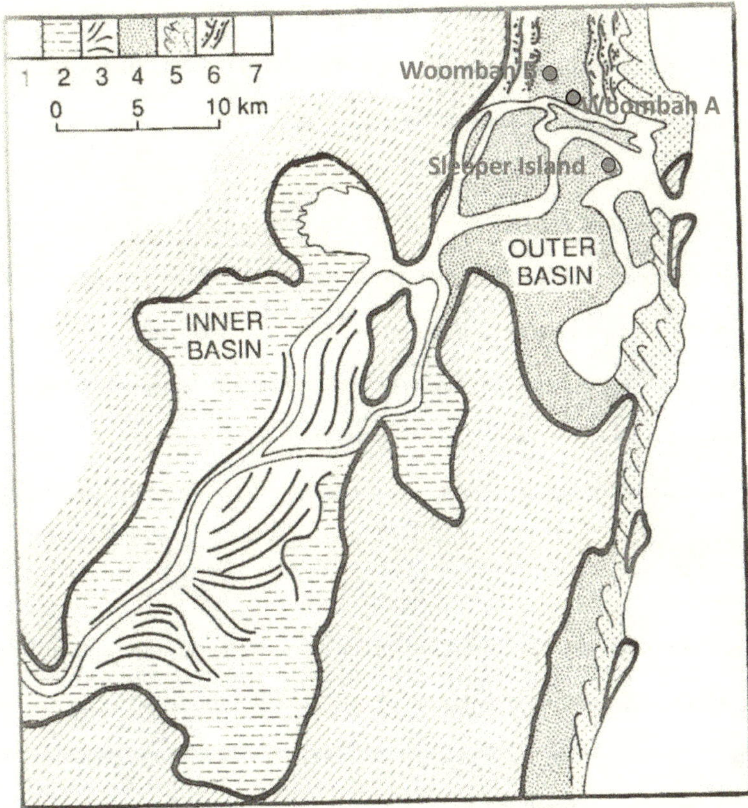

Figure 2.4: Composite estuarine system of the Clarence River showing the location of study sites located within the estuary. Key: 1. Pre-Holocene land surface. 2. Holocene inner basin sediments. 3. Fluvial levee and chute-channel sands. 4. Holocene outer basin estuarine and marine sands. 5. Coastal dune barrier complex. 6. Relict Pleistocene barrier. 7. Estuarine channels and lakes. Source: Carter and Woodroffe, 1994.

Roy (1984; 1994), Roy and Boyd (1996) and Roy *et al.* (2001) recognise four geomorphic zones in south east Australian estuaries. The marine tide delta zone is located in the estuary mouth and is influenced by tidal currents and wave action. Sediments include moderate to well sorted quartzose sand derived from the open coast and minor amounts of mud. High energy environments are restricted to the seaward-most part of the entrance channel, whereas low energy environments are best developed on the delta surfaces and along the inner sides of the barriers. The Clarence River estuary barrier is composed of a soil landscape referred to by Morand (2001) as the Bundjalung Dunefield (see Coastal Sediments and Geomorphology for a description).

Central mud basins, the second zone, consist of dark grey-black mud rich in estuarine shells, foraminifera and organic material (Roy, 1981). The source of this fine silt- and clay-sized sediment is the adjacent river, and it is supplied mainly during floods. Molluscs, polychaete worms and crustaceans are responsible for extensive bioturbation to depths of 15-20 cm, and this has implications for the preservation potential of artefacts (discussed in the following review of taphonomic processes affecting shell material). Central mud basins are found in low energy deeper parts of the estuary as well as in narrow slopes that border their sides.

As an estuary matures its central mud basin reduces in size due to progradation of the fluvial delta. Morand's (2001) soil study showed Clarence delta sediments are present not only on the estuary islands but also on the surrounding mainland. The presence of estuary sediments at the periphery of the Clarence River estuary indicates a relict estuarine landscape. By mapping the distribution of estuarine sediments Morand (2001) has shown that the Clarence River estuary once had a broader range and is thus maturing.

Rivers and streams enter estuaries at the fluvial delta (third zone) and this is a complex landscape containing subenvironments such as river and distributary channels, mid-channel shoals and distributary mouth bars, interdistributary bays, levee banks and crevasse splays. Floodplain sediments are important components of the fluvial and deltaic depositional system – crevasse splays themselves can be reworked (O'Brien and Wells, 1986) and this must be considered when examining the context of Aboriginal shell midden deposits.

The fluvial delta of the Clarence River has an elongated bird's-foot morphology (Carter and Woodroffe, 1994), where progradation of the delta causes outgrowth of natural river levees, forming a finger-like pattern (Whittow, 1984). Due to smaller tidal ranges, the fluvial delta zone in barrier estuaries is less extensive than in drowned valley estuaries. Wind-stress induced water circulation is dominant. Sediment types are variable due to the presence of a number of subenvironments and include clean fluvial sand and gravel in channel beds and on river mouth shoals, medium to coarse moderately sorted sand in small crevasse splays (O'Brien and Wells, 1986), poorly sorted mixtures of sand, mud and organics in levee deposits and mud and organic-rich sediments in marginal embayments and brackish swamps. As an estuary matures its delta front progrades, encroaching on the central mud basin (Roy, 1994). This is evident in the bird's-foot morphology of the Clarence River delta and in the cut-off embayments of Lake Wooloweyah, The Broadwater and Everlasting Swamp.

The riverine channel zone grades downstream into the fluvial delta environment. Roy *et al.* (2001) define the upstream limit of the riverine channel zone as "the maximum landward extent of brackish conditions during droughts" (p. 361). River discharge controls fresh and brackish water conditions in this zone. Sandy point bars occurring at meander bends usually correspond with undercutting and bank collapse of the opposite bank. Incision of riverine channels into relict estuarine muds is common and these channels are now lined with sand. Main sediment types comprise fluvial sand and muddy sand (Rochford, 1951) and are remobilised periodically by flood flows. As an estuary matures its riverine zone migrates seaward, along with the surrounding alluvial plain (Roy and Boyd, 1996).

Morand (2001) identifies two soil landscapes – estuarine/deltaic and estuarine/deltaic-lacustrine – in the Clarence River estuary (Figure 2.6). These soil landscapes both belong to the Clarence Delta physiographic region. The type location for the estuarine/deltaic soil landscape is

Romiaka Island. This landscape includes tidal flats and saltmarshes within the Clarence Delta. Topsoils often contain very high organic matter and these cover unknown depths of Holocene marine sands, clays and muds. Soils are permanently saturated as the region is dominated by tidal activity and saline water. The estuarine/deltaic soil landscape has an extremely low relief of <1 m and simple slopes range from 0-1%. The intertidal (daily tidal inundation, muds and sand flats), supratidal (infrequent inundation, saline watertable at shallow depths) and extratidal zones (inundated in exceptional storm/cyclonic tides) (Isbell, 1996) form extremely low, level tidal flats. Within the intertidal zone soils are deep (>100 cm), saturated Intertidal Hydrosols (Solonchaks); marine sand is also present in this zone. Within the extratidal and supratidal zones soils are deeper (>200 cm) and are composed of poorly drained Sulfidic/Sulfuric Extratidal and Supratidal Hydrosols (Humic Gleys).

The type location of the estuarine/deltaic-lacustrine soil landscape is the western side of The (Clarence) Broadwater. It contains marine and alluvial landscapes of unknown depth with tidal flats, swamps and plain being common landscapes. Elevation is 0-2 m with slopes at 0-1% and local relief is absent. The Broadwater is a large overflow basin formed by progradation of the Clarence River delta (Roy *et al.,* 2001) and water levels are influenced by tides and overland flow. Soils are deep (>200 cm) and are composed of very poorly drained Intertidal and Extratidal Hydrosols (Solonchacks; Humic Gleys). Very poorly drained Redoxic Hydrosols (Gleyed Podzolic soils) are found within limited areas of cattle grazing.

2.1.5.3 *Alluvial sediments and geomorphology*

The Clarence River lowland alluvial plains are present over two fluvioestuarine basins described earlier. The complex, fluvially dominated floodplain of the inner basin (Carter and Woodroffe, 1994) will be the focus of the next section. A brief description of the Alluvial-

Estuarine/Deltaic soil landscape (Morand, 2001) is also included, although the type location for this landscape is located in the outer basin.

Following the Pleistocene-Holocene Postglacial marine transgression vertical and regressive estuarine sediment was capped by alluvium (Roy, 1984). The prograding fluvioestuarine plains behind the coastal sand barrier share facies with the deltaic system. Due to the tectonic stability of the region, the Clarence River fluvioestuarine system is starved of fluvial sediment, thus much of its Holocene sediment originates offshore (Roy, 1984).

The main Clarence channel and its backwater swamps are separated by active channel features with complex chute-channels, crevasse splays and palaeochannels (Roy, 1984). Overbank flood flows contribute significantly to floodplain accretion. Pre-Holocene alluvial facies lie at 8-14 m depth and infilled palaeochannels contain fine textured mildly organic sediments; brackish estuarine facies underlying ~5 m of fluvial beds are present on the Pre-Holocene margins of the active fluvial channel zone. Backwater basins have a thin alluvial cover over organic muds (Roy, 1984).

The Alluvial-Estuarine/Deltaic soil landscape of Morand (2001) is the dominant soil landscape of the Clarence Delta physiographic region. Estuarine/Deltaic and Estuarine/Deltaic-lacustrine soil landscapes are also present in the Clarence Delta region and these have been discussed in the previous section. The type location for the Alluvial-Estuarine/Deltaic soil landscape is Palmers Island, situated in the outer basin of the Clarence River Estuary; other locations include Harwood and Chatsworth Islands and parts of Maclean.

The deltaic plain is extensive (10-15 km wide) and is level to very gently inclined. Holocene marine sediments of undetermined depth underlie 1-2 m of alluvium derived from inland sediments. Relief is 0-3 m, elevation ranges from 1-3 m and slopes are generally 0-3%. Numerous channels create a network of islands within the estuary and abandoned channels and floodways are common. The migrating Micalo Channel/Oyster Channel drainage system has caused erosion on Palmers Island, bringing marine sediments closer to the surface. A terrace scarp commonly separates the main plain from the floodplain.

Soils of the Alluvial-Estuarine/Deltaic (Morand, 2001) landscape are poorly drained with low wet bearing strength at field capacity. They are commonly saline or acidic and subsoils have a high acid sulfate potential. Deep (>200 cm) Melacic Sulfidic/Sulfuric Redoxic Hydrosols consisting of Black Kandosols overlie wet Sulfidic/Sulfuric D horizons.

The Clarence River is laterally constrained until it enters the zone of tidal influence – the site of extensive floodplains; the width of the floodplains greatly expands in this zone to a maximum of ~11 km. The average floodplain width is ~6 km (Huq, 1995). Huq (1995) divides the Clarence River lowland plain between Grafton and Maclean into several floodplain zones based on channel orientation and patterns of the floodplain surface. He further differentiates each floodplain zone into a series of geomorphic units, summarised in Figure 2.4.

Passing through the Grafton-Maclean lowland plain, the Clarence River's main channel is straight to slightly sinuous with occasional anabranches, the most prominent being the South Arm. Moderately well vegetated point and longitudinal bars are present (Huq, 1995). Benches, levees and crevasse splays occur occasionally at channel margins (O'Brien and Wells, 1986; Huq, 1995). The average thickness of fluvial deposits in the Grafton-Maclean floodplain region is approximately 5 m and is influenced by the network of distributary and flood channels; it is not always a function of distance from the main channel. Fluvial deposits are thin to absent in estuarine regions and near valley margins (Huq, 1995).

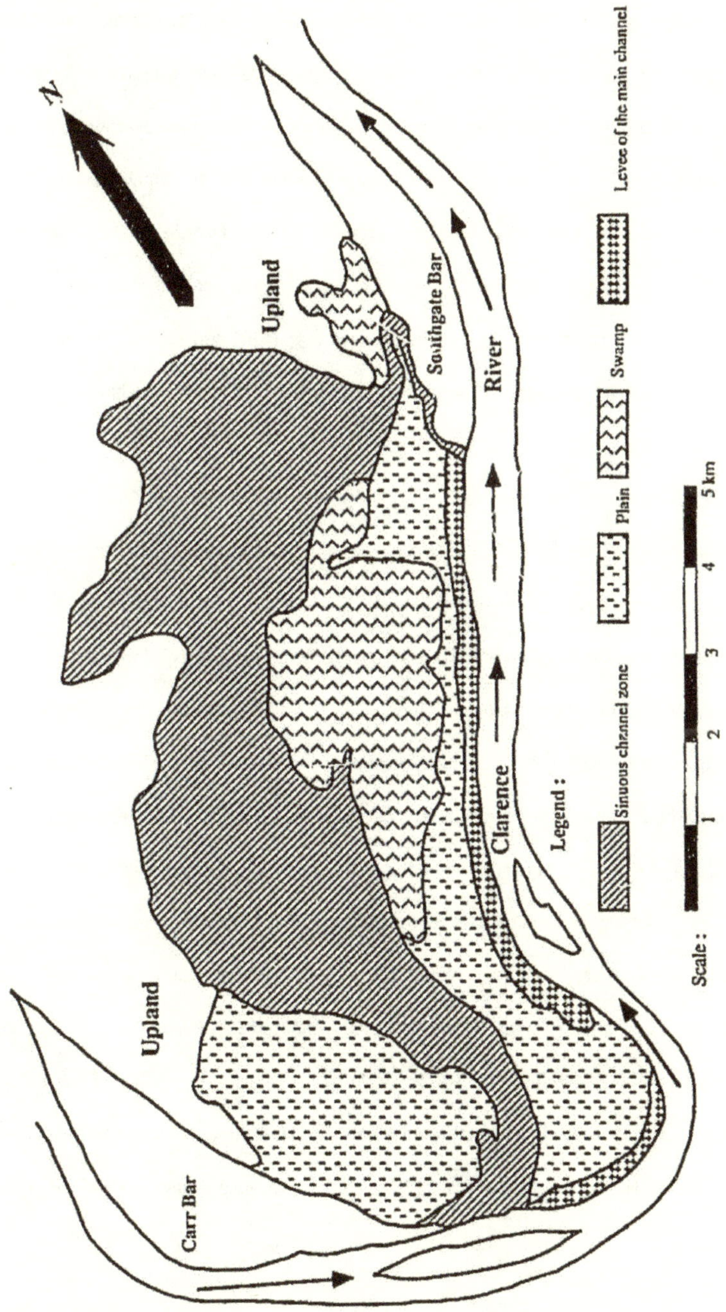

Figure 2.5: Geomorphic subdivisions of the Grafton floodplain.

The type locality for Morand's (2001) Alluvial soil landscape is located along the Maclean-Bluff Point Ferry Road at Cowper. This landscape comprises levees along the main Clarence River channels on the Clarence alluvial plain. Holocene estuarine sediments are overlain by fine-grained alluvium composed mainly of clays and silts with some sand lenses. This alluvium is present to depths >2 m. Elevation ranges from 2-6 m, local relief is 1-5 m and slopes are 0-6%. Major levees along the Clarence River channel and smaller levees along tributary channels form undulating to rolling plains. Land is completely cleared and soils are deep (>200 cm), well drained Brown Dermosols and Brown Kandosols. These erodible soils are strongly acidic and have low permeability.

2.1.6 **Local Resources and Land Use**

The Clarence River system is the largest coastal river catchment in New South Wales, spanning an area of 22 700 square kilometres. The majority of the local population and resources are supported by the Clarence River's extensive alluvial floodplain. The catchment is host to more than 250 sugar cane farms and a mill and refinery are located on Harwood Island. The local sugar industry contributes $103 million to the local economy each year (Clarence Valley Council, 2007). Farm land in the Clarence Valley also supports beef cattle, dairying and other general farming and accounts for 81.5% (8 507.5 square kilometres) of the current land use zonings for the Clarence Valley Council (Clarence Valley Council State of the Land, 2007). Aquatic resources are also important to the local economy; the second largest commercial fishery in New South Wales is located in the region and the industry contributes an estimated $27 million to the local economy each year (Clarence Valley Council, 2007). Timber production is also a significant contributor to the regional economy and the region contains both State Forests (199.4 square kilometres) and Joint Venture Freehold Hardwood Plantations (2 890 hectares) (Clarence Valley Council State of the Land, 2007).

The Clarence Valley also contains Protected Lands and land under Voluntary Conservation Agreements, wildlife refuges and land for wildlife (Table 2.1). Protected Lands include National Parks, which account for an area of 78.6 km^2, Nature Reserves, covering an area of 25.6 km^2, and State Conservation areas covering 17.1 km^2. A total of 239.7 Ha of land is under Voluntary Conservation Agreements, while a total of 11 wildlife refuges (12 747 Ha) and 27 other areas of land for wildlife (1 220 Ha) are contained within the Clarence Valley (Clarence Valley Council State of the Land, 2007). Rural Residential, Residential, Urban and Industrial areas only account for 0.81% (80.6 square kilometres; see Figure 2.5) of the current land use zonings for the Clarence Valley Council (Clarence Valley Council State of the Land, 2007).

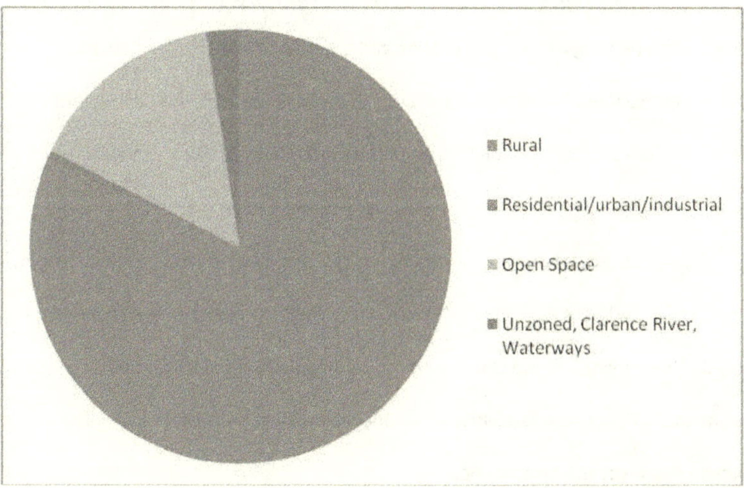

Figure 2.6: Clarence Valley Council current land use zonings. (Data source: Clarence Valley Council State of the Land, 2007).

Table 2.1: Area of Protected Lands, land under Voluntary Conservation Agreements, wildlife refuges and other land for wildlife in the Clarence Valley. (Source: Clarence Valley Council State of the Land, 2007).

Land Type	**Total Area (Ha)**
National Park	78 614
Nature Reserve	27 572
State Conservation Area	17 112
Wildlife Refuge	12 747
Land for Wildlife	1 220
Voluntary Conservation Agreement	240
Total	**237 505**

As the majority of the land in the area is used for farming (Figure 2.5), impacts such as loss of riparian vegetation (leading to riverbank erosion and other flood impacts), acid sulphate groundwater, compaction of soils, loss of topsoils and damage resulting from use of farming implements must be considered in the context of the vulnerability of Aboriginal midden sites in estuarine and riverine environments. As only a small amount of land is zoned residential/urban/industrial these may represent future areas of rapid and concentrated growth. Consideration of disturbance associated with industry, construction and increased population density must also be made. As the Clarence Valley is a popular tourist destination, impact on Aboriginal midden sites of such recreational activities as boating, bushwalking, camping and beach four-wheel-driving must also be examined.

Morand observed disturbance in areas of the Clarence Valley during his 2001 soil landscapes study. The following table (Table 2.2) summarises the data presented in this study with regards to observed disturbance in different environments and soil landscapes in the Clarence Valley region. Land use in different soil landscapes is also included. The following map (Figure 2.6) shows general locations of the different soil types.

Table 2.2: Land use by soil type. (Data from Morand, 2001).

Soil Type and Environment	Name and Type Location of Soil Landscape	Land Use	Degradation/ Disturbance
Alluvial	Cowper (cw), type location along Maclean-Bluff Point Ferry Road and includes parts of Maclean and Lawrence.	Grazing, sugar cane, seasonal cropping, flood refuge for livestock.	Original open- to closed-rainforest has been almost completely cleared. The Rainforest Reserve at Maclean is the sole remaining patch of original Clarence River floodplain subtropical rainforest. Streambank erosion is present.
Alluvial – estuarine/deltaic	Palmers Island (pa), type location on Palmers Island, soil landscape present on the deltaic plain of the Clarence River downstream of Maclean.	Some grazing, several prawn farms on Palmers Island. Includes villages of Harwood, Palmers Island, Chatsworth and parts of Maclean.	Soil structure decline in cultivated soils, acid sulphate soils widespread at depth >1 m. Area includes SEPP no. 14 coastal wetlands and isolated stands of *Casuarina glauca* (swamp Oak).
Estuarine/deltaic	Romiaka Island (rm), type location on Romiaka Island, soil landscape present on tidal flats and salt marshes within the Clarence delta.	Land generally unused as soils are saline and saturated throughout the year. Crown Reserves, Crown Land and several oyster leases.	Some urban encroachment at Yamba and Iluka. Area includes SEPP no. 14 coastal wetlands.
Estuarine/deltaic – lacustrine	The Broadwater (bd), type location on western side of The Broadwater near Broadwater Creek. Soil landscape includes The Broadwater and relict estuarine sediments surrounding it.	Uncleared swamp and mangrove complex containing some areas of extensively cleared swamp complex. Cleared areas support some beef cattle grazing, whilst uncleared land remains generally unused. The Broadwater is an important fishing ground.	Minimal amount of cleared land, no degradation or disturbance mentioned.
Beach/barrier	Angels Beach (ab), type location on Angels Beach, soil landscape also present at Evans Head Beach, 10 Mile Beach and Yamba Beach.	Predominantly recreational uses. Land includes Iluka Nature Reserve (World Heritage listed) and Broadwater, Bundjalung and Yuraygir National Parks.	Exposed to summer storms which can severely erode and reshape beaches. Beaches prone to severe wave attack during high seas and wind erosion causing blowouts particularly in beach access areas. Bitou Bush and Lantana are firmly established in most dune

			systems. Extensive sand mining has occurred in the past along beaches and hind-dunes. Dunes at Weapons Range have been extensively bombed. during military drills.
Aeolian	Iluka (il), type location at Iluka, soil landscape present as Quaternary sand sheets within the Bundjalung Dunefield and Clarence estuarine plain.	Some grazing and sugar cane between Broadwater and Woodburn. Urban areas at Iluka, Yamba and Broadwater. Includes parts of Bundjalung National Park and Iluka Nature Reserve. Otherwise uncleared lands, including Crown Lands.	Minor sheet and wind erosion in some cleared/urban areas. Bitou Bush and Lantana are common woody weeds. Area includes parts of World Heritage listed littoral rainforest at Iluka Nature Reserve.
Swamp	Angourie (an), includes swamps within transgressive dunes and swales of the Bundjalung Dunefield.	Includes parts of Broadwater, Bundjalung and Yuraygir National Parks and Dirrawong Reserve. Crown Land at Angourie.	No observed land degradation.
Alluvium	Brushgrove (bh), includes parts of the alluvial plain of the lower Clarence River. A variant (bha) occurs as a sand mass on Munro Island.	Beef and dairy cattle grazing, sugar cane.	Original open- to closed-forest has almost completely been cleared (see Cowper).
Alluvium	Calliope (cp), includes narrow, elongate swamps along flood chutes and distributary channels on the Clarence alluvial plain.	Mostly unused, some grazing.	Original closed-forest (swamp forest) completely cleared.
Lacustrine/chenier plain	Wooloweyah (ww), lacustrine/chenier plain bounding the west and south sides of Wooloweyah Lagoon.	Generally unused, some beef cattle grazing and sugar cane.	Acid sulphate soils.

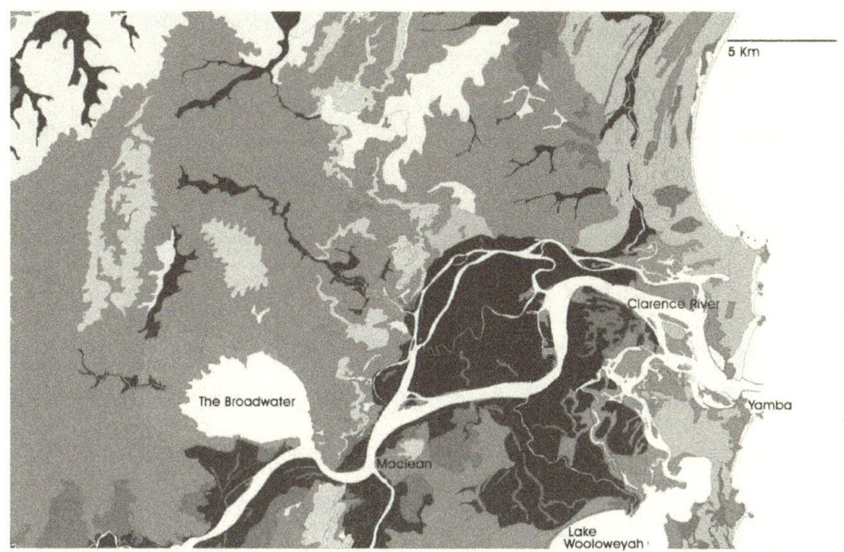

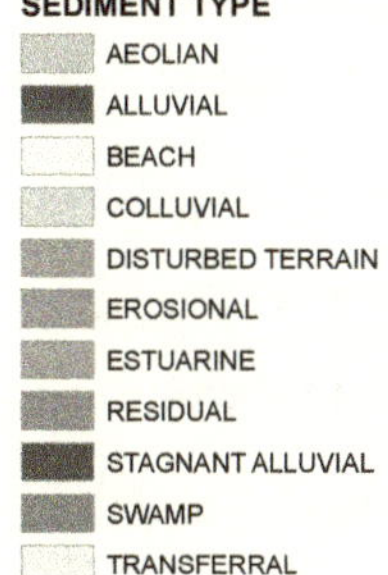

Figure 2.7: Locations of Morand's (2001) soil landscapes in the study area.

2.2 SITE FORMATION PROCESSES AND THE SYNTHESIS OF A GEOARCHAEOLOGICAL FRAMEWORK

2.2.1 **Introduction**

The current project focuses on understanding site formation processes acting in different geomorphic settings in the Clarence Valley. Such an understanding is essential if effective site- and environment-specific conservation guidelines and practices are to be implemented. Site formation processes are physical, chemical, biological and anthropogenic factors which not only act to preserve a site, but which also cause it to degrade (Ward and Larcombe, 2003). Central to the study of site formation processes is an understanding of the local geomorphic and anthropogenic factors which potentially disturb sites, as outlined in the previous section, and knowledge of how these factors act on a site. This section reviews literature on site taphonomy and links it with its causes.

2.2.2 **Site Formation Processes**

Figure 2.7 provides an outline of the contexts in which transformations, or taphonomic processes, occur at an archaeological site. It can be seen that site formation is affected by cultural and natural transformations, although Waters (1992) does not appear to acknowledge post-burial contexts. These are, in fact, of great importance in the Clarence Valley (see 'Local Resources and Land Use') and, indeed, the majority of cultural sites. Human activity may exacerbate natural processes, such as erosion, deposition and deflation, and may also cause other hazards such as acid sulphate groundwater and soil compaction.

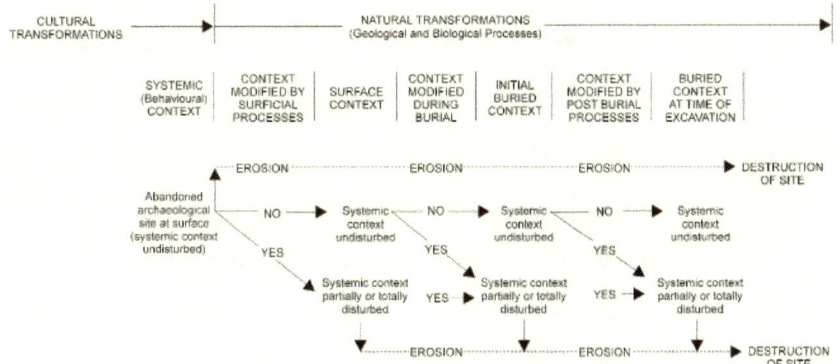

Figure 2.8: A flow chart for site formation. Source: Ward & Larcombe, 2003.

Another important point when considering anthropogenic and environmental factors involves separating the initial cultural context of a site from taphonomic, anthropogenic and environmental processes. Patterns produced as a result of natural formation processes may be mistaken for cultural patterning; this biases interpretation of site function, spatial organisation, chronology and stratigraphy (Erlandson and Rockwell, 1987). Tanner (2005) highlights some of the problems:

- Change of environmental setting: past shellfish may have lived in a habitat different to that of today. An understanding of the palaeodistribution of species and the palaeoenvironment at the time of deposition can effectively remedy this problem.
- Size of excavation/sampling strategy: samples from a single occupation horizon need to be taken from the whole site for a proper representation of site variability. As the focus of the current project involves site conservation strategies such as stratigraphic correlation (from small cores) between cores and with cores from the surrounding non-archaeological sediment, and accurate stratigraphic diagrams drawn from vertical exposures, are sound methods for assessing the integrity of, and variation within, a site.

- Temporal resolution: the more time represented in a single occupation layer the greater the overprint of patterns. Effects of environmental change and human behaviour merge and become difficult to isolate. Thorough stratigraphic studies and ^{14}C chronosequences of a site can aid in determining whether it has been reworked.

Sandweiss (2003) highlights the usefulness of archaeological deposits in palaeoclimatic reconstructions if their integrity can be shown to have remained intact. Sites along the Peruvian coastline with long occupation histories contained well preserved and easily dated sediment, soil signatures of past conditions and marine fauna providing a geochemical record (Sandweiss, 2003) for oxygen isotope studies and amino acid racemisation chronology. Studies of palaeoclimatic conditions and climate conditions since European occupation can help build a picture of susceptibility of Aboriginal midden sites in the Clarence Valley to climatic factors.

The study area, situated along the coastal reaches of the Clarence Valley, is host to a variety of coastal environments including coastal dunes and areas of the Clarence River floodplain adjacent to the Clarence River, estuary and associated swamps. Following is a review of aeolian disturbance processes and disturbance processes associated with alluvial landscapes. Bioturbation is considered separately due to its important in a variety of landscapes.

2.2.3 **Aeolian Processes**

The beach/barrier landscape of the northern NSW coastline is highly susceptible to wind erosion, resulting in blowouts (Morand, 2001). Coutts (1972) describes blowout deposits. A blowout can occur in the side of an unconsolidated sand dune and has the effect of scattering the material contained within the dune over its eroded face. Such surface collections of material are of limited value as chronological and cultural associations among the material have become obscured. (Goldberg and MacPhail, 2006) consider deflation the principal risk for an archaeological deposit in a windblown area. Exposure to wind erosion of unconsolidated or very loosely consolidated deposits containing clasts of various sizes can result in the formation of lag deposits (Garner, 1974). Fine-grained sediment is removed by deflation, leaving behind those clasts too heavy to be transported by the action of wind (Ahnert, 1998). Thus, lag deposits can form from either anthropogenic or natural shell accumulations. Characteristics of lag deposits include segregation of larger or heavier particles (Bloom, 1978), erosional interclasts and imbricated specimens, and condensed and concentrated shell accumulations (Grazhdankin & Seilacher, 2002). Wave-sorting can also produce lag deposits, as it is able to remove finer sands, therefore concentrating heavier material (Millard, 2003).

Rick's (2002) study of coastal dune middens on San Miguel Island, California, USA, found that wind can significantly disturb subsurface deposits to a depth of at least 200 mm. Field observations led Rick (2002) to suggest some key features of deflated midden deposits, although he acknowledges that artefact movement by aeolian processes in dune environments is very complex. Key features include: a higher density of more fragmented shellfish in upper strata, exhibiting angled, faceted, polished and etched surfaces primarily on the side of the shell exposed to the wind, and the presence of charcoal in lower layers of the deposit while it is absent in upper strata. Erlandson and Rockwell (1987) also note that wind abrasion may obscure features of artifacts valuable in determining their use at a particular site or sites.

Frederick, Bateman and Rogers (2002) used optically stimulated luminescence (OSL) dating to gauge the integrity of a site in the sandy uplands of east Texas. OSL results ruled out *in situ* weathering by demonstrating that the unconsolidated sands contained in the deposit had been exposed to significant sunlight prior to mid-late Holocene deposition. Chronostratigraphy is another useful dating technique when assessing site integrity. In an undisturbed midden it would be expected that the ages of shell would show they have accumulated over time (Stone, 1995). If shells of different ages are found at random within a deposit (that is, the deposit has an anomalous chronostratigraphy) it is likely to have been reworked (Erlandson and Rockwell, 1987; Stone, 1995).

2.2.4 **Storm Reworking**

Storm activity can cause disturbance in coastal and alluvial landscapes. Whilst wave erosion is common as a result of summer storm activity along the northern NSW coastline (Morand, 2001), flood discharges and raised estuarine water levels can disturb sites located on river banks. Shick (1987) suggests deposits found in high energy conditions, such as the beach/barrier landscape of the Clarence coastline, are likely reworked. But it is important to assess each site individually, as the degree of reworking will vary between sites (Shick, 1987) and may be related to factors such as amount and nature of dune vegetation, frequency of storm events and frequency of use for recreation.

Hughes and Sullivan (1974, Hons) characterise a midden that has been reworked by storm event(s) as containing shells of species and sizes not thought to have been eaten by Aborigines, water worn shells, rounded pebbles, pumice and marine shell grit with no sorting of material between layers. Rarely are rounded pebbles >5cm in diameter found in undisturbed middens, particularly if the type of rock is unsuitable for use in the manufacture of implements (Hughes and Sullivan, 1974). Pieces of pumice too large to be blown by the wind are common in wave reworked middens and the marine-derived shell grit found in such deposits is usually sub- to well-rounded as a result of abrasion in the surf zone (Hughes and Sullivan, 1974). In contrast, Statham (1892) argues that the presence of pumice within a shell assemblage indicates it was contemporaneous with a period of volcanic activity. Large floods may reverse alluvial sedimentary sequences, thus producing a unit with reversed grading, coarsening from silts to sand or gravel (Brown, 1997); they can also lead to the formation of gravel fans (Goldberg and MacPhail, 2006).

2.2.5 **Other Alluvial Processes**

It is not easy to generalise about the effects of geomorphic processes on archaeological sites in alluvial and wetland locations; variations in sediments and stratigraphy cause variable groundwater transmission rates (Brown, 1997). Meandering and avulsing channels create lateral variability due to movement of sediment (Guccione *et al.,* 1998). Hydrologic events also cause vertical movement of sediment. Sediment type, volume and movement all affect the integrity of archaeological sites in alluvial environments.

Although channel avulsion causes lateral variability in the stratigraphy of floodplain sites (Brown, 1997) it can cause the river course to become abandoned and thus protected from erosion, as is the case with Late Prehistoric (0.5 – 1.0 Ky) archaeological sites located along the Red River, Arkansas, USA (Guccione *et al.,* 1998). In locations meander migration and aggradation have produced overlapping scroll bars sites may be both laterally extensive and vertically stratified (Brown, 1997).

In their study of site preservation along the Red River, Arkansas, Guccione *et al.* (1998) found landforms to be obvious and, as such, geomorphic relationships were more useful than radiocarbon dates in determining the age of landforms and archaeological sites. The formation of diagnostic landforms is controlled by the meandering, migration and avulsion of the Red River and flooding of older floodplain areas deposited a veneer of younger overbank sediment. In such cases Guccione *et al.* (1998) recommend the age of land surfaces be used only as a minimum date for their associated landform. Guccione *et al.* (1998) suggest that vertical floodplain changes may not be as significant as lateral changes in channel position for archaeological site preservation along actively meandering and avulsing rivers such as the Red River, Arkansas.

The integrity of sites located in fluvial contexts is related to the tempo, magnitude and duration of hydrologic events (Petraglia and Nash, 1987). Such events affect the movement of sediment and associated artefacts. Wood and Johnstone (1978) define movement of archaeological materials downslope as 'graviturbation'. The process is fundamentally related to gravity and occurs with the aid of wind, flowing water and trampling (Erlandson and Rockwell, 1987). Stratigraphic anomalies and patterned distributions of artefacts and archaeofauna can be a result of graviturbation (Erlandson and Rockwell, 1987).

Sheetwash is common on slope crests and can transport dissolved and fine-grained loads (Goldberg and MacPhail, 2006), possibly biasing the archaeological record by removing finer and lighter constituents. Sheetwash also has the potential to rework archaeological deposits, thus affecting site integrity. Colluvium, forming slope deposits, is generally massively bedded and poorly sorted and at the slope bottom it is deposited as laminated, water-lain sediment (Goldberg and MacPhail, 2006). The colluvial footslope/valley bottom interface is characterised by interdigitation of colluvial and alluvial deposits – such locations may be identified as poorly sorted silts interfingering organic-rich clays (Goldberg and MacPhail, 2006). The stratigraphy of archaeological sites buried at such locations needs to be carefully interpreted.

After conducting experiments on hydrologic disturbance of stone artefacts Schick (1987) found such disturbance affected the assemblage composition and spatial configuration of stone artefacts. He identified greater proportional losses with successively smaller artefacts and this biased the record, leaving behind a seemingly higher proportion of cores and heavier artefacts. Trends in spatial configurations include:

- relatively core-rich deposits in vicinity of original site
- downstream deposits containing high proportions of debitage – spatial gaps within final deposit

- downstream gradation (coarse to fine)
- changes in material associations
- 'stretching' of site downstream
- reconcentration of site materials downstream (mirrors flow regime and sediment movement in river)
- cementation of site materials in fine-grained sedimentary substrates. Cementation of artifactual materials within substrate without evidence of burial by influx of fluvial or lacustrine sediments per se. Wetting and drying of sediments during and after bouts of rain had cemented artifacts fairy solidly within the drying muds.

Preservation and site integrity are closely related to the rate and intensity of erosion and deposition. At sites where erosion has been dominant since the time of occupation the preservation of sites is unlikely (Guccione *et al.,* 1998). Sites which are covered quickly, however, are more likely to be preserved. The erosional environment can be helpful to researchers in that it has the potential to expose deeply buried sites (Guccione *et al.,* 1998) although management of sites that are susceptible to erosion then becomes a pressing issue. Due to shifting stream beds is it unlikely to find intact human artefacts, other than those associated with intrusive features, in contemporary meander channel deposits (Guccione *et al.,* 1998). In such settings archaeological prospecting should be aimed at palaeochannels (Guccione *et al.,* 1998) and topographically elevated areas such as channel islands or banks and parts of the floodplain some distance from a channel (Schick, 1987). Guccione *et al.,* (1998) found in their study of archaeological sites along the meandering Red River, Texas, that vertically accreted overbank deposits were the dominant type of surficial deposit associated with cultural material. Laterally accreted channel deposits were rarely associated with archaeological sites. Channel deposits in the area showed an overall fining upwards trend. This may indicate slower deposition rates than the vertically accreted sediment which may have covered archaeological sites rapidly, preserving their integrity.

Organic-rich soils (A Horizons) can start to form once alluviation decreases or stops because the rate of soil development on floodplains is inversely proportional to the rate of overbank deposition (Brown, 1997). These palaeosols are useful in determining past floodplain conditions. Mature soils may not form at sites with continually high rates of deposition but such sites have the advantage that it is easier to distinguish multiple occupations, as they will be distinctly separated by sediment. Conversely, sites with low rates of deposition show multiple occupations that are hard to distinguish from one another (Goldberg and MacPhail, 2006).

Floodplain stripping is another geomorphic characteristic indicative of disturbance in an area. Floodplain stripping can occur as a result of secular hydrologic regime change from a drought-dominated regime (DDR), where flood frequency and magnitude are relatively lower, to a flood-dominated regime (FDR), characterised by frequent, high magnitude floods (Warner, 1997). Warner (1995) argues these natural changes are based on secular shifts in climate, but have been further complicated by effects of European settlement such as removal of dense floodplain forests and direct channel modifications. Both of these processes have occurred in the Clarence River estuary, with only small areas of original vegetation (for example, Iluka Nature Reserve) remaining, and the construction of drains on many of the estuary's islands (Morand, 2001).

Warner (1997) determined that the Clarence catchment contains a wide variety of stripped surfaces. These predominantly comprise convex bank bars and chutes. The convex bank chutes commonly occur across meanders but are sub parallel in some instances. Chutes channels occur as a result of high level flood flows passing across an extensively alluviated meander apex; incision of fine alluvium down to basal gravels can be seen (Warner, 1997). Bar gravels are exposed, having been exhumed from under fine alluvium. Another field indicator of floodplain stripping is the presence of extensive surface spreads of gravels and sands, often 5-10 m thick. Hummocky relief on floodplain surfaces, however, is often a result of localised erosion rather than floodplain stripping (Warner, 1997).

2.2.6 **Bioturbation**

Bioturbation is an extremely important taphonomic processes acting in a variety of environments. An understanding of the mechanisms of bioturbation, and the disturbance it causes, is essential when interpreting archaeological sites. Bioturbation affects the structure and maturity of soils, and influences a wide variety of sites including mounds, stable upland sites and floodplain terraces and flats. The activity of bioturbating agents is retarded under certain conditions.

Bioturbation can be defined as "the interaction between animals, plants and soil materials during which soil fabric is altered by additive or subtractive processes" (Grave and Kealhoffer, 1999; P. 1240). Animals participate in numerous processes of soil formation including mounding, mixing, forming and backfilling voids, forming and destroying peds, regulating soil erosion, movement of water and air, decomposition of plant litter, nutrient cycling and biota and production of special constituents (Hole, 1981). Both exopedonic (outside the soil) and endopedonic (inside the soil) animals influence archaeological site formation processes (Hole, 1981).

The presence of deep burrowing earthworms can affect soil structure and infiltration, impacting on soil surface segregation (Shuster, Subler and McCoy, 2000). Mackay and Kladivko (1985), Blanchart (1994) and Ketterings, Blair and Marinissen (1997) have observed earthworm activity to improve water filtration in soils however Shuster *et al.* (1999) have observed a process by which earthworm activity degrades the soil surface. Surface crusts or seals can form when the amount of surface coarse organic matter, which protects the soil surface, is reduced. A lack of surface coarse organic matter also increases exposure of the soil surface to weathering.

Stein (1983) used the Carlston Annis mound in Kentucky, USA, as a case study in recognising bioturbation caused by earthworms. An archaeological site in which surface-casting species are present is likely to exhibit a concentration of larger objects beneath the surface, as fine-grained matrix is brought to the surface by the activity of these earthworms. The activity of subsurface-casting species mixes the matrix of a deposit below the surface only (Stein, 1983) and this can cause homogenisation of a deposit (Erlandson and Rockwell, 1987). In both cases earthworms are responsible for reworking the matrix of a deposit, distorting the archaeological record. Erlandson and Rockwell (1987) also note that surface-casting earthworm action causes selective removal of fine sediment beneath large objects resulting in their burial. Objects found out of context, for example buried burnt rock lacking associated elements such as charcoal, ash or fire pit features, are indicative of bioturbation (Erlandson and Rockwell, 1987). Burrowing action of subsurface-casting species and subsequent accumulation of castings can also bring heavier archaeological material to the surface (Erlandson and Rockwell, 1987). Deposits affected by bioturbation often present a bimodal distribution of coarse and fine material (Erlandson and Rockwell, 1987).

Other larger burrowing species such as rodents create easily detectable burrows which, after abandonment, fill with material from a different soil horizon and can thus be easily recognised (Stein, 1983). The burrows of smaller species such as earthworms, ants, crickets and spiders are less easily detected (Stein, 1983) and may require, in addition to the observations mentioned in the previous paragraph, analyses of soil morphology. Grave and Kealhofer (1999) used several techniques to investigate the role of bioturbation at the Omkoi 14 earthwork complex in northwestern Thailand. Firstly, the results of a radiocarbon analysis were used to establish the onset and rate of sediment deposition. Secondly, sediment macro- and micromorphology was used to identify and assess the extent of percolation and insect and root activity. The upper stratum contained randomly distributed clasts and charcoal, while the lower stratum contained charcoal fragments oriented horizontally. Comparison of these strata indicated the lower stratum was undisturbed by bioturbation while the upper stratum was disturbed. Insect burrows and galleries were identified as extending both horizontally and vertically through the deposit and were infilled by faecal pellets. Orange clay infilling of burrows was also observed, indicating termite activity. Mixing of the A and B soil horizons was evident. Comparison of thin sections from the disturbed and undisturbed strata also highlights the effects of bioturbation in the disturbed stratum at Omkoi 14 (Grave and Kealhofer, 1999). Relatively coarse well-sorted grains were evident in undisturbed areas, while fine, poorly sorted sediments were characteristic of areas where termite galleries were present. The thin sections also showed evidence of percolation of fine water-borne sediments. The lower part of pore spaces show clay coatings forming crescentic laminations (Figure 2.8).

Balek (2002) also studied thin sections from bioturbated soil. Thin sections taken from the Sangamon Soil in western Illinois show faecal pellets and biogenic sorting of mineral grains by size (Figure 2.9). Fining in grain size can be seen with increasing distance from the faecal pellets. The Sangamon Soil forms part of a stable upland site and Balek's (2002) study shows even apparently stable sites located away from forms of geomorphic disturbance can be susceptible to biological disturbance.

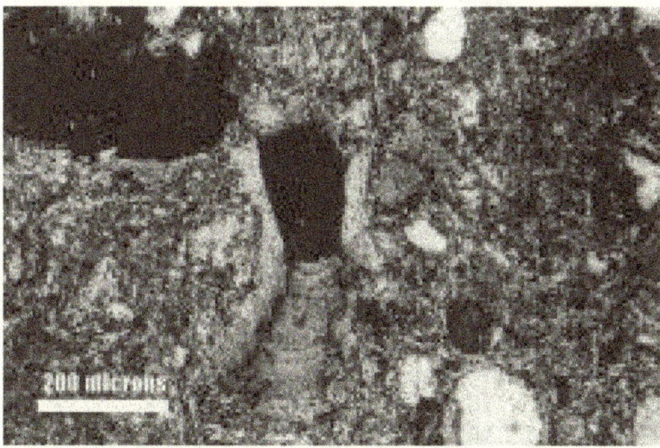

Figure 2.9: Percolation of fine sediments is indicated by the presence of crescentic laminations on the clay coating under the pore space in the centre of the image. Source: Grave and Kealhoffer, 1999).

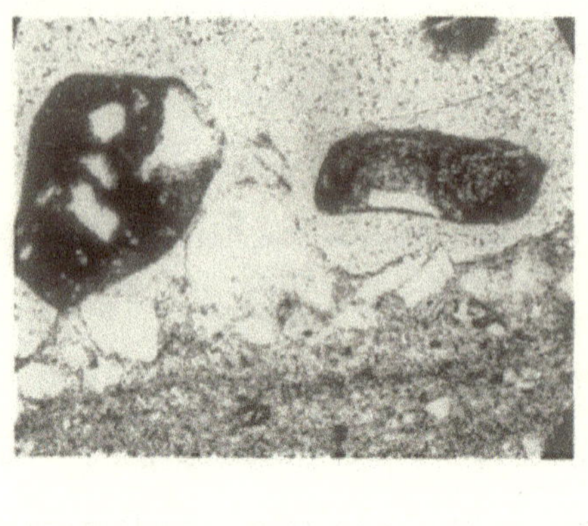

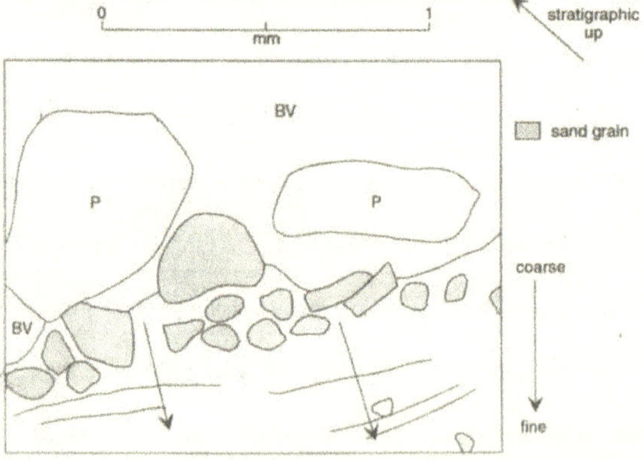

Figure 2.10: Thin section taken from the Sangamon Soil in western Illinois showing biogenic sorting of mineral grains by size. Source: Balek, 2002.

The third technique employed by Grave and Kealhofer (1999) to investigate bioturbation at Omkoi 14 involved an analysis of phytoliths. Each sample contained a full range of phytoliths sizes which suggests the sediment column has been churned by bioturbation. If the sediment had been unaffected by bioturbation it would be expected that phytoliths may be sorted by their size, mirroring the distribution of other sediment particles in the undisturbed stratum.

There are several conditions which exacerbate or retard bioturbation due to earthworm activity. High annual precipitation and temperature (Nye, 1955; Maldague, 1964), as well as mixed or loamy textures and high organic matter input (Brown, 1997), are conditions preferred by earthworms. Brown (1997) suggests that in alluvial environments the locations most densely populated by earthworms are generally terrace surfaces and floodplain flats. High sedimentation rates and very acidic (pH <3.5) and permanently waterlogged conditions inhibit earthworm activity (Brown, 1997).

Knowledge of the habitats of bioturbating agents, coupled with analysis of stratigraphy and soil morphology, is essential when assessing an archaeological site for biological disturbance.

2.2.7 **Synthesis of a Geoarchaeological Framework**

As shown in the studies outlined above, there is a need within archaeological and broader earth science research for a practical geoarchaeological framework. Geoarchaeology can be defined as "The application of geological and geomorphological techniques to archaeology and the study of the interactions of hominins with the natural environment at a variety of spatial and temporal scales" (Brown, 2008, p278). The core characteristic of geoarchaeological studies is the use of geomorphic techniques to place site formation processes into a regional context, thus allowing comprehensive interpretation of the cultural material they contain. Apparent information loss at a site can be investigated in terms of the processes which caused it; this information is often vital for accurate representation within archaeological reconstructions.

Various recent studies have refined highly useful geoarchaeological techniques to reinterpret and add to the volume of knowledge at archaeological sites around the world. Ward *et al.* (2006) integrate archaeological evidence from rock shelter and open site excavations in the Keep River region in north western Australia, after finding depositional and postdepositional processes cause differences in artefact assemblages and occupation chronology.

Reinterpretation of surface stone artefact scatters in western New South Wales, Australia, in a geomorphic context has yielded much useful archaeological information (Fanning *et al.*, 2009; Fanning, Holdaway and Rhodes, 2008; Fanning and Holdaway, 2001). Fanning and Holdaway (2001) measured the horizontal integrity of surface artefact scatters through the application of experimental geomorphic studies based on the movement of nonartifact clasts on hillslopes. This technique allows postdepositional movement of stone artefact scatters on very low slope gradients to be determined over a much larger area than archaeological quantification techniques such as refitting and analysis of microdebitage. Fanning and Holdaway (2001) found horizontal postdiscard movement of stone artifacts on low gradient land surfaces to be minimal, and suggested the broader application of this technique in assessing integrity of surface artefact scatters world-wide.

The geoarchaeological study of Fanning *et al.* (2009) demonstrates the use of geomorphic techniques to build a chronological framework for artifact surface scatters in western NSW. By placing the deposits in a regional geomorphic context, they show that variability in erosion and deposition leads to a variability in land surface age. This information facilitates reinterpretation of the age of surface artifact scatters, showing that artifact deposits which appear to have similar characteristics are not necessarily of a similar age. This study also highlights the reason why the archaeological record of the south east Australian arid zone is rarely found in buried deposits but is rich on the surface.

Geoarchaeological techniques have also been used to resolve ancient settlement patterns in central Tonga. Dickinson and Burley (2007) have shown that a number of geomorphic and geologic factors have influenced the ancient population distribution of central Tonga. Volcanic islands were a source of lithic resources and also the origin of tephra blankets which formed over the non-volcanic limestone islands. Weathered tephra blankets formed rich agricultural soil on these non-volcanic islands, and their terrigenous sand is was a resource used in the making of Lapita ceramics. Forearc uplift and subsidence influenced the diverse morphology of the non-volcanic limestone islands; configuration of evolving shorelines was influenced by Last-Interglacial and mid-Holocene sea level highstands (Dickinson and Burley, 2007). Also in the Pacific islands region, Anderson *et al.* (2006) have linked the sedimentary history of Fiji's Sigatoka Dunes with Fijian archaeological theory. They have shown that OSL and radiocarbon age determinations support the stratigraphic interpretation of the archaeological sequence of three stable dune phases associated with periods of Late Holocene dune stability.

Several recent studies in North America also effectively use geoarchaeological techniques to obtain greater archaeological resolution. Punke and Davis (2006) addressed the lack of evidence of inland migration of humans from initial colonisation of the northwest coast of North America by interpreting subregional tectonomorphic processes along the tectonically active Oregon coast. They found preservation and accessibility of Pleistocene stream terrace deposits is largely influenced by local, upper-plate tectonic structures; identification and understanding of these processes and structures better informs archaeologists as to the possible locations of cultural sites within coastal river valleys in tectonically active areas.

Interpretation of sedimentary structures and grain size distribution to resolve the interaction of aeolian, fluvial and local runoff processes in the arid-land Colorado River Corridor has been undertaken by Draut *et al.* (2008). Results show aeolian deposition has been a significant preservation agent over the last millennium, and that since the construction of the Glen Canyon Dam the absence of sediment-rich floods has reduced the preservation potential of cultural sites located in this area.

Cremeens and Lothrop (2009) studied the distribution of regolith materials and associated soil characteristics to interpret the stratigraphic context of eroded Native American shell middens containing multiple occupation events. Understanding the geomorphic processes affecting the vertical distribution of shells at the site allows for a more thorough interpretation of the cultural material. Also in West Virginia, USA, Cremeens, MacDonald and Lothrop (2003) showed that archaeological materials buried in weakly developed soils of the upland landscapes of the unglaciated Appalachian Plateau provide evidence of short periods of landscape stability in between catastrophic storm events. In addition to using geomorphic techniques to expand our understanding of the context and scope of archaeological sites archaeological information, such as that found by Cremeens, MacDonald and Lothrop (2003) can be integrated into the broader scientific data pool. In this case the authors suggest its application to conceptual models of temporal occurrence and classification of mass movements in co-alluvial settings. Similarly, a geoarchaeological study of the sedimentary record of an archaeological mound in Kinet Hoyuk, Turkey, used artifacts to characterise and date sedimentation in the area. Beach and Luzzadder-Beach (2008) found that artifacts from the mound, as it grew, had eroded into the strata of the surrounding alluvial plain, thus providing further information on the possible time period of erosion and deposition of alluvial sediments.

Ghilardi *et al.* (2008) further highlight the application of chronostratigraphic data in the interpretation, and reinterpretation, of archaeological material. They combine chronostratigraphic data, archaeological evidence and ancient literary sources to reconstruct landscape evolution and shoreline displacement during the past 5 millennia on the Thessaloniki Plain, Greece. Results obtained from the chronostratigraphic data led to a re-evaluation of landform definitions in the ancient literature and, thus, a reinterpretation of the mid-late Holocene landscape.

A practical geoarchaeological framework involves the synthesis of geomorphological techniques for analysing chronostratigraphy, hillslope erosion, regional erosion and deposition rates and sedimentary, geologic, tectonomorphic and pedogenic processes. The recent publication of many geoarchaeological studies incorporating analyses facilitated by these techniques highlights the importance of understanding site formation processes within regional and subregional geomorphic contexts. Previous study of archaeological sites in and around the Northern Rivers region of New South Wales has focussed on site survey and largely ignored site formation processes. The synthesis of a practical geoarchaeological framework facilitates in-depth study of site formation processes at recorded and previously unrecorded Aboriginal shell midden sites.

2.2.8 **Previous Archaeological Studies and Identification of Potential Research Sites**

Several archaeological surveys have been undertaken in the Maclean region but these are largely focused on National Parks land (Starling, 1974; Mcbryde, 1982; Byrne, 1985; 1986; James & Conyers, 1995). While Starling's (1974) survey was the most comprehensive, providing tabulated lists of site type, contents, dimensions and map references, recommendations concerning the conservation of sites were minimal. Although admitting dune middens in the Angourie Point – Iluka area (directly east of Maclean) have the potential to be easily disturbed, Starling (1974) states that their location in a National Park affords them protection. This may be true for human impacts such as recreation and development, however natural processes causing dune destabilisation, such as aeolian sediment movement (Rick, 2002) and storm events (Hughes & Sullivan, 1974) still have the potential to alter or destroy vulnerable sites. Reducing the impact of these processes through careful monitoring and stabilisation of dunes is essential to reduce site vulnerability.

Byrne's (1985) report targets Aboriginal sites in the Ulmarra Shire adjacent to the Shire of Maclean. As a proportion of this land is located outside the area of National Parks, he suggests the activities most damaging to Aboriginal sites will be related to agriculture and construction in riverine areas and sand mining and development of coastal villages in coastal zones. Byrne (1985) also notes that the most common sites located in sensitive areas within the Ulmarra Shire are shell middens, and that these sites are vulnerable to the action of natural forces such as wind and wave action in addition to those aforementioned.

A large number of recorded midden sites situated in the foredunes and inner barrier dunes within Maclean Shire are likely to have been reworked, or are vulnerable to reworking (Byrne, 1986; James & Conyers, 1995). Some deposits have become deflated as a result of the action of wind eroding the sediment in which they have been deposited, and others may have been reworked due to storm events or covered with sediment from the Clarence River estuary (Byrne, 1986). While burial of a cultural deposit by estuarine sediment can assist its preservation (Brown, 1997), a rise in water level can also displace shell and artifacts (Byrne, 1985). Identification of vulnerable and reworked sites in these areas is essential if effective conservation methods are to be developed. Other likely agents of disturbance affecting Aboriginal shell midden sites in the Maclean Shire include sand mining, levee construction, agricultural practice (leading to acid sulfate soils which potentially degrade shells), recreation/tourism, urban development, drainage works and animal damage including bioturbation (Byrne, 1986; James & Conyers, 1995).

James & Conyers (1995) undertook an extensive review of Aboriginal sites recorded in northeastern New South Wales as part of a NRAC funded Aboriginal Archaeology Project. They found, however, that records for many of the sites were sub-par, limiting the amount of information that could be gained from them. Twenty one percent of recorded Aboriginal shell middens showed signs of disturbance due to the agents mentioned in the previous paragraph. James & Conyers (1995) also highlight the need for further study in northern New South Wales both to ascertain whether or not significant disturbance has altered Aboriginal midden deposits and to discover new archaeological deposits. They suggested that the value of disturbed sites may be reduced and therefore the conserved sites may represent a skewed sample. The survey of previously unsurveyed land will no doubt yield Aboriginal sites, decreasing the bias of sampling that exists primarily along the open coast.

Several means were employed when identifying potential sites for research. Firstly, consultation with local Aboriginal communities identified midden sites known to be under threat from erosion. Secondly, the National Parks and Wildlife Aboriginal Sites Register (Aboriginal Heritage Information Management System, or AHIMS) contains information on midden sites and their locations. After consultation with local Aboriginal communities it was found there were site locations registered with National Parks and Wildlife of which they were unaware; consequently, they were enthusiastic to assess risk and implement conservation measures at these locations. Previously unrecorded sites known to the Yaegl Local Aboriginal Land Council were also included in the study and registered with the National Parks and Wildlife Service. Studies discussed above have included some of the sites logged in the register and several impacts have been identified. Further study of the nature of these and other impacts allows the formulation of effective site- and environment-specific conservation guidelines in consultation with local Aboriginal communities. Table 2.3 identifies the study sites and summarises the age range of each midden deposit based on information available from previous archaeological (Woombah sites A and B; McBryde, 1982) and geological studies (Sleeper Island, Plover Island, Minnie Water and Wooli; Troedson and Hashimoto, 2008). The following chapter presents general information, including land use, geomorphology, vegetation and cultural material, on the study sites.

Table 2.3: The study sites, their geomorphic context and age.

SITE	GEOMORPHIC CONTEXT	AGE RANGE	REFERENCE
Woombah A & Woombah B (WA and WB)	Riverbank and creekbank, respectively. Adjacent to the deposits in McBryde's (1982) Woolpack Creek study.	2600-3000 BP; 1400-1800BP	McBryde, 1982.
Sleeper Island (SI)	Estuarine plain.	Holocene	Troedson and Hashimoto, 2008.
Plover Island (PI)	Exposure of Coramba Beds (Figure 2.1). Adjacent shell middens located in coastal barrier foredunes.	Carboniferous bedrock (source material for stone artifact quarry, see Chapter 3); Holocene coastal barrier dunes.	Troedson and Hashimoto, 2008.
Minnie Water (MW)	Rocky Point headland an exposure of Coramba Beds. Midden deposit spans sediment stratigraphically overlying this bedrock as well as adjacent coastal barrier dunes.	Carboniferous bedrock; Holocene coastal barrier dunes.	Troedson and Hashimoto, 2008.
Wooli (WL)	Coastal barrier.	Holocene.	Troedson and Hashimoto, 2008.

3. SITE DESCRIPTIONS

3.1 SLEEPER ISLAND

3.1.1 **Land Use and Geomorphology**

Sleeper Island is a small (~8 km^2), flat, low-lying island located in the Clarence River estuary (S29°24.609', E153°19.540', Figures 3.1, 3.2, 3.3). It is connected to Palmers Island by a cement bridge (Figures 3.4 and 3.6). The portion of Palmers Island adjacent to Sleeper Island is privately owned and is used predominantly as a cattle farm. Evidence on Sleeper Island suggests cattle from the adjoining farm are let onto the island periodically (Figure 3.4, box). Sleeper Island is separated from Palmers Island by a tidal channel 5-7 m wide and the cement bridge which connects the two islands has prevented the flow of water from one side of the channel to the other. Stagnant pools of water can be seen on either side of the bridge (Figure 3.7).

The banks of Sleeper Island are eroding and face daily inundation at high tide. At low tide the western bank of the island falls sharply into the water with only minor sediment deposited from the estuary (Figure 3.8, arrow). The position of this bank in relation to the flow of water in the estuary may account for the lack of observed sedimentation, in an effect similar to that seen on the outside bank of a river meander. The eastern bank, however, shows a much greater exposure of sediment at low tide (Figures 3.1 and 3.9). Deposition due to the position of the bank in the estuary channel may also account for this observation, having a similar, depositional effect as flows on the inside bank of a river meander. Movement of sediment (erosion and deposition) as a result of this and other mechanisms may have changed the shape of the channels between the estuary islands, altering flows and thus impacting on bank erosion (see Chapter 7). Although sedimentation rates and loads may vary between the east and west banks of Sleeper Island bank erosion is considered to be the major geomorphic factor impacting on this island. A subsequent site survey performed two years after the initial investigation showed the bank has been undercut by a further 0.6 m at the site of the midden deposit.

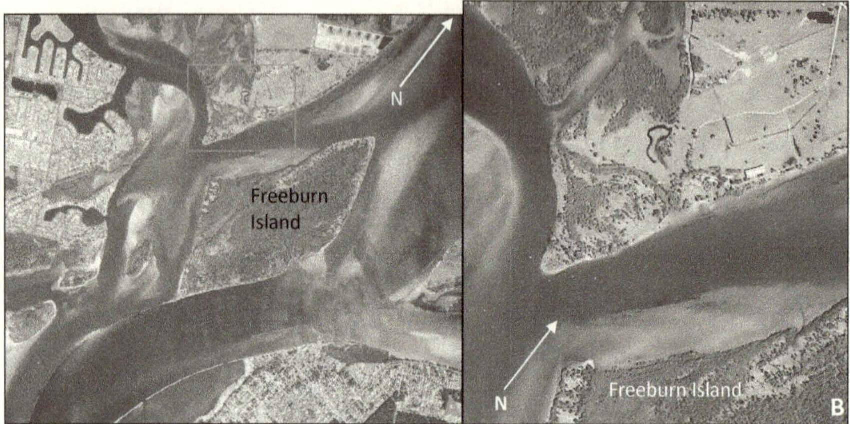

Figure 3.1: A: Aerial photograph of a section of the Clarence River estuary showing Sleeper Island (box). **B:** Close up of Sleeper Island showing location of Aboriginal shell midden (X).

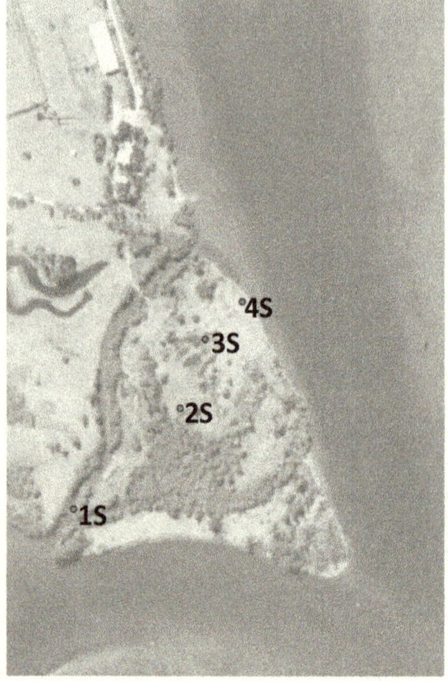

Figure 3.2: Sleeper Island, adjacent to Palmers Island, showing locations of core samples. Scale = 1:5,600

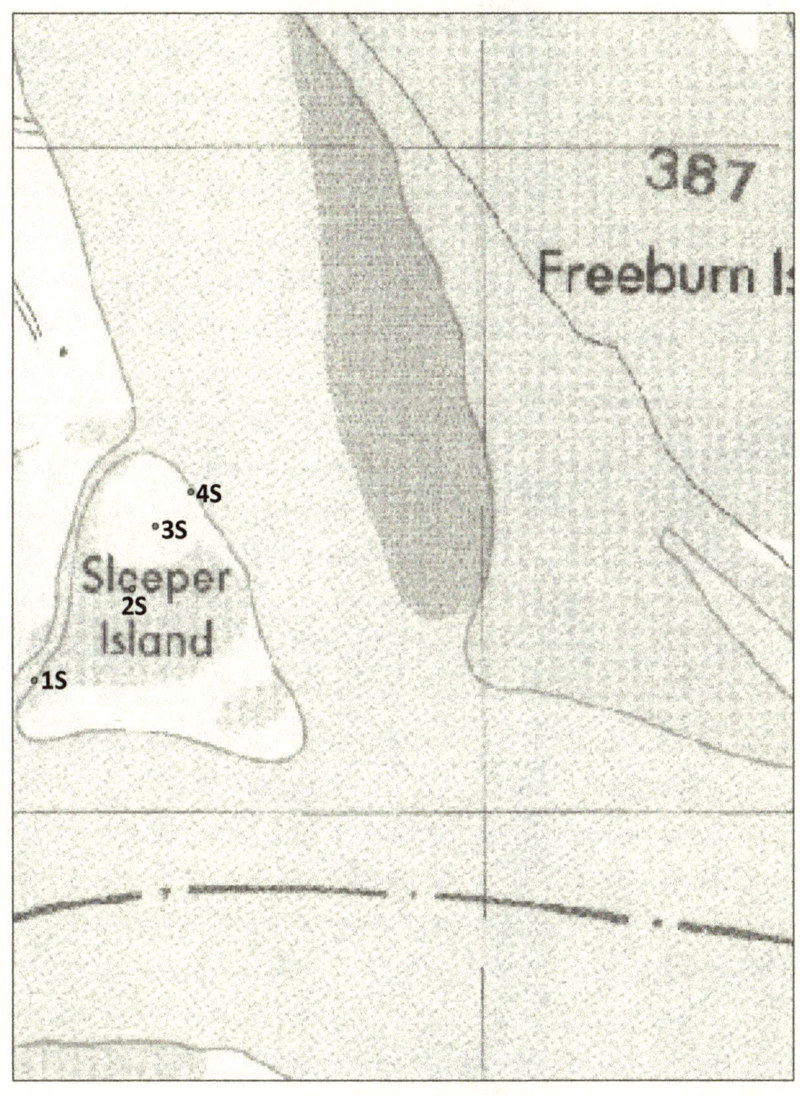

Figure 3.3: Topographic map of Sleeper Island, adjacent to Palmers Island, showing locations of core samples.

Scale=1:5,600

Figure 3.4: Cattle hoof prints on Sleeper Island.

Figures 3.5 & 3.6: Bridge connecting Sleeper and Palmers Islands.

Figure 3.7: Pooled water in the channel between Sleeper and Palmers Islands.

Figure 3.8: West bank of Sleeper Island, showing bank erosion.

Figure 3.9: East bank of Sleeper Island.

3.1.2 **Vegetation**

Vegetation on Sleeper Island comprises native and exotic species. Mangroves are present in and around channels. Many propagules were observed on the eastern, southern and western beaches of the island however the banks are devoid of mangroves. Water couch covers the whole island from the centre to the banks. *Casuarina* is the most common tree on the island. Some large bottle brush and Cyperaceae are also present. Exotic vegetation includes *Cinnamomum camphora* (Camphor Laurel), *Amyema* sp. (mistletoe), *Ipomoea* sp. (Morning Glory) and *Datura ferox* (Common Thorn Apple). Volunteers from the local Aboriginal community are systematically removing these weeds.

3.1.3 **Cultural Material**

There is one cultural deposit on Sleeper Island – an Aboriginal shell midden. The deposit lies 0.30-0.40 m below the soil surface and the dimensions of its exposed face are 0.10 m X 22.5 m long. The vast majority of the cultural material has eroded out of the deposit, which sits in a channel bank (Figure 3.10), and coring suggests the thickness of the *in situ* deposit is negligible at ~ 0.10 m (Figure 3.11). The contents of the midden include bivalve and gastropod molluscs, a vertebrate jawbone and stone tools (see Chapter 6, Plates 1, 6 and 7). A small piece of charcoal (1.50 X 1.50 cm) was found *in situ* in the channel bank deposit.

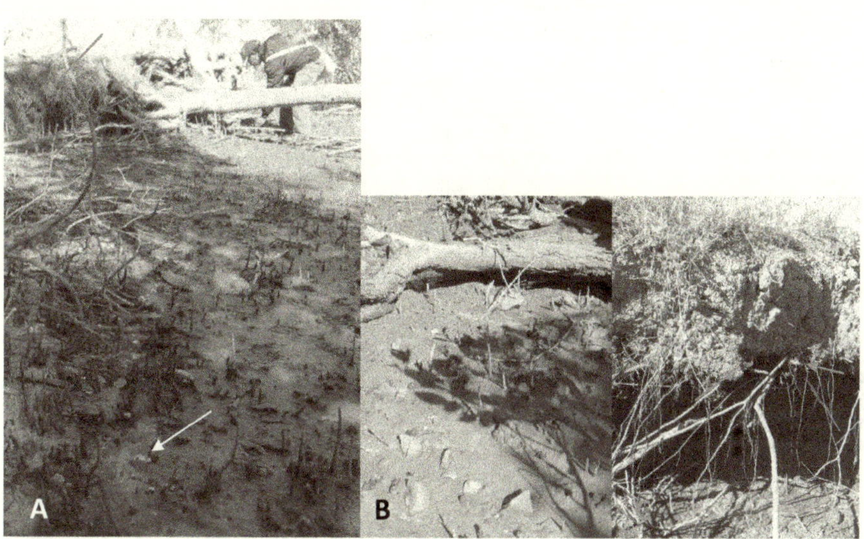

Figure 3.10: A: Site of the cultural deposit on Sleeper Island. Red arrow indicates *in situ* deposit and white arrow indicates lag deposit. **B:** Part of the lag deposit showing stone tools. **C:** Part of *in situ* deposit with arrows showing shell material.

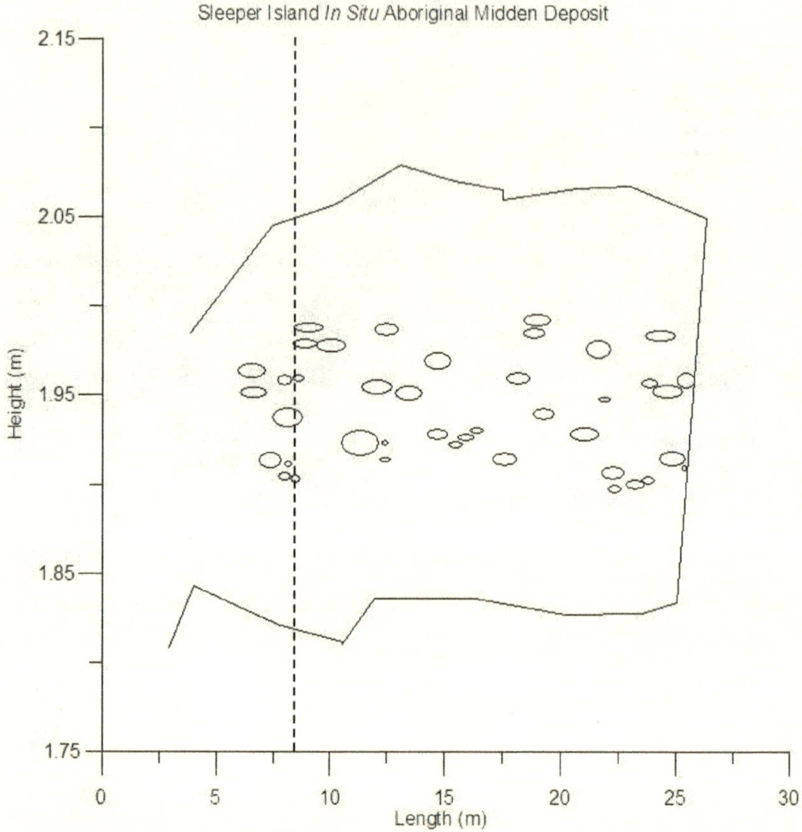

Figure 3.11: Sleeper Island *in situ* Aboriginal shell midden deposit. Dashed line shows the location of core 1S.

3.2 WOOMBAH

3.2.1 **Land Use and Geomorphology**

The Woombah midden complex is located at S 29°22.075', E 153°17.328' on the northern bank and floodplain of the Clarence River estuary's North Arm (Figures 3.12, 3.13, 3.14). It is referred to as a midden complex as there are many discrete Aboriginal shell middens in the area (Roger Mehr, DECCW, personal communication). This study focuses on two deposits – the first, referred to as Site A, is a riverbank *Crassostrea* deposit and the second, Site B, is a creek bank midden exposure (Figures 3.12, 3.15, 3.16, for full species composition details refer to Chapter 6, Biological and Taphonomic Analyses). In addition to these shell deposits there is a thin layer of fragmented shell covering parts of the area (see A_p layer, core diagrams W1a-W5b – Appendix 1). This shell material is clearly reworked.

Although the site B creek bank midden is identified with a sign put in place by the local Aboriginal community and Council, this is a fairly recent addition. The surrounding land is privately owned and has supported orchards and cattle in the past, however it currently does not support crops or livestock. The source of fragmented shell material in the A_p layer is clearly a result of the use of farming equipment. At the eastern end of the study area soil containing fragmented shell material from the A_p layer has been piled into mounds for use as bike jumps. As this shell material was most likely sourced from previously degraded material on the property it is unlikely this activity has caused disturbance to *in situ* cultural material.

The topography of the area is flat, as both deposits are situated on a floodplain. The floodplain at Woombah extends landwards (north) from the channel ~150 m before reaching a gently sloping levee. Directly north of this levee is a 50 m wide tract of trees and a road which runs parallel to the riverbank and levee. The tract of trees marks the northern limit of the study site. The riverbank marks the southern boundary of the study site, while the eastern limit of the site is a small creek running perpendicular to the main channel, and the creek bank site B marks the western boundary (Figures 3.17 & 3.18).

3.2.2 **Vegetation**

The majority of the floodplain within the study area is covered by domestic lawn. Tall, native grasses and reeds grow in the area immediately bordering the creek bank site B and the creek itself supports mangroves. Mangroves also line the riverbank and the creek at the eastern edge of the study area. The tract of trees marking the northern edge of the study site contains Eucalypts, ferns and Lantana.

3.2.3 **Cultural Material**

Both the site A and site B deposits contain only shell material (see Chapter 6 for species list, Plate 1). No artifacts were found at these sites, although other sites in the Woombah midden complex were found to contain artifacts (Mcbryde, 1982). The deposits occur at approximately the same depth. Site A is a riverbank deposit containing almost solely *Crassostrea* shells. It is located in the northern riverbank of the North Arm of the Clarence River approximately 20 m west of the eastern border of the study site. Shell material is eroding from the deposit and forming a lag at its base (Figure 3.15, 3.16). The exposed shell lens extends from 0.48 m to 0.67 m depth; its length is ~30 m.

Site B is a midden exposure present in both banks of the narrow (2.0 m wide) creek marking the western border of the study site. The southern end of the deposit lies 40 m north of the riverbank and the deposit extends north along the creek ~32 m. Coring on either side of the creek bank has shown the *in situ* deposit to extend 10-12 m east of the eastern creek bank and 3 m west of the western creek bank. Cultural material is found between 0.07 and 1.2 m depth in the exposed creek bank and between 0.00 and 0.24m at its eastern extent. At the western extent of the midden shell fragments are found at a depth of 0.00-0.35 m and whole shells from 0.35-0.65 m. It is possible the original deposit extended much further than this, and that the impact of farming machinery has disturbed large areas of it.

Figure 3.12: A: Aerial photograph of a section of the Clarence River estuary showing the Woombah study site (box). **B:** Close up of the Woombah study site showing locations of the Aboriginal shell middens (X).

Figure 3.13: Close up of red box in Figure 3.10A showing the location of core samples. Scale = 1:4,000

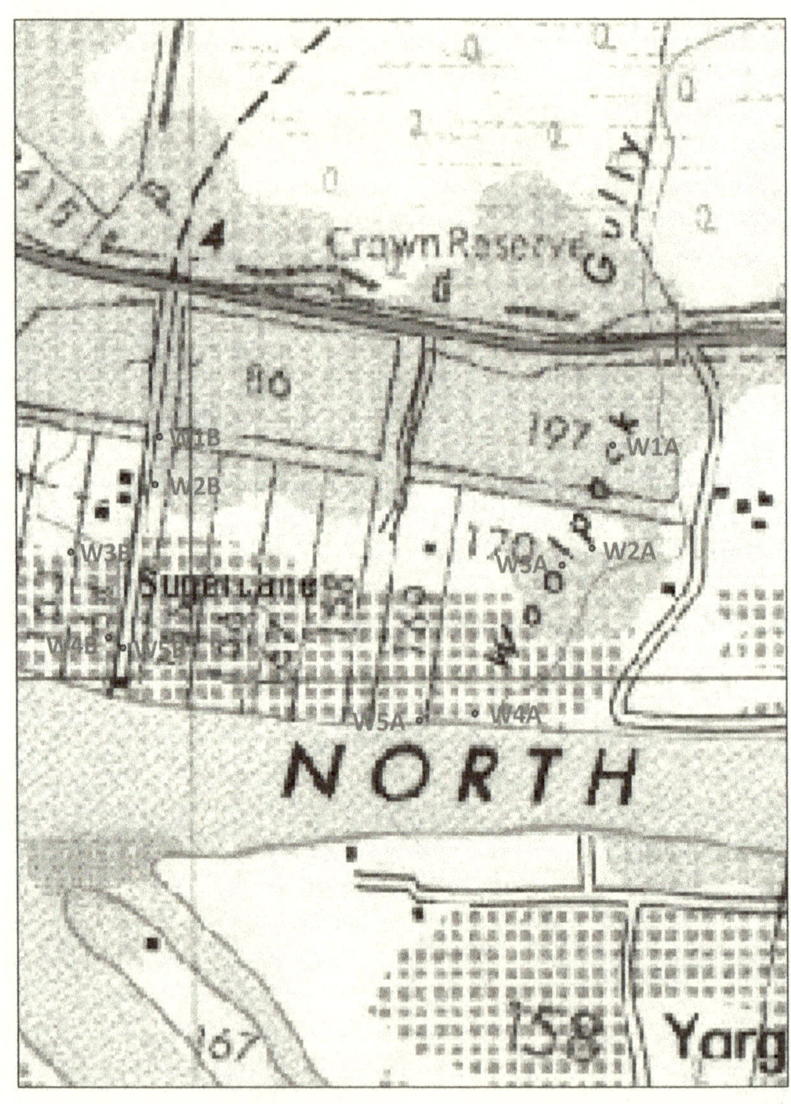

Figure 3.14: Topographic map of Woombah sites A (east) and B (west), showing the location of core samples.

Scale = 1:4,000

Figure 3.15: Section of Woombah Site A riverbank deposit. Scale= 0.50 m.

Figure 3.16: Shell material eroding from the Woombah Site A riverbank deposit.

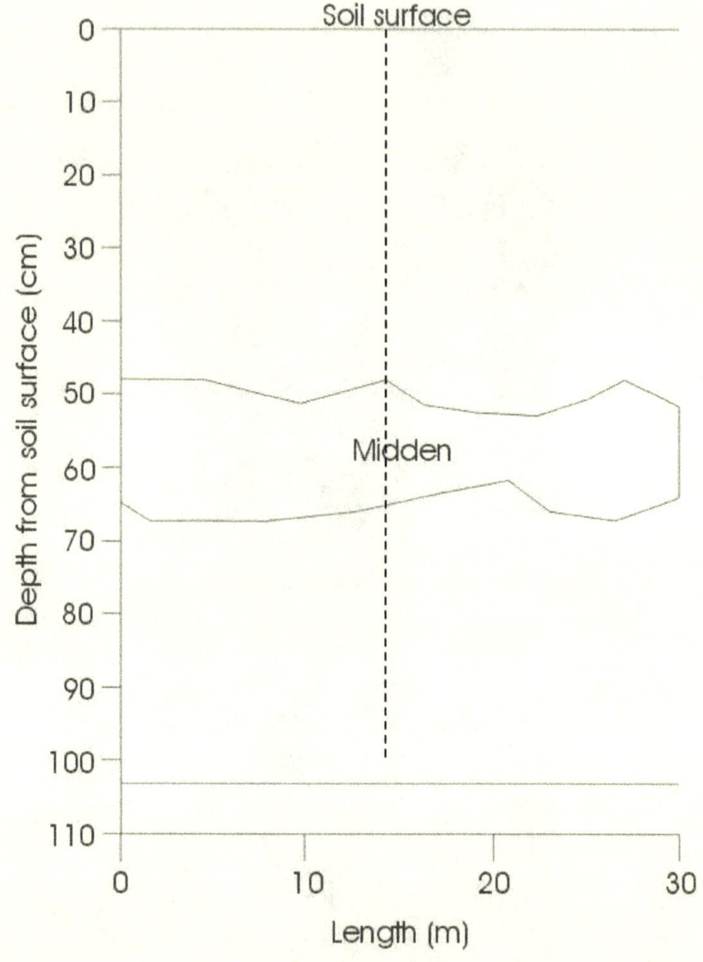

Figure 3.17: Woombah Site A Aboriginal midden deposit. Dashed line shows the location of core 5A.

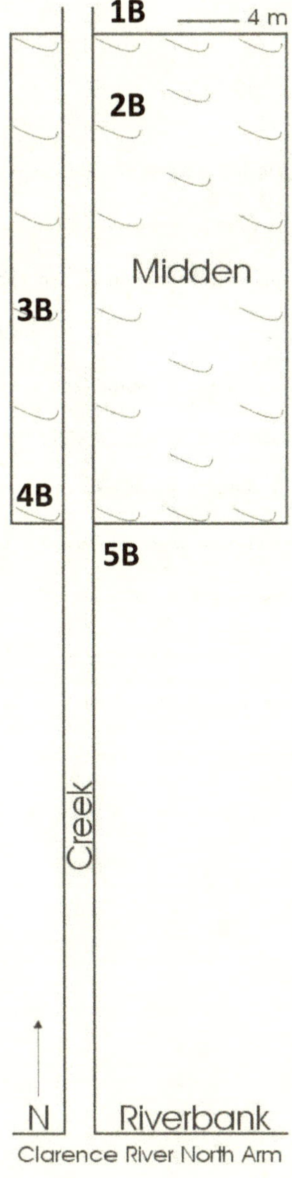

Figure 3.18: Woombah Site B Aboriginal midden deposit.

3.3 PLOVER ISLAND

3.3.1 **Land Use and Geomorphology**

Plover Island is a small (~8,324 m^2), rocky island located on the north side of the mouth of the Sandon River (S 29°40.335', E 153°19.811', Figures 3.19, 3.20, 3.21, 3.22, 3.27) and connected to the mainland by a tombolo. It has a maximum elevation of 7.1 m above present sea level and is exposed to winds around its entire circumference. The adjacent beach and camping ground are located south of Broom's Head, a small but popular surfing and holiday destination. Plover Island, the Sandon River camping area and surrounds are located within the Yuraygir National Park and access to the north side of the mouth of the Sandon River is via a 10 km unsealed road connected to Broom's Head road. Access to Sandon Village, which is located on the south side of the Sandon River, is restricted to a 12 km 4WD track which can be accessed from the Illaroo camping ground north of Minnie Water. Access to Plover Island from the south side of the Sandon River is by boat only. Recreational fishing off the rocks at the base of Plover Island is a popular local activity however this usually requires people to walk around the base of the island rather than over the top of it where the cultural deposits are located. Narrow walking tracks around the island indicate the island is also used for recreational walking and sightseeing (Figure 3.23).

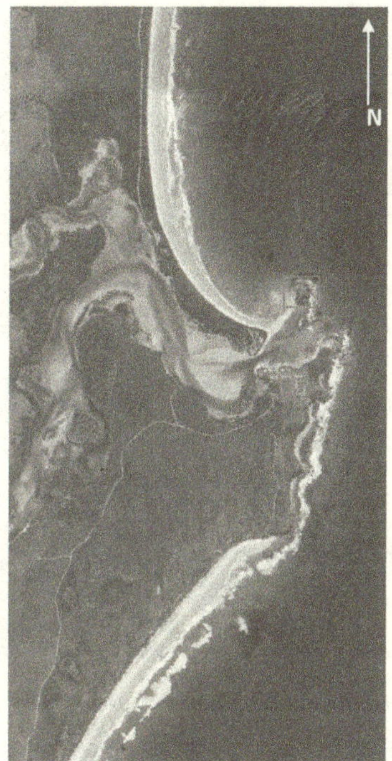

Figure 3.19: Aerial photograph of the mouth of the Sandon River showing Plover Island to the north (red box).

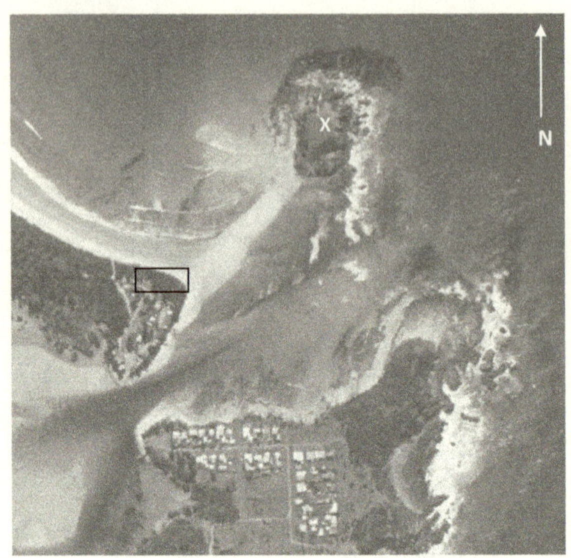

Figure 3.20: Close up of Plover Island showing the locations of the *in situ* stone artifacts (red cross), surface scatter (white cross) and managed Aboriginal shell midden deposit (black rectangle).

Figure 3.21: Plover Island showing the location of core 1P (red dot). Scale = 1:4,000

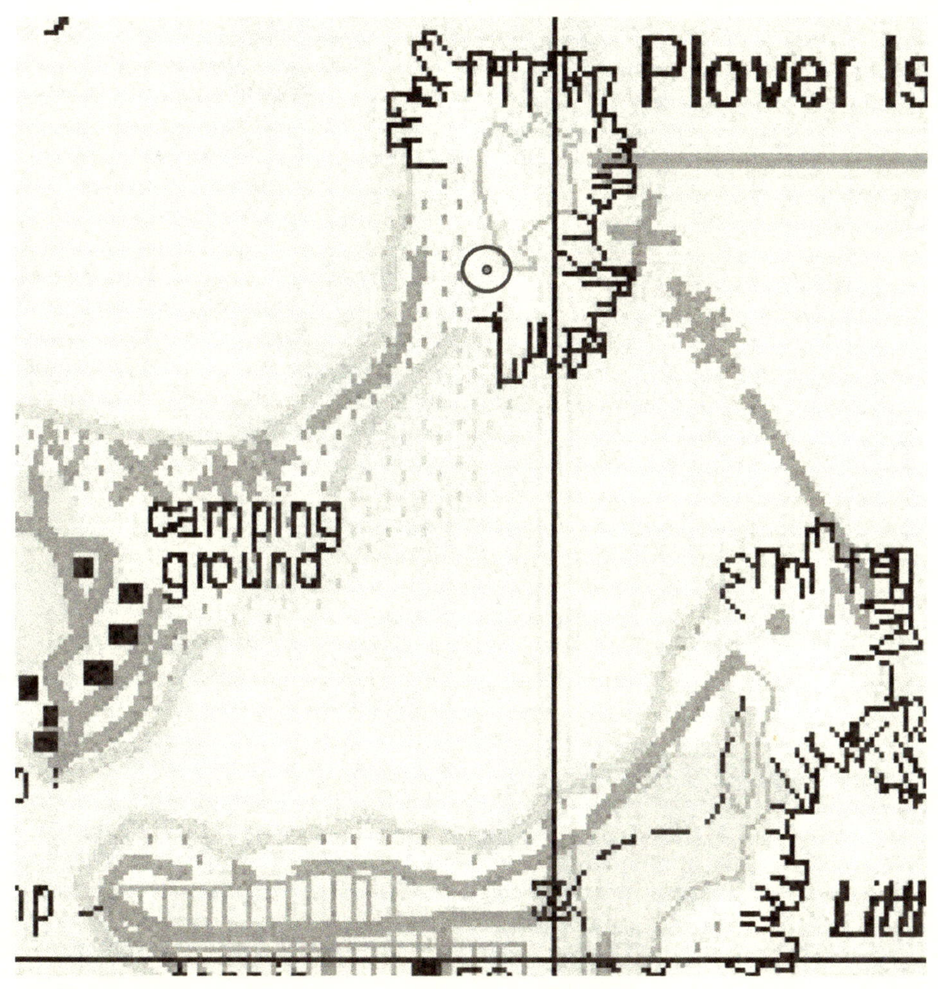

Figure 3.22: Topographic map of Plover Island showing the locaton of core 1P (circled red dot). Scale = 1:4,000

Figure 3.23: Walking track worn partially through the surface scatter of Aboriginal stone tool artifacts on Plover Island.

3.3.2 **Vegetation**

A thin layer of soil (Appendix 1 – core diagram PI) supports grasses, shrubs and small trees on Plover Island. Grasses (Poaceae) are shorter and thicker towards the seaward side of the island and shrubs are virtually absent here. This suggests the prevailing winds come from an easterly direction; their first point of contact with land is the seaward side of Plover Island. Shrubs and small trees are present around the north, west and south edges of the island and include *Acacia* sp., *Casuarina* sp., *Banksia integrifolia*, *Pandanus pedunculatus* and *Scaevola calendulacea*. A climber, *Stephania* sp., is also found with these shrubs and trees.

3.3.3 **Cultural Material**

Plover Island is the site of an Aboriginal stone quarry. Some stone artifacts are found in an *in situ* lens on the western side of the island (Figure 3.20, red cross; Figure 3.24, Plate 5) but most cultural material, including stone cores and flakes, is found in a surface scatter on the opposite side of the island (Figure 3.20, white cross; Figure 3.25). The *in situ* stone artifact exposure is 7.70 m long and sits at a depth of 0.35-0.43 m. The surface scatter is present as an arc following the shape of the eastern side of the Plover Island and is ~20.00 m long and 1.50 m wide (Figure 3.21). The surface scatter is partially covered with thick grass and partially exposed where a walking track has been worn around the perimeter of the island. Plover Island constitutes part of the Coramba Beds (Troedson and Hashimoto, 2008; Figure 2.1), predominantly comprising lithofelspathic wacke (Geoscience Australia, 2008). Stone artifacts from the Aboriginal quarry on the island share this lithology.

A lag deposit containing very well-rounded shells and cobbles is present at the base of the island on its north side (Plate 5). The origin of this deposit is uncertain as no *in situ* material has been found on the island above this deposit (see Chapter 6 for further discussion). The soil is clearly exposed around the circumference of Plover Island and is devoid of shell material.

An Aboriginal shell midden is present in the dunes adjacent to Plover Island in very close proximity to the Sandon River camping area (Figure 3.20, black box). Members of the local Yaegl Aboriginal community have been involved in the protection and preservation of this site by constructing retaining walls, revegetating dunes and advising new locations for campsites (Figure 3.26). A sign has also been erected informing campers and other tourists of the significance of the area to Yaegl people. The work done on this midden is a prime example of the effectiveness of a grass roots approach including community consultation and involvement. While the midden at Sandon is considered stable with a very low susceptibility to destruction, the quarry on Plover Island is in need of further management and thus comprises one of the study sites of this project. Even though it is not strictly a shell midden site the presence of a midden site in close proximity to the Aboriginal stone quarry on Plover Island ensures the area retains its significance as an important Aboriginal cultural site of multiple resource use.

Figure 3.24: *In situ* stone artifact lens, Plover Island. Dotted line indicates position of core 1P.

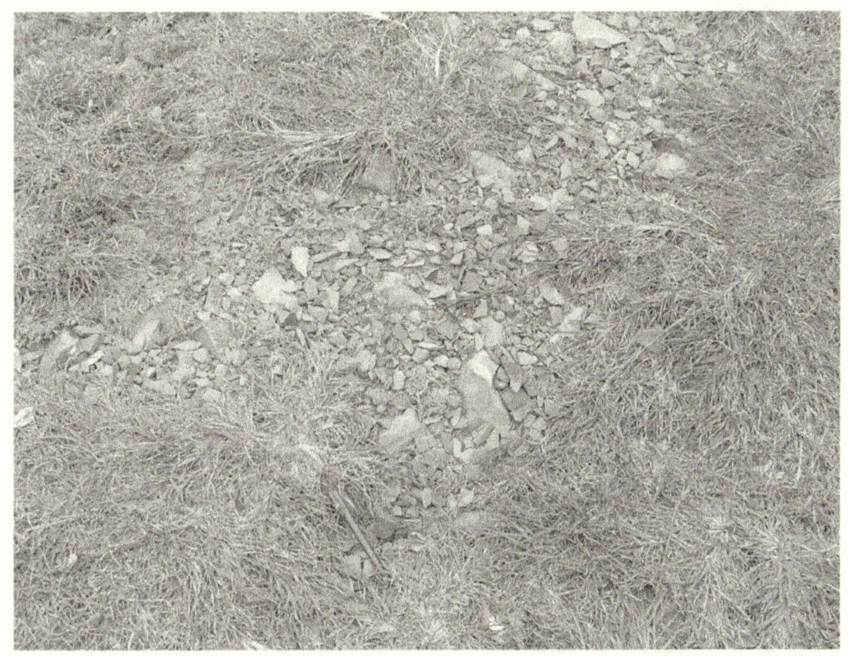

Figure 3.25: Portion of the stone artifact scatter on Plover Island.

Figure 3.26: Retaining wall at the Aboriginal shell midden site, Sandon River camping ground.

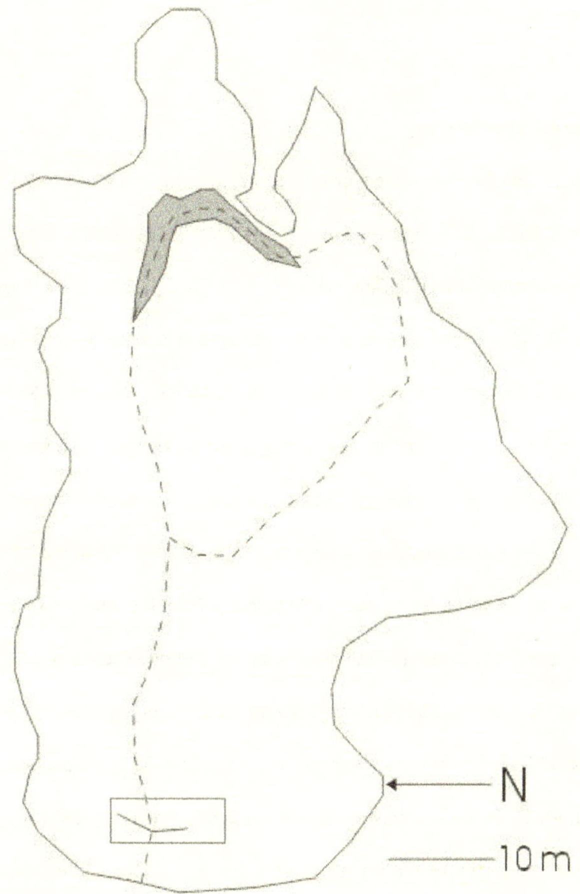

Figure 3.27: Plover Island, showing the location of the *in situ* artifact deposit (red box) and the surface artifact scatter (grey shaded area). The dotted lines show the walking track around the island.

3.4 MINNIE WATER

3.4.1 **Land Use and Geomorphology**

Rocky Point is a small rocky outcrop located at the northern end of the beach at Minnie Water (S 29°45.882', E 153°17.847', Figure 3.28A). The outcrop lies adjacent to beach foredunes forming an arc with a south to east orientation (Figures 3.28B, 3.29, 3.30). These dunes reach a maximum elevation of ~20 m above present sea level and extend ~1.6 km south along the length of the beach. The study site is located 1 km north of the town of Minnie Water and 500 m and 1.3 km from the main beach access points. Rocky Point is located within Yuraygir National Park; the Ilaroo camping ground, also located within Yuraygir National Park, lies 1 km north of the study site. Minnie Water can be accessed via the 15 km sealed Minnie Water Road or the 25 km unsealed 4WD track from Sandon. Access to the beach on the north side of Rocky Point is confined to a narrow walking track through the foredunes 10 m west of the rocky outcrop. Although access to Minnie Water is better facilitated than Sandon and Plover Island, both the Ilaroo camping area and the village of Minnie Water are small and this limits access to the area. Day trips from surrounding areas are possible however these areas are also considered holiday destinations and many of them are relatively small as well. Many of the houses at Minnie Water are holiday rental properties and so an increase in patronage is seen during peak periods such as school holidays.

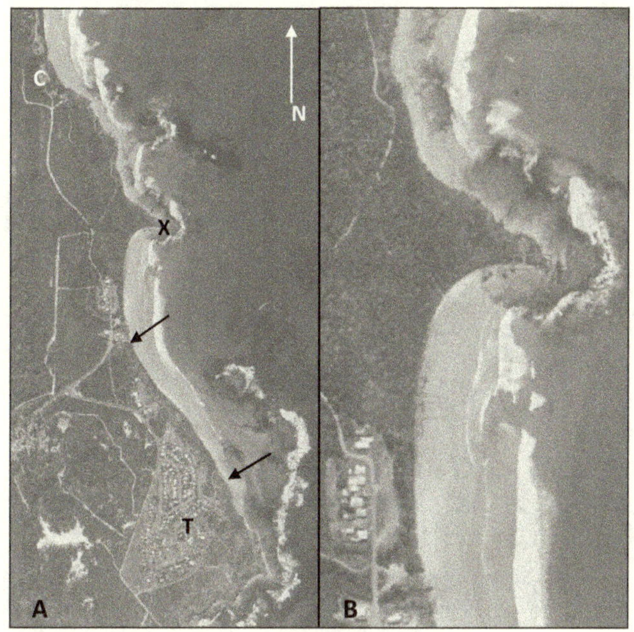

Figure 3.28: A: Aerial photograph of Minnie Water showing the study site (X), town (T), Ilaroo camp ground (C) and beach access points (arrows). **B:** Close up of Rocky Point. Box indicates the location of the midden deposit.

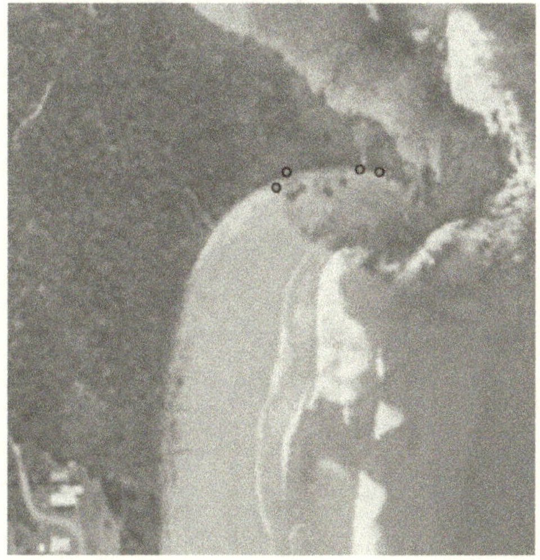

Figure 3.29: Rocky Point Headland (Minnie Water) showing the locaton of core samples. Cores 1MW to 4MW run west to east. Scale = 1:4,000

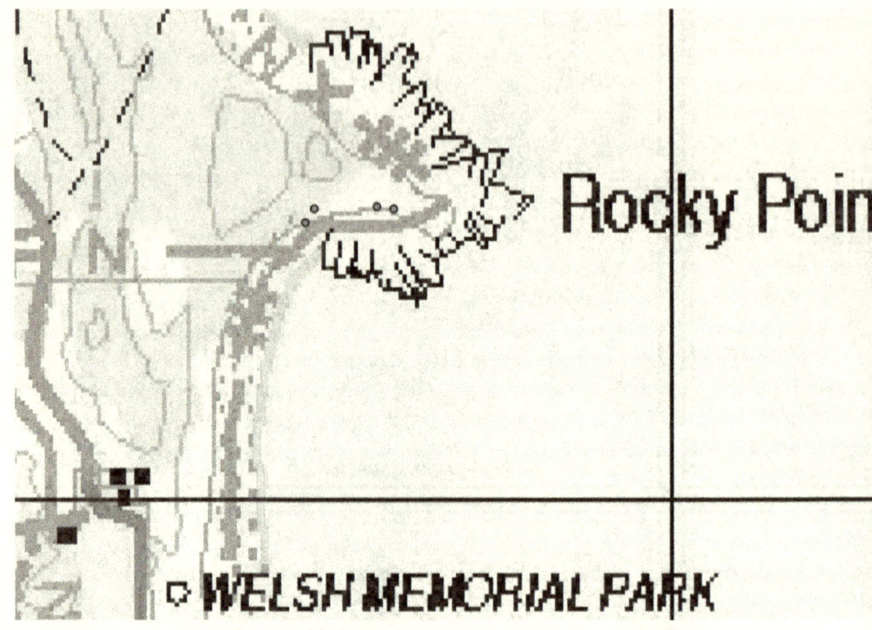

Figure 3.30: Topographic map of Rocky Point (Minnie Water) showing the location of core samples.

Cores 1MW to 4MW run west to east. Scale = 1:4,000

3.4.2 **Vegetation**

Vegetation is present on the Minnie Water foredunes, although the density of coverage is variable. Vegetation present at the Aboriginal shell midden site is similar to that seen at Sandon and Plover Island and likely reflects the similar environmental conditions in the two areas. Vegetation includes grasses (Poaceae), *Casuarina* sp. and *Banksia integrifolia*. The density of trees and shrubs increases from the base to the top of the foredunes. The patchy distribution of trees and shrubs in the dunes closest to the rocky outcrop becomes more uniform with an increased density further away from Rocky Point. Grass coverage is also variable and decreases towards the base of the dunes.

3.4.3 **Cultural Material**

An Aboriginal shell midden deposit (Figures 3.31, 3.32, 3.33, 3.35 & 3.36) containing a variety of gastropod shells is found at the base of the foredunes adjacent to the rocky outcrop at Rocky Point, Minnie Water (see Chapter 6 for species list, Plates 2 and 3). Shell material is eroding out of the exposed face of the deposit and forms a lag deposit at the base of the dunes. The 85.3 m long X 0.09-0.92 m thick X 0.35 m deep *in situ* deposit also contains gravel and pebbles, and shell material appears well-worn, suggesting the deposit may have been reworked by storm waves (see Chapter 6 for further discussion). A stone core was found in the exposed face of the *in situ* deposit (Figure 3.34).

Figure 3.31: A: A section of the exposed face of the midden deposit at Rocky Point, Minnie Water. **B:** The eroding face of the midden deposit showing the lag deposit at its base.

Figure 3.32: Location of the midden deposit at Rocky Point, Minnie Water.

Figure 3.33: Well worn *in situ* shell material at the Rocky Point midden. Scale: 1.5 cm = 1 cm.

Figure 3.34: *In situ* stone core showing points of percussion (red circle). Scale bar = 2 cm.

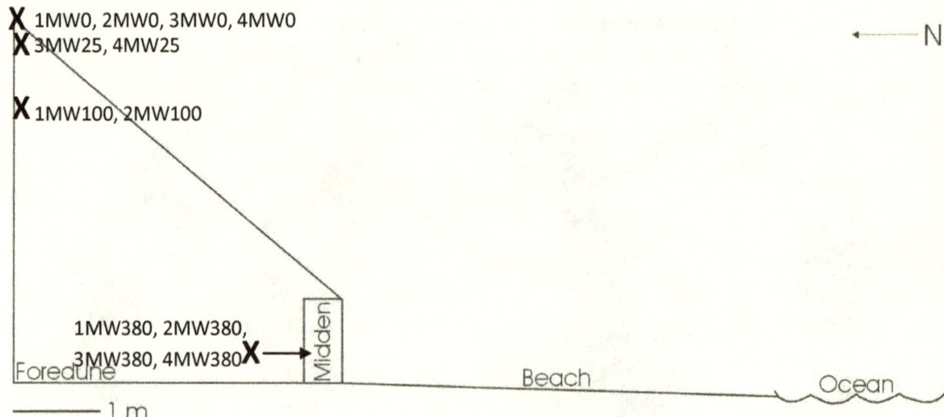

Figure 3.35: Cross section of the location of the Minnie Water Aboriginal midden. Sediment samples were taken at depths of 0 cm, 100 cm and 380 cm for cores 1MW and 2MW and 0 cm, 25 cm and 380 cm for cores 3MW and 4MW.

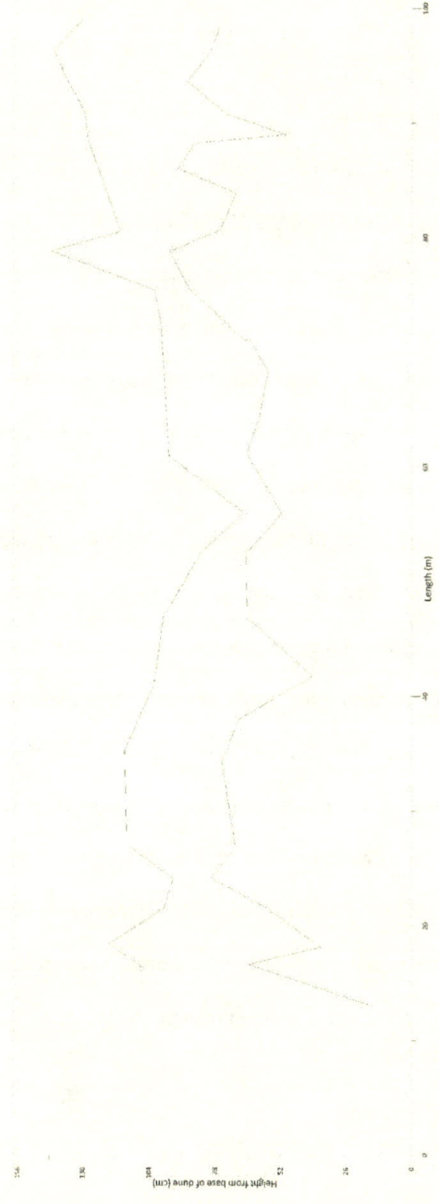

Figure 3.36: Minnie Water Aboriginal midden deposit.

3.5 WOOLI

3.5.1 **Land Use and Geomorphology**

The Aboriginal shell midden deposit at Wooli is located along a section of the western edge of Harold Lloyd Park, Wooli (S 29°52.475', E 153°15.885', Figures 3.37, 3.38). It is orientated north-south and is buried under well-vegetated, gently sloping land which runs parallel to the riverbank of the Wooli River. The width of the river is 100 m at this point and an entrance for small watercraft and people wishing to fish and swim is present over the northern edge of the deposit. This is currently not causing any disturbance to the midden, although continual use will likely erode the surface, potentially exposing the midden deposit underneath. Land use in the vicinity of the midden is recreational however a large portion of the deposit is buried under soil and a thick layer of vegetation on the fringes of the public park so it is unlikely to be continually walked over. Twenty two centimeter deep burrows (Figure 3.39) ranging from 0.05-0.15 m in diameter are scattered along the western side of the midden, although the amount of shell material that has been disturbed is very minimal (see Erosion discussion, Chapter 7). The burrowing agent/s is/are unknown but magpies and bandicoots have been suggested (Clarence Valley Council, personal communication). Wooli can be accessed via sealed Wooli Road from the Pacific Highway north of Coffs Harbour, Grafton or Maclean. As is the case at Minnie Water, many of the houses are holiday rental properties and so an increase in patronage is seen during peak periods such as school holidays, although Wooli has a larger permanent population than Minnie Water.

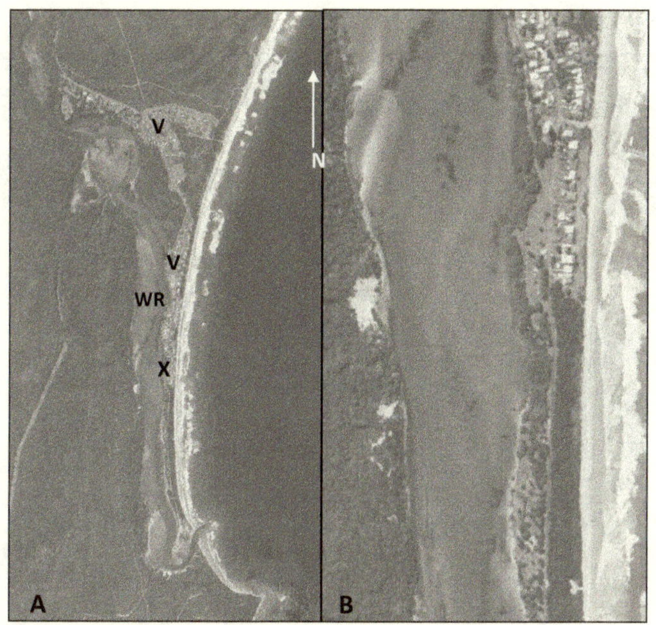

Figure 3.37: A: Aerial photograph of Wooli showing the study site (X), the village of Wooli (V) and the Wooli River (WR). **B:** Close up of Harold Lloyd Park. Box indicates the location of the midden deposit.

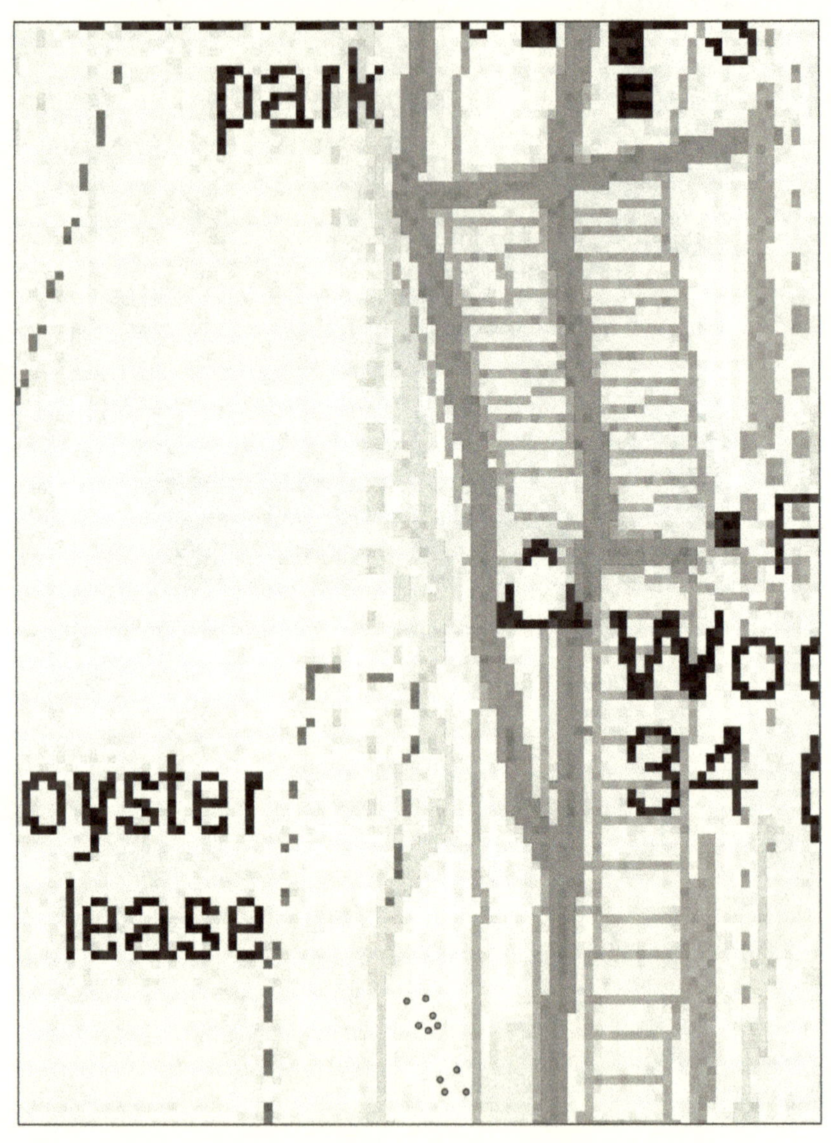

Figure 3.38: Topographic map of the Wooli study site showing the locaton of core samples. See Figure 3.42 for core labels. Scale = 1:1,600

3.5.2 **Vegetation**

The vegetation present on top of the midden deposit comprises exotic species, the most prevalent being Lantana and Buffalo grass. The adjacent, gently sloping riverbank supports dense mangrove growth. The soil lying above the midden deposit is well protected against erosion by thick vegetation coverage, thus protecting the underlying deposit. If the removal of the exotic vegetation is undertaken steps must be taken to ensure rapid re-planting of suitable species in order to preserve the soil which is protecting the midden.

3.5.3 **Cultural Material**

The Aboriginal shell midden at Harold Lloyd Park (Figures 3.40, 3.41 & 3.42) is present at a depth of 0.25 m and reaches a depth of 0.41 m at its thickest point. The deposit extends over an area of ~157 m^2. The major shellfish species present are *Anadara trapezia*, *Pyrazus ebeninus* and *Saccostrea glomerata* (see Chapter 6 for a complete species list, Plate 4). No artifacts were found in the material sampled from the 10 trenches which were dug through the midden for collection of sediment and cultural material. The next chapter outlines the methodology used in this research project. It includes field and laboratory techniques and formulation of the erosion hazard assessment methods.

Figure 3.39: A burrow through the Wooli Aboriginal shell midden showing cultural material which has been brought to the surface as a result of the burrowing process.

Figure 3.40: Photograph of the northern end of Harold Lloyd Park, Wooli. The arrow points to the boat access area discussed above. The approximate position of the northern section of the midden deposit is shown in red. The Wooli River is situated behind the mangroves.

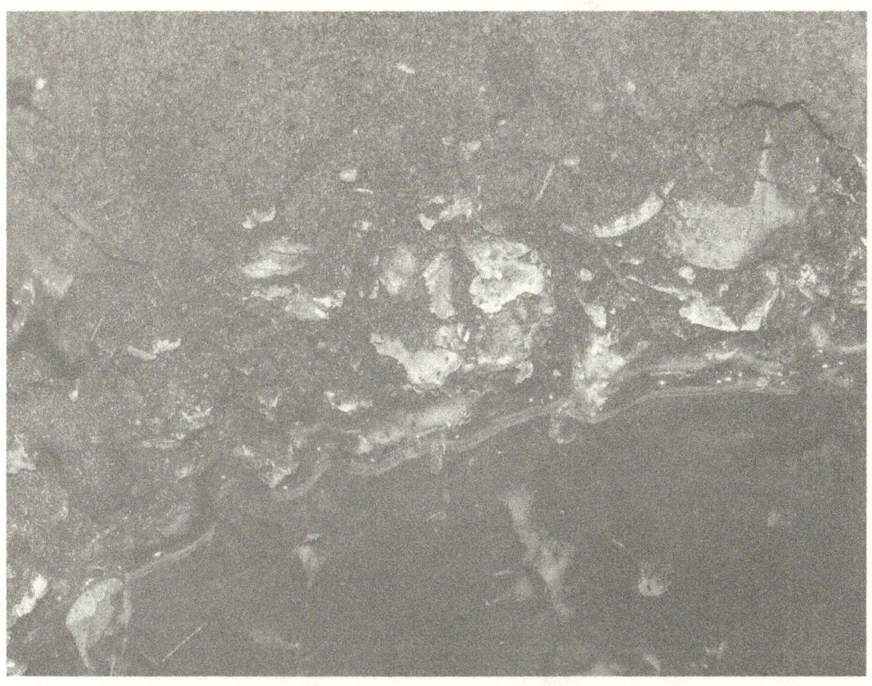

Figure 3.41: Photograph of a section of one of the trenches dug for sample collection at Harold Lloyd Park.

Note the high watertable due to the recent floods (mid-2009). Scale: 1 cm = 2 cm.

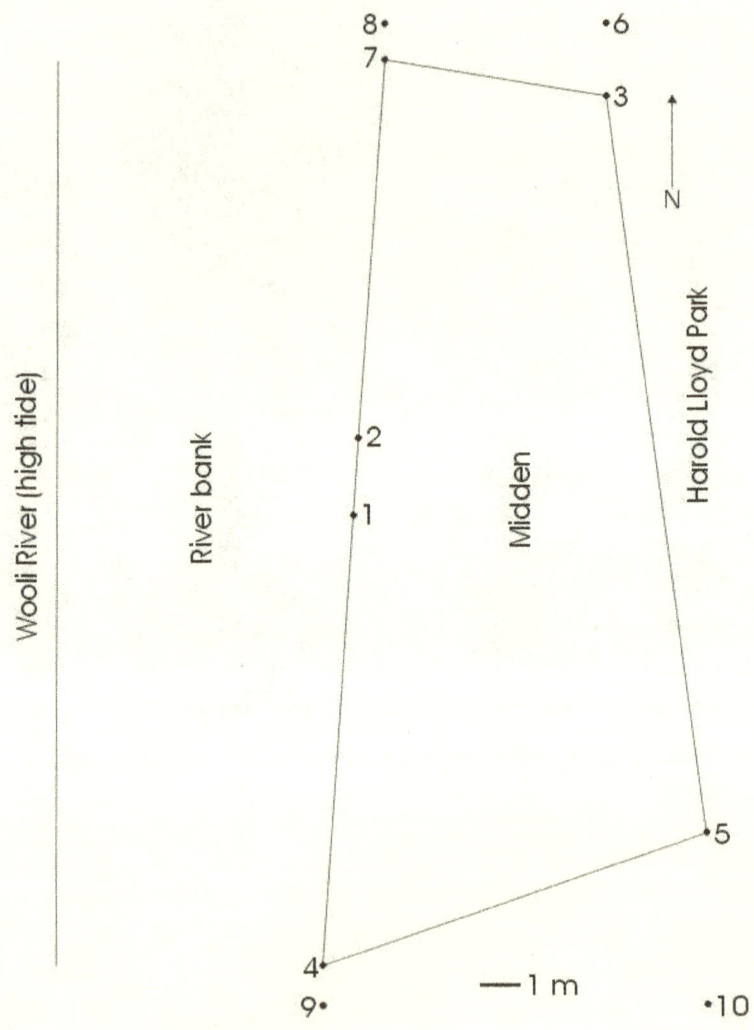

Figure 3.42: Plan view diagram of the Wooli Aboriginal midden deposit showing the locaton of core samples.

1=1WL, 2=2WL, 3=3WL, 4=4WL, 5=5WL, 6=6WL, 7=7WL, 8=8WL, 9=9WL, 10=10WL.

4. METHODOLOGY

This chapter outlines a detailed description of the methodologies used in the research project including field work, laboratory analyses and formulation of the erosion hazard assessment models. A Section 87 Permit was obtained from the NSW National Parks and Wildlife Service, Department of Environment, Climate Change and Water (DECCW)[1], prior to the commencement of field work.

4.1 FIELD METHODOLOGY

4.1.1 **Woombah**

4.1.1.1 *Shell sample collection*

A total of six *in situ* shell samples were collected from two locations at Woombah – three from one location at site A and three from one location at site B. A bed of oysters (23 m X 40 cm surface) is exposed along the riverbank at site A. Shells have eroded out of the exposure and are present as a lag deposit on the shoreline. *In situ* shells were collected for comparison with shells found at the site B midden (see Biological Analyses, Chapter 6). The purpose of this comparison was to ascertain whether or not the shells found at site A represented a food source and thus formed a natural shell deposit or whether they constitute part of the Woombah Aboriginal midden complex. Shells from site B were preferentially used for comparison over shells found in surface scatters at site A as the site B (see core diagram 3b, Appendix 1) creek bank exposure is denser, more extensive and contains whole valves and is thus believed to be the source of the shell material found in the surface scatters at both sites.

Four hundred and fifty three grams of *in situ* shell material was collected at a depth of 40-80 cm at random from the site A deposit using the pick (pointy) end of a geopick, ensuring not to damage the shells. One thousand four hundred and nine grams of *in situ* shell material was

---

[1] DECCW now operates within the Office of Environment and Heritage

collected from the site B creek bank exposure in the same way, at a depth of 35-69 cm. This depth corresponds to the relatively unfragmented shell material, as ascertained by coring and visual inspection of the creek bank exposure. The material was bagged, labeled and transported to the laboratory.

4.1.1.2 *Sediment collection/coring*

Two methods were used at Woombah to collect sediment for analysis – a corer and a hand auger. Firstly, a coring device was used at site A. The device constituted a handle for turning the corer and a barrel attachment fitted to a shaft. The barrel of the attachment was 300 mm in length and had a diameter of 80 mm. The shoe was 50 mm in length. The barrel comprised two semicircular halves which, once the shoe and shaft were removed, separated so the sore could be removed. Material from the corer was placed in 90 mm wide PVC pipe which was capped, cut into lengths of 1 m then cut in half to make 2 semicircles. The coring process was undertaken 3 times at each core, making a total length of 1 m for each core. Cores were then placed in the PVC half-pipes and wrapped securely with cling wrap.

Due to the difficulties experienced when attempting to unscrew the shoe from the barrel of the corer a different method was employed when collecting sediment at site B. A hand auger was used instead of a hand corer. The barrel of the auger was 1 m in length and tapered from 50 mm wide at the top to 30 mm wide at the tip. Holes were made with this device and the material it contained was scraped out and bagged according to stratigraphy. Separate bags were used for material from different horizons and these were carefully labeled according to depth. Five cores were taken at each site (A and B) roughly parallel to each other and extending from the riverbank north across the floodplain and up onto the first levee. Prior to bagging/wrapping and storing for transport wet Munsell colours (GretagMacbeth, 2000) and field textures were recorded for each horizon in each core sample.

On a return visit to Woombah the stratigraphy of site B was refined using the same hand auger. The augering procedure remained the same however after depths, wet Munsell colours and field textures were recorded the sediment was discarded. Auger holes were made at locations 15.7 m, 29.4 m, 33.6 m and 37.5 m north of the riverbank between core locations 5b and 4b. Another auger hole was made between core locations 2b and 1b on the edge of the floodplain adjacent to the levee rise.

Test cores were also made around the perimeter of the study sites A and B to determine the extent of the disturbed midden material (the area of the A_p layer). This area was then measured and the measurements used in the calculation of ploughing disturbance (see 'Calculation of the effect of ploughing on the Woombah middens').

4.1.1.3 *Surveying*

A survey of sites A and B at Woombah was carried out using a Leica Geosystems TC 600 (http://www.leicaus.com/support/TPS1200/TPS_Legacy_TC_00Manuals.cfm). Survey data was imported into the Grapher 6 program and plan and/or elevation maps were generated (Figures 3.13 and 3.14). Locations of core samples were recorded with a hand-held GPS and added to the GIS model of geomorphic and environmental impacts on sites in the study area (Appendix 6). The slope of the surface above the deposit was measured with a clinometer.

4.1.1.4 *Vegetation coverage estimates*

Percentage tree/shrub and grass cover were estimated at sites A and B using random 1m X 1m quadrats (Barry, 2011). These estimates are used in the erosion hazard risk assessment methodologies.

4.1.2 **Sleeper Island**

4.1.2.1 *Determination of the size of the deposit and collection of cultural material*

An Aboriginal shell midden containing *Crassostrea, Anadara, Pyrazus ebeninus* and stone artifacts is located on the western tip of the island. The contents of this midden are largely present as a lag deposit at the base of a tidal channel bank. Very little material remains *in situ*. The surface dimensions of the *in situ* and lag deposits were measured with a tape. The depth which the deposit extends back into the channel bank was measured by digging test trenches parallel to the bank. The *in situ* material visible in the eroded channel bank was counted by species. Stone artifacts and shell material present in the lag deposit were collected at random by placing 4 25*25 cm quadrats over the deposit and removing the materials inside. Subsequent to collection the material was sorted into shell and stone artifacts and these different types of material were bagged separately.

4.1.2.2 *Sediment collection/coring*

Two methods were used at Sleeper Island to collect sediment for analysis. Sediment was collected at 4 points across the Island from the midden locality on the western tip in a northeast cross section to the eastern side of the island. The first method was used at core sites 1s, 2s, 3s and 4s and the second at core sites 2s and 3s.

The first method involved using a 1.6 m long core barrel with a 50 mm diameter PVC inner tube. The corer was hammered into the ground using a slide hammer and the depth (penetration) recorded. The corer was then removed from the ground using a jack and the inner tube removed. The amount of sediment in the tube (recovery) was recorded and it was cut to size and capped.

At sites where recovery was poor (2s and 3s) a hand auger was used. At site 2s a 35 cm core was collected as described above and then a hand auger was used to collect sediment from 35-100 cm depth. This sample was bagged according to its stratigraphy as at Woombah site B. At site 3s a

26 cm core was collected and then a hand auger was used to collect sediment from 26-100 cm depth. This sample was also bagged according to its stratigraphy as at Woombah site B. When core and bagged materials were unpacked in the laboratory wet Munsell colours and field textures were recorded.

4.1.2.3 *Surveying*

A survey of Sleeper Island was carried out using a Leica Geosystems TC 600. Survey data was imported into the Grapher 6 program and plan and/or elevation maps were generated (Figure 3.9). Locations of core samples were recorded with a hand-held GPS and added to the GIS model of geomorphic and environmental impacts on sites in the study area (Appendix 6). The slope of the surface above the deposit was measured with a clinometer.

4.1.2.4 *Vegetation coverage estimates*

Percentage tree/shrub and grass cover were estimated at the sites of the *in situ* deposit and surface scatter and also over the island as a whole using random 1m X 1m quadrats. These estimates are used in the erosion hazard risk assessment methodologies.

4.1.3 **Plover Island**

4.1.3.1 *Collection of cultural material*

Minimal cultural material was collected from the stone quarry site on Plover Island. Six stone cores were collected from the *in situ* lens on the western side of the island. No cultural material was collected from the stone artifact scatter on the eastern side of the island. The taphonomic processes affecting the deposits on Plover Island could be determined relatively easily without the removal of much cultural material. The soil around the artifacts removed from the *in situ* lens was severely eroded and it is likely these artifacts would not have remained *in situ* for much longer. Collection of these specimens ensures some information is retained from a deposit facing destruction through erosion. As with all cultural material collected from study sites, these artifacts will be returned to the Yaegl community after the mandatory period of storage at the conclusion of this research project.

Stone and shell material was collected from the lag deposit at the base of Plover Island. Random grab samples were placed into snap lock bags and later separated into stone and shell components for further taphonomic study (see 'Taphonomy' and Chapter 6).

4.1.3.2 *Sediment collection/coring*

Examination of the exposed soil on Plover Island indicated its uniformity around the circumference of the island. As it was also relatively shallow (0.80 m) only one core sample was needed. A 1.00 m long hand auger was used to collect sediment at a location on the western side of Plover Island, directly adjacent to the *in situ* stone artifact lens. Wet and dry Munsell colours were noted for the A and B horizons present in the core. Sediment collected using the hand auger was bagged according to horizon (material from the A horizon in one bag, the B horizon in another). Sample bags were then dated, labelled and stored in a refrigerator until laboratory examinations were carried out.

4.1.3.3 *Surveying*

A survey of Plover Island was carried out using a Leica Geosystems TC 600. Survey data was imported into the Grapher 6 program and plan and/or elevation maps were generated (Figure 3.21). Locations of core samples were recorded with a hand-held GPS and added to the GIS model of geomorphic and environmental impacts on sites in the study area (Appendix 6). The slope of the surface above the deposit was measured with a clinometer.

4.1.3.4 *Vegetation coverage estimates*

Percentage tree/shrub and grass cover were estimated at the sites of the *in situ* deposit and surface scatter and also over the island as a whole using random 1m X 1m quadrats. These estimates are used in the erosion hazard risk assessment methodologies.

4.1.4 **Minnie Water**

4.1.4.1 *Shell sample collection*

The shell deposit was present at the base of the foredunes and the lens was clearly visible due to erosion at the site. Shell material was collected at random by placing 10 25X25 cm quadrats over the exposed face of the deposit and removing the materials inside. Shell material present in trench samples (technique discussed below) was also collected. All shell material was bagged and its location clearly marked. Five random 25X25 cm quadrat samples were also taken from separate locations along the beach within 10 m of the midden deposit. This contemporary shelly beach material was collected for the purpose of taphonomic and biological comparison with the *in situ* midden material. Material was then transported to the laboratory for further analyses.

4.1.4.2 *Sediment collection*

The Aboriginal shell midden deposit at Minnie Water sits at the base of beach foredunes up to 5 m in height. As coring through a dune to such a depth presents many challenges an alternative method of sediment collection was employed. As the sides of the dunes were steep it was possible to dig into them at given depths and obtain samples which, when *in situ*, would have been vertically aligned. The first samples were collected with a shovel from the surface (a depth of 0 cm). The next samples were collected at a depth of 1 m (cores 1 and 2) and 25 cm (cores 3 and 4). The final samples were taken at a depth of 380 cm and included midden material. Sediment was bagged and labelled according to stratum and core and transported to the laboratory for further analyses. When bagged materials were unpacked in the laboratory wet Munsell colours and field textures were recorded.

4.1.4.3 *Surveying*

A survey of the midden site at Minnie Water was carried out using a Leica Geosystems TC 600. Survey data was imported into the Grapher 6 program and plan and/or elevation maps were generated (Figure 3.27). Locations of core samples were recorded with a hand-held GPS and added to the GIS model of geomorphic and environmental impacts on sites in the study area (Appendix 6). The slope of the surface above the deposit was measured with a clinometer.

4.1.4.4 *Vegetation coverage estimates*

Percentage tree/shrub and grass cover were estimated at the site of the *in situ* deposit and over the foredunes using random 1m X 1m quadrats. These estimates are used in the erosion hazard risk assessment methodologies.

4.1.5 **Wooli**

4.1.5.1 *Shell sample collection*

As the midden deposit at this location was buried under a 25 cm thick layer of soil, trenches were dug to determine its vertical and lateral extent (see sediment collection methodology below). Shell material from these trenches was collected and bagged in the field in preparation for examination in the laboratory. Shell samples from each trench were bagged separately and labelled accordingly.

4.1.5.2 *Sediment collection*

As the shells were present as a relatively thin lens (<17 cm) and the watertable sat at a depth of <1 m in the study area a corer was not needed to collect shell and sediment samples. Ten trenches of ~30 cm square and to the depth of the watertable were dug with a shovel. Sediment samples were taken from the exposed, *in situ* sediment lining the walls of the trenches. The stratum and trench number was noted on each sample bag and the samples were stored ready for analysis in the laboratory. When bagged materials were unpacked in the laboratory wet Munsell colours and field textures were recorded.

4.1.5.3 *Map measurements*

Due to technical issues the Leica surveying equipment was not used at the Wooli Aboriginal shell midden. Test trenches indicated the perimeter of the deposit and this was measured with a tape and mapped onto graph paper (Figure 3.28). The thickness of the deposit was determined through the test trenches and this information is presented in the core diagrams of the site. Locations of core samples were recorded with a hand-held GPS and added to the GIS model of geomorphic and environmental impacts on sites in the study area (Appendix 6). The slope of the surface above the deposit was measured with a clinometer.

4.1.5.4 *Vegetation coverage estimates*

Percentage tree/shrub and grass cover were estimated over the deposit and riverbank using random 1m X 1m quadrats. These estimates are used in the erosion hazard risk assessment methodologies.

4.2 LABORATORY ANALYSES

4.2.1 **Biological Analyses**

4.2.1.1 *Percentage Composition by Weight, Size Range and Minimum Number of Individuals*

Shells collected from Woombah sites A and B, Sleeper Island, Minnie Water and Wooli were analysed to determine the percentage composition of constituent species by weight. The size range and total weight of shell species was also measured. After collection from the field shells were soaked for 12 hours in a mixture of water and detergent, rinsed and then cleaned with a toothbrush to remove sediment. Samples were then dried prior to weighing. Firstly, all shell material from each collection site was weighed on an electric balance to determine its total weight. Shells were then separated into species and weighed again. The weight of each species was recorded and percentages based on these weights were then calculated. *Crassostrea* and *Anadara trapezia* shells were then separated into upper and lower valves and these samples were also weighed. They were then sorted until the smallest and largest upper and lower valves were found and these shells were measured to determine the size range of the valves from the sample sites. Size range data were collected from whole valves only. Data are presented in Table 6.1.

Two counts were made on *A. trapezia* material. The first set was based on individual shells which had their umbo intact. Counts for the second set of percentage composition by weight calculations involved counting the highest number of hinges of one side to give the MNI (Ulm, 2006). Only upper valves with their umbo intact were included in MNI *Crassostrea* counts and when counting gastropods, only those specimens with their aperture intact were included.

A percentage composition by weight calculation was used to compare the shell deposits found at Woombah sites A and B to account for all the shell material in the samples. Upper and lower *Crassostrea* valves were also weighed separately in order to determine whether or not there was a taphonomic bias for one valve type. Size range was measured for *Crassostrea* valves as an additional means by which to compare the two deposits. Percentage composition by weight and species was used to compare the Minnie Water *in situ* and lag deposits to help give an indication of site integrity. A comparison of taphonomic and species composition characteristics is broad-ranging and therefore increased in accuracy over a comparison of one of these groups of characteristics alone. Other analyses such as percentage total weight per horizon or stratum and soil: shell ratios will be very useful at sites with multiple strata or occupation layers.

In situ counts were made at Sleeper Island (see field methodology – Sleeper Island) and these were then added to the counts of minimum numbers of individuals. Average weights for the three shellfish species contained in the midden were then calculated, however in *situ counts* were excluded in these calculations as their weights were not measured and therefore did not add to the total weights determined for the sample material.

4.2.1.2 *Number of identified specimens (NISP)*

This is a measure of the number of shell fragments identifiable to a particular taxon (Ulm, 2006). Although this method can be limited by the level of identifiability of fragmented shell it can be useful for examining shell fragmentation rates in deposits containing highly fragmented shell (Ulm, 2006). All deposits contained a negligible amount of highly fragmented, unidentifiable shell. Wet-sieving (3 mm sieve) of the matrix surrounding collected shell specimens from these deposits confirmed this field observation, therefore this method was not applied to these deposits.

4.2.2 **Taphonomic Analyses**

Taphonomic, sedimentological and stratigraphic features were documented at each of the study sites and compiled into tables modified after Kidwell (1991) – Attributes of Shell Concentrations (Tables 6.4, 6.5, 6.7, 6.8, 6.9, 6.10). A different table was compiled for each shell deposit. Additional analyses were performed on shell material from the Woombah Site A and B deposits and the Minnie Water midden and lag deposits in order to refine likely site formation processes.

Shell samples from Woombah Sites A and B were analysed to determine the most common region of breakage and also the percentage of fragmented shell material by weight (Table 6.6). Shell material from the Minnie Water midden and lag deposits was analysed to determine the amount of abrasion and biological modification as a percentage of material affected (Figures 6.8 and 6.9).

4.2.3 **Loss on Ignition – measurement of organic content of soil samples**

Subsamples from each horizon present in the core samples were dried in an oven at 110°C for 24 hours. This material was subsequently prepared for the furnace as follows (Heiri, Lotter & Lemcke, 2001). Metal crucibles were weighed to 2 decimal places using an electric balance. A quantity of subsample was then added and the crucibles were re-weighed. All weights were recorded. Subsample weights were then calculated. Subsamples were then heated in a furnace at 430°C for 48 hours to burn off any organic material. After removal from the furnace material was cooled in a closed container for 15 minutes and then weighed immediately to 2 decimal places using an electric balance. These weights were recorded. The difference between the initial weights after drying at 110°C and the final weights was calculated. The difference in these weights indicates the amount of organic matter present in each of the subsamples (Appendix 2).

4.2.4 **Emerson Aggregate Test**

Aggregate stability was determined using samples from A and B horizon soils at all study sites. The method used to determine aggregate stability was the Emerson Aggregate Test (Department of Sustainable Natural Resources Soil Survey Standard Test Method Version 2; Emerson, 1967). Following are a list of steps used in this study for each sample analysed:

1. Three air-dry aggregates 5-10 mm in diameter were placed, equally spaced, in 75 ml deionised water.

2. After 2 and 20 hours aggregate behaviour was assessed. The presence of slaking or swelling was noted along with degree of dispersion.

3. Emerson Class Numbers were then determined.

4. For samples which showed slaking but no dispersion after 20 hours, 30-40 g fresh air-dry aggregate was placed in a mixing bowl and mixed for 30 seconds with sufficient deionised water to increase the soil moisture content to within the plastic range.

5. A 5 mm cube of the soil was moulded using a spatula and placed in 75 ml of deionised water. The degree of dispersion was rated after 2 and 20 hours and Emerson Class Numbers were then determined using the table in Department of Sustainable Natural Resources Soil Survey Standard Test Method Version 2.

4.2.5 **Sand:Silt:Clay Ratio**

4.2.5.1 *Sample preparation*

Following the methodology outlined in Harfield *et al.* (1985), subsamples from each horizon present in the core samples were dried in an oven at 110°C for 24 hours. They were then ground with a mortar and pestle where necessary. The subsamples were then poured through a sample splitter until a final subsample of ~40 g was obtained. This step ensured a representative subsample was being prepared for the particle sizer. The final subsamples were then placed in a beaker to which a 10% solution of H2O2 was added to digest the organic material present in the sediment. The beakers containing the bubbling samples were then covered, placed on a hot plate in a fume hood and heated to ~50°C. Samples were removed from the fume hood when the bubbling had stopped, as this indicated the organic material had been digested. As the sediment had settled, the liquid was then discarded from each beaker.

Samples were then rinsed into labelled centrifuge tubes with distilled water and each cartridge was axially balanced using an electric balance and topped up with distilled water as required. Samples were centrifuged for 10 minutes at 2000 rpm. After centrifugation the samples were removed from the centrifuge and the supernatant discarded. They were then rinsed and the centrifugation process repeated.

After washing into their labelled beakers samples were placed in a fume hood and mixed with a 10% solution of acetic acid to digest any carbonate material that may be present. Bubbling samples were covered and heated on a hot plate at ~50°C until bubbling had ceased, taking up to 72 hours. The centrifugation process outlined above was then repeated twice. After centrifugation samples were mixed with a deflocculating agent and allowed to stand for 24 hours. They were then wet-sieved through a 2000 µm sieve to separate the larger gravel-sized particles from the material to be analysed in the Malvern Mastersizer (www.malvern.com/mastersizer). The gravel-sized portion was then dried and weighed and the results added to the data obtained from the Malvern Mastersizer.

4.2.5.2 *Particle size analysis*

A Malvern Mastersizer was used for particle size analysis. At least three subsamples were run from each prepared sample. Beakers containing sample sediment were placed under an electric mixer for the duration of the sampling process to ensure representative subsamples were analysed. Subsamples were taken from each beaker using disposable 3 ml droppers and placed into the refractive medium (deionised water) drop by drop until the laser obscuration was within range (10-20%). Laser obscuration for all subsamples from each sample was kept as consistent as possible.

After an initial run the first subsample from each prepared sample was treated with ultrasonics, applied by the Malvern Mastersizer for 30 seconds, and run again. Results of the two runs were then compared. If results were in good statistical agreement ultrasonics were not applied to subsequent subsamples unless the results from those subsamples differed significantly from previous runs. Where the two sets of results (treated with ulttrasonics or not treated) differed significantly the results gained after application of ultrasonics were retained. Average results from retained subsample runs were calculated and these data are presented and analysed in this Book.

4.2.6 **Flood and Tide Hazard Analyses**

In order to quantify the flooding hazard at Aboriginal midden sites at Woombah, Sleeper Island and Wooli a method was devised by the researcher which uses information on flood heights and return periods and site elevation. The aim of these calculations was to determine the level of flooding (and thus the return period) to which a site is vulnerable, based on its elevation. The minimum depth of each deposit corresponds to its maximum elevation and this was the level used as a reference flood level, as floods reaching this elevation would totally inundate the deposit. In order to accurately determine the maximum elevation of each *in situ* midden deposit the sites were visited at high tide and a measurement was taken from the water surface to the minimum depth (maximum elevation) of the deposit. This measurement was then added to the known high tide level, giving an elevation in metres above Lowest Astronomical Tide (mLAT), the standard datum for tide height measurements. This elevation was then converted to the Australian Height Datum (mAHD) by adding 0.895, the fixed difference between LAT and AHD at the Yamba tide gauge (see equations 1 and 2 below). Using flood data provided by Manly Hydraulics and the Clarence Valley Floodplain Services (Appendix 4) the flood level matching the maximum elevation of each deposit was located and the corresponding ARI noted (Table 7.5). Thus, the risk of total inundation by flooding was calculated for the sites mentioned above.

1: Distance from high tide water surface to top of *in situ* midden deposit + height of high tide = maximum elevation of deposit (mLAT)

2: Maximum elevation of deposit (mLAT) + 0.895 = maximum elevation of deposit (mAHD)

When assessing the impact of tidal inundation on the Aboriginal shell midden sites at Woombah, Sleeper Island and Wooli two sets of results were generated (Table 7.6). The first set of calculations was based on the 2009-2010 tide predictions for the Yamba and Wooli gauges. The second set was based on the actual occurrence of tides over an 18-20 year period (Appendix 4, data from NSW Department of Commerce, Manly Hydraulics Laboratory).

Tidal predictions for the Yamba tide gauge for the period from July 2009-June 2010 were analysed to determine the predicted frequency of tidal inundation of the sites mentioned above. As tide height is measured in metres above Lowest Astronomical Tide site elevations calculated using equation 1 above were used in the tidal inundation calculations. The maximum elevation of the deposits in mLAT corresponds with the minimum tide height required to fully inundate these deposits. The number of times tide heights greater than or equal to the maximum LAT site elevations were predicted to occur were counted. This gave a predicted frequency of inundation for the twelve months from July 2009-June 2010.

The elevation of Aboriginal shell midden sites at Woombah (A and B), Sleeper Island and Wooli was also used to determine the tidal inundation class of these sites. Tidal inundation classes are based on the frequency of occurrence of measured tide heights over an 18-20 year period and have been formulated by Manly Hydraulics Laboratory. Appendix 4 shows tidal ranges and their corresponding inundation classes. This is a measure of the relative likelihood of tidal inundation of midden sites based on the frequency of tide heights occurring at Yamba and Wooli over the past 18-20 years.

4.2.7 **Calculation of erosion rates**

In order to quantify the erosion clearly visible at Sleeper Island and Woombah river bank site A channel measurements were taken from different sources. Historic parish maps were available for the years 1914, 1915, 1919, 1923, 1926, 1933, 1936, 1943, 1954, 1958, 1961 and 1967 for Sleeper Island and 1912, 1919, 1921, 1931 and 1936 for Woombah (courtesy of the Department of Lands). Topographic maps of the areas dated at 1986 and aerial photographs dated at 2005 were also used.

Measurements of the width of channels between Sleeper and Freeburn Islands, Sleeper Island and the mainland, and Woombah and Yargai Island (part of the North Arm of the Clarence River) were made using a ruler and then converted to distances using the scales provided on the maps and photos.

As there was agreement among the historic sources and among the recent sources the difference between these distances (historic and recent) was used to calculate the difference per year, giving the erosion or deposition rate. Where the channel appeared wider in contemporary measurements the rate calculated represents the erosion rate. Where the channel appeared narrower the rate calculated represents the rate of deposition. The rates calculated are minimum rates; there are no data for the 19 years between 1967 and 1986 so it is not known when the difference in the channel measurements started. Calculation of the erosion and deposition rates using the method outlined above proved inconclusive due to differences in measurements between sources and an absence of data for the 19 year period between 1967 and 1986.

4.2.8 **Calculation of erosion hazard**

4.2.8.1 *Introduction*

Table 4.1 outlines selected methods of erosion hazard assessment. In this context hazard assessment is defined as 'the process of estimating, for defined areas, the probabilities of the occurrence of potentially damaging phenomenon of given magnitudes within a specified period of time. Hazard assessment involves the analysis of formal and informal historical records, and skilled interpretation of existing topographical, geological, geomorphological, hydrological and land use maps' (European Centre on Geomorphological Hazards). Hazard assessment is an essential prerequisite of risk analysis, defined as 'the use of available information to estimate the risk to individuals or populations, property or the environment, from hazards' (European Centre on Geomorphological Hazards).

The methods of erosion hazard assessment outlined in Table 4.1 have a geomorphic rather than archaeological focus and many require complex inputs, algorithms and computer modelling. Of the field-based techniques many are designed for use on agricultural land for impact or suitability assessment; others are formulated for use in specific geomorphic settings such as rivers or riparian zones. The methods used in this study must be standardised in order to gain consistent and reliable results and must be applicable to Aboriginal midden deposits in a range of geomorphic settings.

A number of the methods presented in Table 4.1 use a factorial scoring system where combined impacts are scored and then given an overall ranking corresponding to the degree of erosion impact or suitability for certain land use practices. The factors impacting erosion are themselves largely quantifiable. This ensures reliable data are collected and data on subsequent landscape change can be directly compared with that collected at other points in time. Scoring of these measurements/impacts is somewhat arbitrary and relies on consistent and well-defined methodology. Stocking and Murnaghan (2001) note that development of one's own specific ranking system is appropriate when requiring a specific and comprehensive view of land degradation, providing the system is used consistently.

Three methods have been developed by the researcher to assess erosion hazard at the study sites. The first method assesses factors contributing to erosion using quantifiable and semi-quantifiable outcomes. It has been designed for use by professional archaeologists and geomorphologists. The second method is a rapid, field-based erosion hazard assessment formulated for use by Aboriginal communities as a cultural heritage management tool. This method includes a numerical ranking system, the Erosion Hazard Index, and a set of recommendations for maintenance and conservation of Aboriginal shell midden sites. The third is a GIS model formulated in ArcMap using data on soils, vegetation coverage, slope, Quaternary surface and subsurface sediment age and dominant texture and land use at the landscape scale (Webb *et al.*, 2009). This method also includes a numerical ranking system.

Table 4.1: Selected methods of erosion hazard assessment.

METHOD	DESCRIPTION	ADVANTAGES	DISADVANTAGES	REFERENCE(S)
Landscape processes at archaeological sites located within arid-land river corridors interpreted using analyses of sedimentary structures and particle size distributions.	Investigation of the sedimentological characteristics distinguishing fluvial, aeolian, slope-wash, colluvial and debris-flow-dominant deposits at archaeological sites in the Colorado River corridor, Grand Canyon, Arizona, USA. Identification of depositional facies by combining sedimentary structures with grain size analyses.	• Uses sedimentological analyses in a broader context to gauge contemporary vulnerability of, and risk to, archaeological sites.	• This particular case study focuses on arid zone archaeological sites. • Generation of results requires large-scale field work and extensive laboratory analyses and is thus unsuitable for use in a rapid, field-based methodology designed for use at a grass roots level.	Draut *et al.*, 2008.
Coding system for soil erosion appraisal in the field.	Proforma for recording soil erosion in the field includes climate (rainfall and temperature), vegetation (type, % ground cover and tree/shrub cover), slope characteristics including position and degree of slope, soil characteristics including depth, surface texture and erodibility, and degree of erosion. Accompanying erosion coding system is a numerical ranking from 0 to 5. Each erosion code number is accompanied by a set of indicators.	• Takes into account multiple indicators in a format which can be readily completed in the field.	• Does not take into account that different erosion indicators may be present in different geomorphic contexts.	Morgan, 1995.
Semi-quantitative ranking scale for land degradation	Land degradation and conservation potential based on ranking of sheet erosion,	• Farmer-perspective approach – user-	• Designed to assess agricultural land	Stocking & Murnaghan,

hazard.	rill erosion and crop management considerations. Designed for use by farmers at the detailed field-level. Sheet and rill erosion are given a ranking between 0 and 3 (absent – severe), based on the degree of soil loss as evidenced by field indicators such as evidence of surface wash, pedestal development and root exposure. Crop management considerations are also given a score between 1 and 3, inclusive. These scores are based on the degree to which crop management indicators effectively conserve the soil and act to inhibit erosion. Scores for these three indicators of land degradation (sheet and rill erosion and crop management) are then averaged to produce an overall score between 1 and 3, which corresponds to land degradation hazard	friendly system. • Indicators of land degradation can be assessed, scored and ranked separately with respect to their seriousness – combining indicators gives a more holistic viewpoint and is more likely to include correct weighting of indicators. • Clearly defined method which is well set out.	degradation and conservation – crop management considerations would not be very useful for the current study.	2001; Douglas, 1997.
EHR (erosion hazard rating).	Factorial scoring system for rating erosion risk. Based on 5 categories of erosion: erosivity, cover (mm of rainfall), slope (degrees), erodibility and human occupation (persons/km^2). These categories are rated 1 to 5 in severity of likelihood to cause erosion. Scores for each of these 5 factors are summed to give a total score which is compared with an arbitrary erosion risk classification system. Under this system dominant factors – those with the highest scores within the categories mentioned above – are placed in subgroups. Thus, when areas are mapped according to their erosion risk, subgroups (dominant factors contributing to erosion risk) are also visible.	• Easy to use system. Factorial scoring/classification system. • Can readily include factors which cannot be easily quantified in any other way.	• Although maps show dominant factor subgroups (see Table …), there is independent treatment of each factor (does not allow for interaction between factors). • Factors are not weighted.	Stocking & Elwell, 1973; Morgan, 1986.

Land capability classification.	System developed by the United States Soil Conservation Service and adapted for use in many other countries. It is a semi-detailed assessment of the extent to which erosion risk, soil depth, wetness and climate affect the agricultural potential of the land. Suitability for agriculture and other uses is based on the capability unit, which consists of a group of soils similar in profile form, slope and erosion. Capability units are grouped into subclasses according to their limiting factors and these subclasses are in turn grouped into classes based on the nature of their limiting factor. Each of these land capability classes has been assigned a set of characteristics and accompanying land use recommendations.	• Erosivity data can be combined with information gained from land capability surveys to yield a more detailed assessment of erosion risk.	• Used as an indicator of the potential of arable land. • Used as an indicator of erosion risk due to current farming activity (ie. areas susceptible to agricultural soil erosion). • Attention to recreational use of land is insufficient – according to the capability classification land is only set aside for recreation when it is considered too marginal for farming.	Morgan, 1986.
Rapid assessment technique for determining the physical and environmental conditions of rivers in Queensland.	A relatively simple rapid survey method which can be undertaken by inexperienced staff after a relatively short training period. Catchment waterways are subdivided into small sections using attributes such as geology, stream gradient and land use. Eleven data sheets are used during the survey. Some are completed using existing data and others in the field. Datasets with a similar focus to the current Aboriginal shell midden impacts research include bank condition and scenic, recreational and	• Surveys can be undertaken relatively rapidly by non-scientist laypeople with knowledge of the land. • Framework over which other data can be laid. • Encompasses a broad spectrum of river condition parameters	• Formulae used to derive attributes and weightings are arbitrary, although based on the best available information, and are thus open to debate. • Physical habitat parameters are measured as	Jackson & Anderson, 1994.

	conservation values. Data pertaining to bank condition include the location and extent of any bank instability (erosion, aggradation or slumping) along with factors identified in the field which may be affecting this stability. A subjective assessment of scenic, recreational and conservation values is included in the survey and uses various rating scales to provide overall value assessments for each section. Data contained within the various datasets are then assigned a percentage value which has been appropriately weighted in terms of the importance of each dataset at each survey location. Percentage values can range from 0 to 100%, where 100% represents the standard for local pristine sites or those in very good condition. This allows different standards to be used in different areas. Ratings for individual sections of a river are combined using cluster analysis to give an overall condition rating.	– suitable for ecological and utilitarian management. • Trends or rates of change in condition can be established through follow-up surveys. • Data can be displayed within a GIS. • Ranking scale base on standardised rankings.	indicators of ecological condition and assumptions have been made regarding which parameters are important to measure. • Survey essentially an ecological one – includes some useful parameters for the current study such as bank condition and scenic, recreational and conservation values – along with others which may be less valuable such as water quality and aquatic habitat.	
DEFRA (Department for Environment, Food and Rural Affairs, London) risk ranking scale.	System of erosion risk assessment which aims to be easily understood and implementable by all UK farmers and useable on a field-by-field basis. Soil texture and slope are assessed by the farmer after which a map of ranking from very high to low risk is produced for the farm. A ranking of erosion-susceptible land uses is also provided by DEFRA and this outlines combinations of soil texture, slope	• Designed for non-scientist laypeople with knowledge of the land. • Useable on a field-by-field basis. • Appropriate scale for current research. • Quantitative. • Standardised	• Designed for use on agricultural land. • Doesn't consider the cumulative impact of runoff from a series of connected fields – parcels of land considered in	Boardman *et al.*, 2009.

	and crop type which lead to high risk of erosion.	method.	isolation with regards to field boundary permeability.	
SICOM (site comparison method).	Uses complex algorithms and matrices with many data sources, inputs and variables to generate a COG (comparison group) number. COG numbers range from 0 (high quality) to 5 (low quality) and rank agri-environmental conditions. Results are more likely to be used in political decision-making and to check regional handling and allocation of subsidies rather than to take action to prevent wind and water erosion at a grass roots level. Designed for evaluation of ecological measures at different administrative rather than landscape scales.	• Broad, standardised numerical ranking system which use quantifiable data.	• Many data sources, inputs and variable. • Complex algorithms and matrices are not user-friendly at the grass roots level. • Designed to rank agri-environmental conditions rather than archaeological or broader environmental conditions. • Focus on administrative rather than landscape scales.	Deumlich *et al.*, 2006.
TRARC (tropical rapid appraisal of riparian condition).	A method developed for rapid on-ground qualitative visual assessment of the environmental condition of wet-dry tropical savanna riparian zones. Indicators of riparian zone condition are used by land managers to assess riparian areas in tropical savannas in a consistent and cost-effective manner. These health indicators are grouped into categories which reflect the functions of the riparian zone: vegetation	• Rapid, field-based method. • Health indicators reflect the functions of the riparian zone. • Consistent and cost-effective. • Most appropriate at spatial scales from 1 km to 200 km river	• Focus on savanna riparian zones. • Ranked data format inhibits precise detection of change, thus less suited for multi-temporal analysis, however image data can	Johansen *et al.*, 2007.

	cover and leaf litter, regeneration of native plants, weediness, bank stability and disturbance/pressures. Broad score categories ranging from 0 to 4 (poor to good condition) were created to reduce user variability in visual assessment of riparian health indicators. Each indicator is assigned a score during field survey and these scores are then used to derive a total score out of 100 which reflects the overall condition of the riparian zone studied.	sections.	provide detailed information on gradual change.	
Rosgen Classification and associated Natural Channel Design.	Classifies and predicts the stability and behavior of a river based on its appearance. Morphological, hydraulic and sedimentological data including water surface slope, bedload transport rate, total sediment yield, bankfull mean velocity, shear stress, friction factor and roughness coefficient are calculated and used to classify rivers into different morphological types and stability classes.	• Classification good as a communication tool (types of rivers).	• Very complex requiring advanced formal training courses, even a 2 week course for professional geomorphologists, geologists and engineers. • Past 14 years work, with the exception of Rosgen, 1994, hasn't passed through accepted channels of peer review. • Some peers (Simon *et al.*, 2008; Miller & Ritter, 1996) have issues with classifications	Rosgen, 2008; 1994; Simon *et al.*, 2008; Miller & Ritter, 1996.

			being used in a predictive sense for management purposes – a variety of predicted possible responses is more useful than constrained responses based on Rosgen Classification. • Focus on rivers only.	
BEHI (bank erosion hazard index).	Represents a part of the Pfankuch-Rosgen channel stability rank based on stream characteristics. Measurements of the bank height to bankfull ratio, root depth to bank height ratio, root density (%), bank angle and % surface protection are indexed with a range of measurements falling within each index range. Indexed scores for each of the measurements listed above are then added to give a total score between 5 and 50, corresponding to a hazard or risk rating between very low and extreme, respectively.	• Takes into account a range of quantifiable bank characteristics. • Relatively easy to measure in the field.	• Channel stability ranking only – the current project covers many geomorphic settings.	Rosgen, 2001
ERI (erosion risk index).	Assessment of soil erosion risk using data from soil hydrological characteristics (infiltration-runoff ratio), rainfall aggressiveness and slope. Based on 2 equations incorporating the Fournier Index for determining erosion risk under differing rainfall aggressiveness, and runoff potential as a function of soil structure and soil	• Measured at an appropriate scale for the current research. • Quantitative.	• Too complex for rapid field assessment. • Appears to be designed for use on agricultural land.	Lobo *et al.*, 2005.

	particle size. Used in combination with the PI (productivity index) as a measure of agricultural damage/suitability.			
AUSLEM (Australian land erodibility model).	A computer model designed to predict land susceptibility to wind erosion in western Queensland. It operates on a daily time-step at a 5 km X 5 km spatial resolution. Inputs include grass and tree cover, soil moisture, soil texture and surficial stone cover. Aims to track spatial and temporal variability in dust emissions.	• Daily time-step ie. not static.	• Designed only for measurement of wind erosion. • Complex computer model. • Resolution not tight enough for the current study.	Webb *et al.*, 2009.

4.2.8.2 *Method one: Assessment of disturbance processes, their contributory factors and outcomes*

Appendix 5 shows disturbance processes contributing to erosion of Aboriginal shell middens in the study area. Each process has a set of contributory factors with quantifiable or semi-quantifiable outcomes. Assessment of these outcomes is based on interpretation of field evidence, aerial photographs, current and historic maps, wind rose data and information on tidal flows and flooding. Data sources are also included for each outcome in an adjacent column. Major factors contributing to bank erosion include bank stability, frequency of tidal inundation, position of the bank in a channel and human activity (land and watercourse usage). Factors affecting potential vulnerability to wind erosion include deposit stability (stability of the matrix), exposure to prevailing winds and human activity. Ocean swell is the main factor causing wave erosion. Processes of cultivation and excavation are also considered.

Percentage vegetation cover (grasses and shrubs/trees) was used as a key indicator of bank stability. This variable can be measured relatively easily in the field and supplementary information can be found in aerial photographs. In this study percentage cover of grass and shrubs and trees was calculated in the field. Ground coverage of grasses, shrubs and trees was measured at the base of the plants and is a measure of the vegetation coverage in contact with the ground surface. Vegetation coverage was measured in this way as soil in close proximity to channel banks in the study area appears to be more susceptible to processes such as channel flow, tidal inundation and flooding than to rainsplash. Vulnerability to erosion was then interpreted based on the erosion-cover relationship graph of Stocking (1994, Figure 7.23).

Tide height was used as a key indicator of the susceptibility of a site to tidal inundation. The elevation of the midden deposits was calculated using known tide heights. At high tide the distance between the surface of the water and the top of the midden deposit was measured and this gave a maximum elevation for each site in mLAT (Lowest Astronomical Tide). These values were then used to assign each relevant site a Tidal Inundation Class (calculated using data provided by New South Wales Department of Commerce, Manly Hydraulics Laboratory; Appendices 4 and 5), with classes 1-5 representing most to least often occurring tide heights.

Fetch is a key indicator of wave height and was chosen as it can easily be measured from a topographic map. The width of the channel was measured and this gives a distance over which waves can form on the surface of the water as a result of the action of wind. Bank position in a channel was assessed by looking at the surrounding geomorphology. Whilst not quantifiable, this interpretation can be made relatively easily by studying air photos and topographic maps. Bank position in a channel was divided into 3 possible categories based on geomorphology. The bank could either be situated in an erosional setting on the outside of a meander bend, a depositional setting on the inside of a meander bend, or a sheltered/protected location such as opposite a channel island or in a back channel.

The final key indicator used in the assessment of bank erosion involves a human activity multiplier. Human activity in riverine and estuarine environments of the Clarence River is largely associated with motorised water craft. Boating wash can affect wave height and bank stability and as such, a method was created to include this potential threat in the erosion risk assessment. The human activity component in the assessment of bank erosion involves multiplying the usage intensity by the number of affected factors, in this case wave height and bank stability. A human activity multiplier is also used in the assessment of wind erosion. To calculate the human activity multiplier the intensity of human activity is multiplied by the amount of factors it affects. Intensity of human activity is given a score of 1, 2 or 3. A score of 1 represents minimal activity/impact year round, 2 represents predominantly seasonal usage, such as during the school spring and summer holidays, and a score of 3 corresponds with steady/sustained usage throughout the year. The usage intensity was identified in the field and through informal consultation with the local Indigenous and non-Indigenous communities. Given that the outcome of the human activity multiplier is numeric, it provides a relatively simple, semi-quantitative means of comparison between sites where human activity affects other erosion hazard assessment factors.

Disturbance related to cultivation is a product of human activity. Excavation can be a result of anthropogenic activity or biological activity (bioturbation). Several key indicators are used to assess erosion hazard due to excavation. Anthropogenic excavation is interpreted in this study as any human-induced process associated with the removal of material from an area. The most likely reason for such removal would be building or infrastructure based. Farming is considered separately under the process of cultivation (Appendix 5).

The first key indicator of potential erosion hazard due to anthropogenic excavation involves calculating the percentage of the original deposit remaining *in situ*. This was calculated using a combination of field reconnaissance/survey and examination of topographic maps and aerial photographs and can be summarised in an equation as follows:

Percentage of midden undisturbed = area of *in situ* deposit/area of disturbed shell X 100

The effect of bioturbation at an Aboriginal shell midden sites was calculated in a similar way as illustrated by the following equation:

Percentage of midden disturbed by burrowing = volume of the burrow which has been dug through the midden layer/total volume of the midden layer X 100

If the percentage of the original deposit remaining *in situ* cannot be calculated due to cultural sensitivity and a desire by the relevant land council not to disturb the deposit any further a measurement of the area of apparent disturbance may be used instead. A measurement of the area of apparent disturbance may also be used if a deposit is located in difficult terrain which, for example, can only be surveyed by boat. Information on disturbance as a result of historic anthropogenic excavation can be gained through oral history of past and present landowners, newspaper articles, parish maps and other historic topographic and military maps. In the case of parish maps, however, it must be noted that all historic editions may not be available, leaving information gaps before the first and after the last available editions.

Proximity to roads and Council land use zoning can greatly affect the disturbance potential of a site and hence are included as the final key indicators of potential erosion hazard at Aboriginal midden sites. Proximity to roads can be calculated from current topographic maps by hand or using GIS software. In this study, measurements were taken from hard copy topographic maps and confirmed in ArcGIS. Information on council land use zonings is available from local councils (in the case of this study, the Clarence Valley Council). Midden locations were plotted over a land use zoning shapefile in ArcGIS to determine the zoning of the land on which they are located. It is important to note that while all Aboriginal sites are protected by law in Australia they are often buried in cryptic locations and may not be discovered until excavation works have commenced. In addition, diagnosis of the origin of a shell deposit requires some skill and experience (Attenbrow, 1992); the origin of a shell deposit is not likely to be known by a general observer.

Key indicators used to assess erosion risk due to farming include the area of land clearance or percentage of original deposit remaining *in situ*, slope of the land, distance of crops from the riverbank and history of cultivation in the area. These are similar to the key indicators of human-induced excavation outlined above. The area of land clearance and history of cultivation were measured using the resources described for measurement of these key indicators in the process of excavation. The slope of the land was measured in the field using a clinometer and the distance of crops from the riverbank was also measured in the field by either land- or water-based survey.

The processes of wind and wave erosion were considered at midden sites located close to the coast in areas such as dunes and headlands. Three factors affecting a midden deposit's susceptibility to wind erosion were considered as a part of the erosion hazard assessment performed in this study. They are deposit stability, exposure to prevailing winds and a human activity multiplier. The key indicator for deposit stability is vegetation cover and this is calculated and interpreted in the same way as previously outlined for bank stability.

The key indicators for assessing the effect of prevailing wind at a coastal midden deposit are wind direction and approximate length of daily exposure. Information on regional prevailing wind direction and intensity can be found by examining wind roses, such as those compiled by the Australian Bureau of Meteorology which were used in this study. The closest locations to the study area for which this information is available are Coffs Harbour and Brisbane. These data were used to provide information on regional wind patterns and were validated in the field by observing the characteristics of coastal vegetation (whether it is wind-shaped and in what direction) and the orientation of mobile sand dunes and dune blowouts. Aerial photographs also contain information relating to the local and regional orientation of modern and relict sand dunes.

Wind rose data are broken up into roses reflecting morning (9 am) and afternoon (3 pm) average conditions. As such, the approximate length of daily exposure of a midden site to prevailing winds is given a percentage value of 0%, 50% or 100%. When comparing site orientation with prevailing wind direction as evidenced by regional wind roses and site-specific field evidence, a value of 0% is given to sites which, as their orientation suggests, are sheltered from morning and afternoon prevailing winds. A value of 50% is given to sites which have an orientation exposing them to either morning or afternoon average prevailing winds only. A value of 100% is given to sites which are exposed to morning and afternoon prevailing winds.

Recreational activities associated with tourism in beach environments throughout the study area form the basis for the human activity multiplier associated with the process of wind erosion. Activities such as driving 4WD vehicles on beaches, camping and walking over dunes and headlands for sightseeing or fishing purposes can affect the stability of midden deposits. As previously discussed, this human activity component involves multiplying the usage intensity by the number of affected factors. In this case the affected factor is bank stability.

Ocean swell is the major factor affecting susceptibility of a midden site to sustained or periodic wave erosion. Three key indicators of ocean swell are considered in this erosion assessment methodology. Site elevation and the presence or absence of storm surge deposits and cliffing were recorded in the field. The use of geomorphic indicators that are readily identifiable and measurable in the field is a simple and effective way of ascertaining whether or not wave erosion is affecting midden deposits and their surrounding areas.

4.2.8.3 *Method two: A rapid, field-based erosion assessment methodology*

The development of a straightforward rapid, field-based methodology for assessment of erosion at shell midden sites is an essential cultural heritage management tool. Included in this methodology are an Erosion Hazard Pro Forma and a scoring system using characteristics of field forms and vegetation coverage, taphonomic characteristics of shell material found at a midden site, tidal activity and a standardised template for recording soil aggregate stability (Appendices 3 and 5). Scores obtained in these tables are used to calculate an Erosion Hazard Index for each site which corresponds to a set of recommendations for maintenance and conservation of Aboriginal shell midden sites. Collection of data in this way allows Aboriginal communities and their representatives access to a variety of information pertaining to a site whilst also identifying current and potential destructive impacts.

The layout of the Pro Forma is loosely based on that presented by Morgan (1995) for assessing erosion in the field. Like the Morgan (1995) Pro Forma it contains sections pertaining to land use, vegetation, slope and soil, but is expanded to include landscape characteristics, taphonomy and erosion field forms, in addition to basic information on the location, orientation and contents of a site. The inclusion of these additional characteristics improves its relevance for use in the assessment of erosion as it affects midden deposits.

The first section of the Pro Forma contains information about the location and site type – important background information for any field study. The grid reference for a site can be taken from a topographic map. It is important to note the scale of the map and also the coordinate system (i. e. GDA or MGA in Australia). Alternatively, a GPS reading can be taken at the site. Including an option of either grid reference or GPS reading does not disadvantage communities who don't have access to a hand held GPS. GPS/grid reference conversions can be performed easily using online resources (such as Geoscience Australia's website). The Site Type field requires a brief description of the function of the site, for example open site shell midden with artifacts, open site shell midden without artifacts, open site stone quarry, closed site shelter/cave.

The Current Land Use section gives a list of options for describing the nature of the current land use at a site. More than one box may be checked. The field worker is also required to make a note of the type of farming and recreational activity if applicable. Information on land use is available from a number of sources. Topographic maps contain information on the location of National Parks, State Forests and Crown Land. Land use can also be confirmed in the field. Local Council will have information on land use zoning if a more detailed approach is required.

The next section of the Pro Forma provides a description of the landscape at two scales – the terrain (surrounding area) and the landform (at site). The terrain is measured up to the landscape scale (10 000 km^2; Webb and Phinn, 2009) and includes coastal, estuarine, riverine and hillslope/mountainous environments. A variety of landform options are available within each terrain category and the field worker is required to select one from the list. Larger scale terrain features can be identified using maps and aerial photographs and landforms can be identified in the field.

Vegetation is covered in the following section of the Pro Forma. Characteristics influencing erosion include type and amount of cover. Vegetation type can be identified in the field and a general description is all that is required here. It may include a note on the presence/prevalence of exotic versus native vegetation and the basic type of vegetation association, such as open/closed forest, grassland, woody/herbaceous, established/new, mangroves/riparian vegetation, halophytes. Ground, tree and shrub cover are measured as a percentage of land area. Larger-scale vegetation cover can be measured using air photographs and site-scale coverage can be measured in the field. Field study can also be used to ground truth air photo interpretation.

The Tidal Activity section consists of only one question. Tidal influence has been observed to affect some sites in the current study. If a midden deposit is present in a tidal channel it has the potential to be affected not only by tidal activity but also flooding. The purpose of this section is to highlight potential disturbance of tidal activity rather than gauge the severity of this impact, as this requires more complex calculations based on tide height and frequency. The upper limit of tidal activity is included in topographic maps. Tide prediction charts and local knowledge will also provide useful information for completing this section.

Information on the orientation of the deposit is included in the Pro Forma. It is useful to have this information in case further studies of wave direction and fetch and effect of prevailing winds are required. The orientation of a deposit can be measured in the field using a compass or the sun as a guide. Slope is another characteristic which may contribute to erosion hazard. The angle of a slope can be measured in the field using a clinometer. The shape (cross section) can be described and sketched on the Pro Forma.

It is important to consider the effect of certain soil parameters on erosion at midden sites. The depth, thickness and length of a midden deposit can be measured in the field. Field measurements taken at varying points in time can be compared to ascertain whether or not there has been loss of material due to erosion or burying of material due to deposition. Measurement of field texture (for example, Isbell, 1996; Northcote, 1979) can be carried out in the field or at another location after collection of sediment. It is a far more rapid, straightforward and economical alternative to particle size analysis and can be carried out with minimal training. The Emerson Aggregate Test (Emerson, 1967) is a simple analysis yielding information on soil aggregate stability. The only materials required are deionised or rain water, containers and in some cases easily obtainable aqueous chemical compounds.

Taphonomy can also provide useful information about the depositional history of, and geomorphic processes currently acting at, a midden deposit. Some basic measurements and characteristics are included on the Pro Forma in the section 'Appearance of Shells in Midden'. The percentage of exposed *in situ* versus weathered material can give an indication of actual and potential information loss. Rates of information loss can also be calculated by comparing measurements taken at varying points in time. It is important to remember, however, that the exposed material may only provide a snapshot of the amount of material contained within a deposit. Likewise, the amount of visible material weathered out of the deposit may only represent a portion of the total amount of material that has weathered out of the deposit over time. The condition of shells is also important and the Pro Forma includes a subsection where such information can be recorded.

The final section included in the Erosion Hazard Pro Forma includes descriptions of a number of field forms which, based on their size and extent, can indicate the severity of erosion at a site. They form part of a selection of field forms used by Stocking and Murnaghan (2001) to assist farmers in developing countries assess degradation on their land. They can all be identified and measured in the field using basic equipment. An in-depth explanation of the techniques required in identification and measurement of the parameters set out in the Erosion Hazard Pro Forma is included in a handbook available to Aboriginal communities interested in using the techniques.

Scoring System for Use in Conjunction with the Rapid, Field-based Erosion Hazard Assessment for Aboriginal Shell Midden Sites

Systems which aim to score or rank land degradation rely, to some degree, on assigning arbitrary values to field measurements and other quantifiable data. The scoring system formulated for use in conjunction with the Erosion Hazard Pro Forma is based on several key components rather than assigning arbitrary, unweighted scores to all sections. The information contained within the Pro Forma can be assessed on its own merit as it does not rely on a scoring or ranking system to contextualise the data.

The Erosion Hazard Index developed in this research study is provided as a supplement and may be used to prioritise conservation and management of middens and other Aboriginal cultural deposits (Appendix 3). It is made up of four parts, using information from the Pro Forma, which can be added together to give an overall value linked to the severity of erosion at a site. The first involves scoring the severity of erosion based on characteristics of field forms and vegetation. It is a synthesis of characteristics outlined by Morgan (1995), Stocking and Murnaghan (2001), and Stocking (1994). The next provides scores based on the taphonomic characteristics of shell material contained in a deposit. The third part includes the Emerson Class Numbers for strata within the deposit and is a numerical rank of soil aggregate stability based on the Emerson Aggregate Test. The final part includes a score for tidal activity. All scores are equally weighted with a minimum value of zero and a maximum value of three. This alleviates unnecessary bias as it allows all characteristics at all sites to be scored and compared equally. Vegetation, soil, tidal and taphonomic characteristics were chosen for use in this scoring system as they represent key components in midden degradation due to erosion.

Scores are assigned based on the four components outlined above. These four scores are then averaged to give an overall score of the severity of erosion at a site, the Erosion Hazard Index. When results from different sites are compared, higher scores indicate greater erosional disturbance. These scores can be used as an aid in prioritising site conservation.

Recommendations for maintenance and conservation of Aboriginal shell midden sites are included in the Handbook for Use with the Erosion Hazard Pro Forma (Appendix 3) and correspond to the Erosion Hazard Indices. These are general guidelines only. Information on site-specific processes can be collected by archaeologists and environmental scientists using information collected in the Erosion Hazard Pro Forma as a starting point for further study.

4.2.8.4 *Field Trial of the Erosion Hazard Pro Forma*

The purpose of the field trial was to introduce the system to various stakeholders – the Yaegl Local Aboriginal Land Council, archaeologists and environmental scientists – and compare results obtained by the researcher with results obtained by these groups. The field research groups each contained members of each stakeholder group. After a general briefing and outline of the methodology the groups used the Erosion Hazard Pro Forma to collect data at Woombah A, Woombah B, Sleeper Island, Minnie Water and Wooli Aboriginal shell midden sites. They then used the scoring system to obtain an Erosion Hazard Index for each site.

The groups contained field workers with a variety of educational backgrounds. As a minimum standard all volunteers had a high school education. There were also different levels of tertiary education amongst the groups, from Bachelors and Masters degrees to Doctorates. Whilst field workers with tertiary qualifications in archaeology and environmental science could record requisite information on the Erosion Hazard Pro Forma without needing to refer to the accompanying Handbook, high school educated members of the Yaegl Aboriginal community and scientists not specialised in archaeology and environmental science found the Handbook to be a valuable aid. The tertiary educated archaeologists and environmental scientists were also able to demonstrate the methodology to these volunteers which, through hands-on experience, they picked up with relative ease. Gathering data at multiple sites also increased their confidence in working with the Pro Forma.

As is the case with any data collection system, some training is required before it is able to be used with confidence. The ease with which the Erosion Hazard Pro Forma was understood by tertiary educated specialists and was able to be explained to and practised by high school educated members of the Yaegl community suggests its usefulness as a standardised erosion hazard assessment tool for Aboriginal shell midden sites.

4.2.8.5 *Method three: GIS model*

This model was formulated in ArcMap and shows the interaction of factors contributing to erosion at the landscape scale. Detailed results are presented in Appendix 5; data and maps are also included in electronic form in Appendix 6. Data on soils, vegetation coverage, slope, Quaternary surface and subsurface sediment age and dominant texture and land use are used to assess erosion risk at Aboriginal shell midden sites in the study area. Data from each layer have been assigned numerical risk values of 0 (no/extremely low erosion risk), 1 (low risk), 2 (moderate risk) and 3 (high risk) (Table 4.2). Each factor represents a layer in the model and scores for each layer are averaged to give an overall risk value. Multiple shell midden sites can then be ordered according to the degree of erosion risk and conservation efforts can be prioritised where needed.

Vegetation coverage was digitised from aerial photographs obtained through the New South Wales Department of Lands. Based on the erosion cover relationship graph of Stocking (1994), three categories were generated – 20, 40 and 60. These were then merged into one layer to represent vegetation coverage. Category 20 corresponds to a value of 0-20% vegetation coverage and this is given a score of three, high erosion risk. Category 40 corresponds to a value of 40% vegetation coverage and this is given a score of two, moderate erosion risk. Category 60 represents areas of 60-100% vegetation coverage. It is given a score of one, low erosion risk.

Data in the slope layer were sourced from the digital elevation model DEM NSW 9s, courtesy of the NSW Rural Fire Service. Risk categories in this layer were determined using jenks (natural breaks) in the data. Assigning categories in this way is more reliable than using arbitrary values as the categories accurately represent variation in the natural elevation of the landscape. A slope of up to 5.99° is assigned an erosion risk value of 1, representing low erosion risk. Slopes from 6-14.99° are assigned a value of 2, representing a moderate erosion risk. Finally, land with a slope of 15-43.99° is assigned a value of 3, high erosion risk. The value of 43.99° represents the maximum slope in the digital elevation model throughout the study area and surrounds.

Three soil characteristics are used in the erosion risk model. Laboratory analyses were used to determine dominant texture, total organic content and Emerson Aggregate Number of soil samples from the study sites (outlined earlier in this chapter). Results of soil analyses were set out using the same format as Troedson and Hashimoto's (2008) Coastal Quaternary Geology datasets, compiled for the Geological Survey of NSW. The paucity of data in the study area necessitated the use of field data from the study sites. In any case, use of site-specific data following the format of Troedson and Hashimoto (2008) is recommended to ensure accuracy of results as characteristics of local soils may be highly variable, especially in areas with a variety of land uses.

The dominant texture of soils in the midden strata at the study sites was determined using a Malvern Mastersizer (see 'Laboratory Analyses'). Three categories – sand, silt and mixed – were assigned risk values based on their relative erodibilities as outlined in Evans (1980), Lal and Elliott (1994) and Troedson and Hashimoto (2008). Where sand was the dominant texture, these soils were assigned the low risk value of 1. Soils with a mixed texture were assigned a risk value of 2, corresponding to a moderate erosion risk. Soils containing predominantly silt-sized particles were assigned a high risk value of 3.

The total organic content of soils at the study sites was determined in the laboratory (see 'Laboratory Analyses'). These data were then divided into low, moderate and high risk categories. The soils dataset of Troedson and Hashimoto (2008) defines soils with an organic content greater than or equal to 7.50% as having a high organic content. Soils from the study sites which fell into this category were assigned a low erosion risk value of 1. Based on this same dataset, soils with an organic content between 4.00 and 7.49% were assigned a moderate erosion risk value of 2 and soils with a low organic content, between 0.00 and 3.99%, were assigned a high erosion risk value of 3.

The Emerson Aggregate Test (Emerson, 1967; see 'Laboratory Analyses') was also performed on soil aggregates from the midden strata at the study sites. Soils with an Emerson number of 1 or 2 were assigned a high erosion risk value of 3, as these are the most unstable aggregates (Emerson, 1967). Soils with an Emerson number of 3 were assigned a moderate erosion risk value of 2, as these aggregates are stable until soaked to field capacity (Emerson, 1967). Soils with an Emerson number of 4, 5 or 6 were assigned a low erosion risk value of 1 and soils with an Emerson number of 7 or 8, the most stable aggregates (Emerson, 1967), were assigned a very low erosion risk value of 0.

Troedson and Hashimoto's (2008) regional map of Quaternary surface and subsurface sediment age and dominant texture was included in the model as a measure of potential shoreline erodibility. Induration of Pleistocene dunes greatly improves their stability and thus their ability to withstand sea level fluctuations (Troedson and Hashimoto, 2008). Middens located within these sediments are therefore less susceptible to erosion than those located in younger, unconsolidated dunes.

Locations where Holocene age surface sediments overlie Holocene subsurface sand and sand-mud were placed in the high risk category and given a value of 3. Where Holocene surface sediments overlie Holocene subsurface mud a moderate risk value of 2 was used. A low risk value of 1 was assigned to locations where Pleistocene surface sediments overlie Pleistocene subsurface sediments of a variety of textures.

Council land use zoning (data courtesy of the Clarence Valley Council) was also included in the model. Erosion risk values were assigned to different zones based on the nature and scale of development which is prohibited within a zone. National Parks were assigned a value of 0 as development is prohibited within these areas. Small-scale National Parks and Wildlife Service developments undergo strict approval processes. Land use zones assigned a low risk score of 1 include areas of low-density residential development, open space, environmental protection and proposed National Parks. Commercial and industrial development, as well as development affecting environmental processes and wildlife habitats is prohibited within these zones. Rural zones, medium-density residential zones, commercial and village zones were assigned a moderate erosion risk value of 2. High-density residential development, industrial development affecting the value of agricultural land is prohibited within these zones. Rural land set aside for urban expansion, industrial and residential tourism zones were assigned a high erosion risk value of 3 as industry, agriculture and high-density housing are all permitted within this zone, making this land the most intensively used by humans.

Table 4.2: Standard Definitions for GIS Erosion Risk Categories.

LAYER	CATEGORY	RISK	DEFINITION & REFERENCE/SOURCE
VEGETATION COVER	20 40 60	High Moderate Low	0-20% 40% 60-100% Stocking, 1994 Data source: Digitised from NSW Dept. of Lands aerial photographs
SLOPE	Low Moderate High	Low Moderate High	0.00-5.99° 6.00-14.99° 15.00-43.99° Jenks (natural breaks) used to determine categories. Data source: DEM NSW 9s, courtesy NSW Rural Fire Service
SOILS (Dominant Texture)	Sand Mixed Silt	Low Moderate High	Evans, 1980; Lal & Elliott, 1994; Troedson & Hashimoto, 2008 Data source: Malvern Mastersizer (field samples)
SOILS (Total Organic Content)	Low Moderate High	High Moderate Low	0.00-3.99% 4.00-7.49% ≥7.50% Troedson & Hashimoto, 2008 Data source: laboratory analysis
SOILS (Emerson Aggregate Number)	Emerson No. / Risk Score 1 / 3 2 / 3 3 / 2 4 / 1 5 / 1 6 / 1 7 / 0 8 / 0		Emerson, 1967 Data source: laboratory analysis
QUATERNARY SURFACE/SUBSURFACE AGE & DOMINANT TEXTURE	Holocene Surface/Holocene Subsurface Sand Holocene Surface/Holocene Subsurface Sand-Mud Holocene Surface/Holocene Subsurface Mud Pleistocene Surface/Pleistocene Subsurface Sand Pleistocene Surface/Pleistocene	High High Moderate Low Low	Holocene surface sediments overlying Holocene subsurface sand and sand-mud. Holocene surface sediments overlying Holocene subsurface mud. Pleistocene surface sediments overlying Pleistocene sands and Pleistocene various (mixed texture) sediments.

	Subsurface Various		Data source and definitions: Troedson & Hashimoto, 2008
LAND USE	8a (national parks)	None	*Prohibited:* All development with the exception of National Parks developments (require consent).
	2a (low-density residential) 5a (special uses) 6a (open space) 7a (environmental protection, conservation/habitat) 7b (environmental protection, ecological significance) 7e (environmental protection, escarpment/scenic) 8b (proposed national parks)	Low	*Prohibited:* Commercial and industrial development, development affecting and affected by coastal processes, development adversely affecting significant vegetation and wildlife habitats, development in geologically hazardous areas. *Subject to consent:* low-density housing, forestry, construction of public utilities, clearing of land.
	1a (rural, agricultural protection) 1b (rural, general rural land) 1f (rural forests) 1i (rural investigation) 1w (rural waterways) 2b (medium-density residential) 3a (commercial) V2 (village zone)	Moderate	*Prohibited:* High-density residential development, industrial development, development affecting conservation value of land, farming prohibited in commercial zone. *Permitted:* agriculture, forestry, recreational and commercial fishing, development of tourist facilities not resulting in environmental degradation, development providing a wide variety of community housing options.
	1e (rural, urban investigation) 2t (residential tourism) 4a (industrial)	High	*Permitted:* Industry, agriculture, development of tourist facilities and high-density accommodation, agricultural land set aside for urban expansion. Data source: Clarence Valley Council

5. STRATIGRAPHIC INVESTIGATION AND INTERPRETATION

5.1 CHARACTERISTICS OF QUATERNARY STRATA

This chapter contains a discussion of Quaternary strata along the mid to north coast of NSW and the southern coastal areas of Queensland. Characteristics, likely formation processes and dates of relevant strata are reviewed, and links are made with stratigraphic data collected in this research project and previous archaeological studies in the Clarence Valley. Contextualisation of the stratigraphy of the study sites enables further interpretation of site formation processes and forms the basis for the development of the erosion hazard assessment methods.

Current research indicates that most dunes in coastal New South Wales have formed since the Penultimate Interglacial period (200 000 – 250 000 yrs BP, Oxygen Isotope Stage 7) (Bryant *et al.*, 1994). Dune barrier plains are present at a number of sites along the east coast of Australia, including the Newcastle Bight, Port Stephens-Myall Lakes region, Evans Head (NSW), and North Stradbroke Island and Rainbow Beach (QLD) (see Table 5.1 for dates and references). The dune barriers identified at Evans Head extend south to the Clarence River. Two near-coastal dune barriers have been identified in the study area: an inner, Pleistocene barrier and an outer, Holocene barrier (Langford-Smith, 1971; 1972; Warner, 1971; Marshall and Thom, 1976; Pickett *et al.*, 1989; Bryant *et al.*, 1994).

Dunes comprising the Pleistocene Inner Barrier system at Evans head are parabolic, with a south to southeast orientation reflecting prevailing wind trends at their time of formation (Thom *et al.*, 1994). The near-coastal Pleistocene Inner Barrier dune system is highly podzolized; a humate (lithified B horizon) stratum is overlain by an A2 horizon composed of leached incoherent quartz sand which is in turn overlain by a peat horizon in areas where channels have been incised through the dunes (Thom, 1965; Warner, 1971; Bryant *et al.*, 1994). Entrenched channels are likely to have been incised through dunes during a period of sea level lower than present (Thom, 1965). Bryant *et al.* (1994) identify a thin (~20 cm) layer of iron nodules forming a crust on top of underlying humate at a site in Jervis Bay, New South Wales. The presence of this crust indicates the humate was exposed subaerially prior to being covered by sands forming the A2 horizon.

Podzolization is thought to have occurred within the Inner Barrier as soil particles from vegetated dunes became mixed with the sand lying below the soil. The period of transgression leading to the Last Interglacial (Oxygen Isotope Substage 5e) caused the watertable to rise and subsequently a hardpan was formed from the layer containing sand and humic material. The hardpan is referred to as humate or sandrock (Ward *et al.,* 1979; Thom *et al.,* 1994). The Outer Barrier, by contrast, is only weakly podzolized (Thom *et al.,* 1994). Dune soils of the early Holocene (~6000 – 9000 years BP) contain comparatively shallow A horizons and only moderately developed B horizons with incipient light yellow to dark brown columns and pipes, unlike the thick humate rich columns and concretions found in sandrock of the Inner Barrier dune system. Thom (1965) noted that no hardpan was present beneath the ridges of this system in the Myall Lakes area and that the watertable lies below the surface of its swales.

The Holocene Outer Barrier also differs from the Inner Barrier in other ways. It is commonly separated from the Inner Barrier by a tract of shallow lagoon or swamp and blowouts are a common feature of the foredune ridge. The removal of sand from these foredunes creates a mobile sand sheet which is blown inland by onshore winds (Thom, 1965).

5.2 AGE DETERMINATIONS

Table 5.1 lists dates obtained from materials located within the Inner Barrier dune complex along the east coast of Australia. The age determinations in Table 5.1 focus on the Pleistocene Inner

Barrier, as McBryde (1982) observed mid-Late Holocene shell middens in the Woombah area situated behind these dunes and stratigraphically overlying possible hardpan sediments associated with them. Angourie is situated along the Clarence coastline, south of the Clarence River and work was undertaken by Warner (1971) in this area. He dated three consecutive strata – the basal humate platform, the grey (leached) sand stratigraphically above the platform and the overlying peat. The dates indicate the strata formed just prior to the Last Glacial Maximum, set at 22 000 years BP (Bard *et al.,* 1990), however the result obtained for the humate platform indicates a younger age than the overlying strata. No replicate determinations were made and Warner (1971) acknowledges the sample taken from this layer may have been contaminated. Also, these dates are reaching the upper age limit of the conventional radiocarbon dating technique (~30 000 years) and contamination can occur in older materials (Thom, 1973).

Evans Head lies to the north of the Clarence River and is located at the mouth of the Richmond River, New South Wales. Dates have been obtained for several Pleistocene strata including offshore sediment contained within the continental shelf at a depth of 53 m (Colwell and Roy, 1983; Table 5.1). Plant root material dated by Colwell and Roy (1983) was considered by the authors to have come from muds associated with interdunal swamps which were a feature of the landscape during the Last Glacial Maximum. The age determination of 18 070±280 years BP (Table 5.1) supports this idea. Organic material from the Inner Barrier sandrock at Evans Head was dated by Langford-Smith (1971; Table 5.1) at 34 000 +1200 -1000 years BP using conventional radiocarbon dating. Another conventional radiocarbon date of 25 900±1100 years BP was recorded by Gill (1967) for the same stratum in the same location. These determinations both indicate formation of the Inner Barrier dunes at a time prior to the Last Glacial Maximum and correlate (within 1 standard deviation) with the age obtained for the grey sandy layer at Angourie. The Evans Head Inner Barrier dates are, however, approaching the limit of reliability for the conventional radiocarbon dating method. Scleractinian corals collected from the Gundurimba Clay, Evans Head, were dated using the Uranium Series Disequilibrium technique (see Table 5.1 for researchers and dates). The Gundurimba Clay is a formation which is widely distributed in the Richmond River Valley (Pickett *et al.,* 1989), however it is not mentioned in the stratigraphic literature pertaining to the Clarence Valley so no direct comparison of dates can be made. A revision of the dates of Drury and Roman (1983) and Marshall and Thom (1976) by Pickett *et al*. (1989) suggests the Gundurimba Clay is most likely Last Interglacial (Oxygen Isotope Substage 5e) in age.

A date obtained from Inner Barrier sandrock at Rainbow Beach, southern Queensland (31 000 +3200 -2200 years BP; Langford-Smith, 1972) is consistent with other radiocarbon ages obtained for sites in Northern New South Wales (Table 5.1). Thermoluminescence age data from the Newcastle Bight area also appear to be consistent with the radiocarbon determinations for the Inner Barrier at Angourie, Evans Head and Rainbow Beach (Table 5.1). Sand dunes at North Stradbroke Island, Southern Queensland, however, are much older and appear to be associated with the Penultimate Glaciation (Oxygen Isotope Stage 6; Table 5.1). A thermoluminescence determination of 76 600±18700 years BP was obtained by Bryant *et al,* (1994) from barrier dunes at Cape Hawk, Myall Lakes, New South Wales but it was suggested by the authors that this deposit had been reworked.

5.3 DEPOSITIONAL SEQUENCE – NEAR-COASTAL INNER BARRIER DUNES

Using age determinations and palaeoenvironmental data presented in the papers appearing in Table 5.1, a possible depositional sequence for near-coastal Inner Barrier dunes in mid-northern New South Wales and southern Queensland is presented. Last Interglacial barrier dunes formed as a result of progradation associated with a sea level similar to, or higher than, the present level. During the Last Glacial Maximum extensive aeolian reworking created dune instability and incorporated younger sediments into the barrier. Progradation associated with the subsequent Postglacial Marine Transgression saw increasing dune stability and a rise in the groundwater table resulting in formation of a humate hardpan, and thus, podzolization. As the Inner Barrier dunes became increasingly vegetated a rich peat deposit formed capping the Inner Barrier system at Rainbow Beach and Angourie (Ward *et al.,* 1979; Warner, 1971).

5.4 STRATIGRAPHIC INTERPRETATION

5.4.1 **Woombah**

Study of the Quaternary stratigraphy of the Clarence Valley allows the archaeological deposits studied in this research, and those previously studied, to be placed in context and provides key information regarding age and stratigraphic integrity of such deposits. The Woombah midden complex is situated on the landward side of the Pleistocene Inner Barrier at various locations along the north bank of the Clarence River's North Arm. McBryde (1982) studied a midden belonging to this complex in depth in 1963 and 1964. The site, which she termed Woombah 1, is located on the eastern site of Woolpack Creek. She also notes the presence of middens in a similar location to those forming a component of the current study however these were not excavated. McBryde (1982) made various notes on the stratigraphic context of the Woombah 1 deposit, however as the study was archaeological in nature and there was a large amount of material to interpret, some details regarding depths of strata are missing. Archaeologically sterile layers were not thoroughly analysed to determine their exact location in the Quaternary depositional sequence. Some notes on the possible palaeoenvironment are included but McBryde (1982) is careful to note the limitations of the study.

Examination of aerial photographs of the Myall Lakes region (Thom, 1965) and the current study location reveals backswamp areas landward of the Inner Barrier dune system. These backswamp areas are likely to have formed during a period of higher sea level than at present. A shallow lagoon-type environment would have been favourable for lithification of lagoon sediments and formation of a crust on top of this layer. This is consistent with the stratigraphy observed by McBryde (1982). Directly underlying the midden strata is a thin white sandy layer which rests on top of a white sandrock deposit. This sandrock deposit is capped by a thin cemented crust. Depths of the archaeologically sterile layers are not noted. Ward *et al.* (1979) define sandrock as being "composed of quartz sands cemented with organic matter" (p. 305) however organic matter appears to be absent from the white sandrock described and photographed by McBryde (1982). If sediment was lithified in a lagoon environment it is unlikely to be overlain by mature solum from which to derive organic material, and organic material on the lagoon bed may also have been minimal. This may explain the lack of organic staining found in McBryde's (1982) white sandrock.

Mcbryde (1982) suggests this white sandrock stratum may have formed during the Last Interglacial and, since the Holocene midden deposit rests directly on this stratum in the excavation area, it may have been formed at this time when a lagoon was present in the area. There are a couple of problems associated with this interpretation. Although the midden deposit is found in close proximity to Woolpack Creek the Clarence River alluvial sediments appear to be absent from the stratigraphy as seen in the excavation pits. This leads McBryde (1982) to suggest occupation at the site whilst it was still a lagoon. As formation of the lagoon would have required sea levels at or above the present level this indicates it would most likely have formed during the Last Interglacial (Oxygen Isotope Substage 5e) as present conditions are alluvial. Midden strata were radiocarbon dated between 2600-3000 and 1400-1800 years BP. Rather than occupation during lagoonal conditions the apparent gap in alluvial sedimentation may be due to erosion from floodwaters or agricultural disturbance, as both these processes are very active in the Clarence Estuary. McBryde (1982) does note a thin layer of brown soil below the dense midden layer which contains only a few shells. This may have been deposited alluvially and some mixing may have occurred with the overlying midden stratum resulting in the presence of a minimal amount of shell material in the otherwise archaeologically sterile soil layer. Also, the matrix of the midden itself may have been deposited alluvially. The excavated Woombah midden comprises shellfish species primarily of estuarine habitat (McBryde, 1982) and this could suggest proximity to an estuary at the time of resource utilisation.

A black sandrock layer stratigraphically below the white sand/sandrock stratum was exposed by McBryde (1982) in a cutting through the Woolpack Creek bank. She suggests this stratum may correlate with the humate platform described at Angourie by Warner (1971). This stratum was radiocarbon dated at 24 810 +1190 -1010 years BP (see Table 5.1 and previous discussion of dates). If these strata are analogous the white sandrock which stratigraphically overlies the black sandrock will be younger than the humate platform. A minimum age for the white sandrock is, however, uncertain due to the aforementioned problems associated with the date obtained by Warner (1971) for the humate platform.

Both the Site A riverbank and Site B creek bank midden deposits in the current Woombah study area are thinner and less extensive than those studied by McBryde (1982), and they are located in a low-lying floodplain area; excavations were undertaken to a maximum depth of 1.0 m. The stratigraphic sequence observed by McBryde (1982) is not seen at Woombah sites A and B. There is no white or black sandrock and no podzolisation. Morand's (2001) soil landscapes map (Figure 2.6) clearly shows sediment associated with Pleistocene Inner Barrier dunes separated from more recent Holocene dune sediments by patches of swampland analogous to that seen by Thom (1965) in the Myall Lakes region of NSW. Orange areas in Figure 2.6 represent Inner Barrier sediments. Swampland is represented by mid-blue and bright yellow areas along the coast represent Holocene Outer Barrier sediments. Aerial photographs of the Clarence River estuary also show patches of swampland between Inner and Outer Barrier dunes as well as areas of alluvium as discussed below.

Although the Woombah study site is situated in an area predominantly comprising Pleistocene Inner Barrier sediments its proximity to both the Esk River and the North Arm of the Clarence River suggests the dominance of alluvial sediment. In his soil landscapes study, Morand (2001) found alluvium overlying Holocene marine sediments in the Woombah study area. He named this sediment type pa (Palmers Island) and noted that it occurred on the deltaic plain of the Clarence River (Figure 2.6). As sediments of this nature lie adjacent to Pleistocene beach ridge plains and their associated sediments (Morand, 2001) this may account for the difference in observed stratigraphy between the middens studied by McBryde (1982) and those in the current study area.

Coring undertaken at the Woombah study site revealed some features of interest. As expected the core taken closest to the riverbank (5.0 m in from edge, core 5b, Appendix 1) contained clayey alluvial sediments with a relatively high organic content compared with other strata (Appendices 1 and 2). However other core samples taken in a northwards facing transect at site B across the width of the floodplain yielded very sandy sediment. Troedson and Hashimoto (2008) also found the Clarence River estuarine-deltaic plain to be a relatively sand-dominated system and they suggest this reflects the geology of the catchment. All cores collected from Woombah site B contained sandy sediments (Appendix 2). Particle size analysis highlights a trend of reduced clay, silt and superfine sediments and an increase in sand-sized sediment with depth. Results also show a thinning of the top, clayey stratum in a northward direction across the floodplain away from the river; in most cases this stratum is underlain by consecutively sandier strata containing reduced organic content (Appendices 1 and 2). This is indicative of a shift from reducing to oxidising conditions with a move north away from the river. Also, the clay appears to be sealing the reduced deeper strata and this is a characteristic conducive to acid sulfate groundwater conditions. Acid sulfate groundwater conditions are not currently considered to be a major impact at this site as the midden deposits are situated above the watertable. A rising watertable could potentially impact the shell midden deposits. The relative thinness of alluvial sediments on a floodplain in such close proximity to a flood prone channel is considered somewhat unusual and may have an impact on the midden deposits at the site. Lack of alluvial sedimentation can leave cultural deposits exposed and thus vulnerable to erosion and disturbance from farming processes.

Cores 5.1b and 5b represent strata at the bottom and top of a levee slope at the edge of the floodplain, respectively (Appendix 1). Sand is present in all strata to a depth of 0.56-0.60 m where the watertable is present. At 15.7 m north of the riverbank, strata seen in core 5.1b lie in relatively close proximity to the river channel, however the thinning clay layer present in cores 4b-1b is absent here. Thus, the extent of alluvial clays on this part of the floodplain is minimal. As Morand (2001) identified Inner Barrier dune sediments directly north of the study site the sandy nature of the floodplain sediments may be a product of their proximity to the dune sands.

A trend towards decreasing organic content with depth is seen in the cores from Woombah Site A, taken at the eastern edge of the study area, although particle size analyses show negligible change in grain size by depth for cores 1a-4a (Appendix 1). Clay could not be identified in the field texture of these sediments, however particle size analyses show minimal clay- and silt-sized particles in cores 2a and 3a (Appendix 2). A possible explanation for this is that loamy soil may have been built up in the area to support agriculture, as the top strata are similar to the strata present in core 1b, taken from the western edge of the study location in an area previously used for farming. Lack of alluvial sediment is a feature of the eastern side of the study area also, and to an even greater extent than the western side (cores 1-5b). Core 5a was taken in close proximity to the riverbank and particle size analysis (Appendix 2) confirms the nature of the sediment in this core differs from that of the other cores taken at Woombah Site A. A much higher percentage of clay- and silt-sized particles, along with superfine particles, are present in this core – characteristics seen in sediment from the Site B floodplain cores.

5.4.2 **Sleeper Island**

Morand (2001) identified sediments on Sleeper Island as belonging to his 'rm' (Romiaka) soil landscape which he describes as extremely low to level tidal flats and saltmarshes within the Clarence Delta containing Quaternary marine and fluvial sediments regularly inundated with tidal waters. He found the area to have a permanently high watertable. Data obtained from coring (Appendix 1 – core diagrams 1-4s and Appendix 2) support Morand's (2001) findings of deep, very poorly drained Humic Gleys, organic and waterlogged saline soils with low wet bearing strength. Field observations confirm the island's banks are highly erodible. Morand (2001) also found potential and actual acid sulfate soil materials throughout the 'rm' landscape. Currently, the Aboriginal midden deposit on Sleeper Island lies above the watertable however this was measured at a depth of 0.21 m in the middle of the island, a low point covered in water kooch; a rise in the watertable may impact on the midden if acid sulfate conditions are present.

Associated with the 'rm' soil landscape is the 'rma' landscape comprising tidal delta sand masses (Morand, 2001). This occurs opposite the eastern and southern sides of Sleeper Island (Figure 2.6) and indicates areas of deposition of Quaternary marine and fluvial sediments. As noted in the Site Descriptions section these areas of deposition lying opposite areas of erosion on Sleeper Island may be indicative of channel dynamics similar to those seen on opposite banks of a river meander bend. Aerial photographs (Figure 3.1) of the Clarence River channels around Sleeper Island show these sediments as areas of deposition opposite the eastern side associated with Freeburn Island and opposite the southern side associated with the mainland.

Cores taken on Sleeper Island show a trend in field texture with depth and across strata. All sediment contained some clay and there is a trend from loamy material in the top stratum through light and heavy clays to sandy clays with increasing depth (Appendix 1 – core diagrams 1-4s). Strata can be traced across the island (Appendix 1). Depths of the Light Clay stratum correspond between cores 2s and 3s, located in the middle of the island, and cores 1s and 4s, taken close to the island's western and eastern banks. When adjusted for elevation, the depth of the Light Clay stratum corresponds neatly between cores. Similarly, depth of the Sandy Clay stratum corresponds between cores. Thus, stratigraphic integrity has been maintained across Sleeper Island. Most of the midden material, however, does not remain *in situ*. Erosion has greatly disturbed the midden, as evidenced by the accumulation of shells and artifacts in a lag deposit at its base. The minimal remaining *in situ* material has likely not been disturbed, but is at immediate threat from erosion, as the tidal channel where it is situated is inundated daily.

There is no trend in organic content with depth or across strata (Appendix 2). The organic content does not appear to be associated with field texture either. Sleeper Island sediments have a higher organic content than those collected from Woombah and this is in keeping with Morand's (2001) findings. As strata on Sleeper Island were relatively easy to distinguish through field texture this was seen as the most appropriate method of studying the stratigraphy at this location. Strata have been correlated across the island for the purpose of investigating the integrity of its midden deposit.

5.4.3 **Plover Island**

Plover Island is a rocky outcrop overlain by a relatively thin (0.80 m) layer of soil. The soil consists of a 0.52 m thick A horizon containing a stone artifact lens at a depth of 0.35-0.45 m and a pedal B horizon at a depth of 0.52-0.80 m (Appendix 1 – core diagram PI). The A and B horizons can clearly be traced around the circumference of the island and bedrock is present below a depth of 0.80 m. The relative thinness of the solum may indicate its youth; exposure to coastal winds will likely lead to removal of topsoil, even in the presence of grasses and shrubs.

The Bare Point Soil Landscape map (Department of Environment, Climate Change and Water, 2010) indicates the soil at this location belongs to regolith class R2 – unconsolidated sands originating from quartz sandstone parent rock. These sediments have a low coherence, increasing their susceptibility to erosion (Hazelton and Murphy, 2007). Field texture results show the A horizon is a loamy sand and the B horizon a clayey sand (Appendix 1 – core diagram PI), showing there may be minor localised variation in the composition of the parent rock. Organic content decreases with depth (Appendix 2).

Troedson and Hashimoto (2008) found headlands north of Plover Island are composed of Triassic to Cretaceous sedimentary rocks of the Clarence-Moreton Basin. Despite low data resolution for the area between Broom's Head and Wooli (due to limited accessibility) geological maps indicate this area is part of the Clarence-Moreton Basin (Troedson & Hashimoto, 2008). The composition of local headlands, coupled with the underlying regional geology, suggests the presence of similar sedimentary rocks of the Clarence-Moreton Basin on Plover Island. As is the case with neighbouring headlands, Plover Island sits adjacent to a Holocene coastal barrier system which, although typically narrow and poorly developed regionally, is present between Iluka and Evans

Head, Brooms Head and Sandon, and other various locations between Yamba and Brooms Head (Troedson & Hashimoto, 2008).

5.4.4 **Minnie Water**

The Aboriginal shell midden site at Minnie Water is located at the base of the dunes adjacent to a rocky outcrop, Rocky Point, at the northern end of Minnie Water Beach. Geological maps show Rocky Point is part of the Clarence-Moreton Basin (Troedson & Hashimoto, 2008 and references therein) and sediment analyses yield similar results to those obtained at Plover Island (Appendix 2). Field texture varies laterally across the midden deposit and overlying strata (Appendix 1 – core diagrams 1MW-4MW). Narrow, unstratified Holocene dunes present along Minnie Water Beach (Troedson & Hashimoto, 2008) terminate at Rocky Point and it is at this location that field texture, aggregate stability and Munsell soil colour of the A horizon soil are the same as at Plover Island (Appendix 2). B horizon soils at Plover Island and Minnie Water adjacent to Rocky Point also have similar characteristics. Although adjacent to Holocene dunes they both contain clay and their Aggregate Stability Class is identical. Munsell colour is also similar. These common characteristics within parts of the soil profiles at Plover Island and Minnie Water may indicate the presence of a similar parent rock at the two locations. The Bare Point Soil Landscape map (Department of Environment, Climate Change and Water, 2010) indicates the soil at this location belongs to regolith class R2, the same as at Plover Island, consistent with the site's coastal location.

Another feature of Rocky Point which was also observed at Plover Island is the presence of coffee rock. This commonly occurs within Pleistocene barrier deposits in the study area and is a result of cementation of subsurface sand grains by organic matter and iron, leaving near-surface horizons leached to white (Troedson & Hashimoto, 2008).

Grain size distribution at the base of the dunes (cores 1MW380, 2MW380, 3MW380 and 4MW380) is variable and also includes a variable proportion of gravel (Appendix 2). The presence of poorly sorted sands and a variable amount of gravel may be a result of reworking due to wind or wave activity. Surface sands sampled from the foredunes (cores 1MW0 and 2MW0) are well sorted, as are sand samples taken at a depth of 1 m (cores 1MW100 and 2MW100). There is a strong correlation between grain sizes of these samples. There is also a strong correlation in grain size distribution between cores 3MW0 and 4MW0, which were taken east of cores 1MW and 2MW (Appendix 2), adjacent to the rocky outcrop at Rocky Point. The grain size distribution differs from cores 1MW0 and 2MW0 and includes a clay fraction. The distinct difference in grain size distributions between cores 3MW0 and 4MW0, and 3MW25 and 4MW25 is indicative of two distinct soil strata, which cannot be seen in the adjacent dunes (1MW and 2MW cores). Results from soil analyses support Troedson & Hashimoto's (2008) observations of narrow and regionally poorly developed Holocene barrier dunes backed to their landward side and/or underlain by Pleistocene barrier deposits.

There is a trend towards reduced organic content with depth in 1MW, 2MW and 3MW cores, although organic content varies between these cores (Appendix 2). There is some lateral consistency between cores 1MW0, 3MW0 and 4MW0 but organic content in core 2MW0 is approximately double the level seen at this depth in the other cores. These variations, coupled with the lack of a trend in reduced organic content with depth in 4MW cores, may be due to small scale variations in vegetation cover and/or soil permeability, and may provide further evidence of the mixed origin of sediments at this site, as highlighted by the results of the grain size analysis.

5.4.5 **Wooli**

The Wooli Aboriginal shell midden is located parallel to the bank of the Wooli River at a depth of 0.25-0.41 m. Geological maps show Wooli is also part of the Clarence-Moreton Basin (Troedson & Hashimoto, 2008 and references therein). Narrow, unstratified Holocene dunes overlie Holocene subsurface sediment, as at Minnie Water and Plover Island (Troedson & Hashimoto, 2008). Similarly to Minnie Water, the majority of core samples across the midden and adjacent sediment comprise sands with a low organic content, however the size-sorting of sediment follows a different pattern at both of these sites. Sands are very well sorted throughout all of the Wooli cores (Appendix 2). Sediment located at the top of the Minnie Water dunes is well-sorted, while sediment located at the base of the dunes is poorly sorted, containing many coarse sand- and gravel-sized particles (Appendix 2). The difference in particle size distribution at these two sites, a low energy riverbank deposit and a high energy aeolian coastal deposit, reflects a difference in their depositional histories.

The presence of poorly-sorted sediment in conjunction with well-rounded shells and pumice at the base of the Minnie Water dunes indicates the Minnie Water midden deposit is likely to have been reworked. At Wooli, the presence of well-sorted fine- to medium-grained sands and fully buried whole shells in relatively good condition indicates a well preserved midden deposit.

Placing the study sites into a stratigraphic context facilitates further investigation into site formation processes. Studying the species composition and taphonomy of the shells present in the midden deposits consolidates understanding of site formation processes. Results and discussion of species composition and taphonomic analyses at the study sites are presented in the next chapter.

Table 5.1: Age determinations obtained from materials located within the Inner Barrier dune complex along the east coast of Australia.

LOCATION	STRATUM	AGE DETERMINATION (yrs BP)	DATING METHOD AND MATERIAL DATED	REFERENCE
Northern NSW – Angourie	Humate platform	24810 +1190 - 1010 (GaK – 2818)	^{14}C, wood	Warner, 1971
	Grey sand stratigraphically above the humate platform	28600 +4400 - 2600 (GaK – 2817)	^{14}C, charcoal	
	Peat bench stratigraphically above the grey sand layer	26800 +1600 - 1300 (GaK – 2816)	^{14}C, peat	
Northern NSW – Evans Head	Offshore (continental shelf 53 m below MSL)	18070±280 (HV-10783)	^{14}C, plant root material	Colwell and Roy, 1983
	Gundurimba clay, widely distributed in the Richmond River Valley	119000±4000 (MMF20572, MMF20602)	$^{230}Th/^{234}U$, Scleractinian corals	Pickett *et al.*, 1989
	Gundurimba Clay	124000 (WRC39143) 128000 (WRC39157)	$^{230}Th/^{234}U$, Scleractinian corals	Drury and Roman, 1983
	Gundurimba Clay	112000±9000 (74630127) 127000±18000 (74630130)	$^{230}Th/^{234}U$, Scleractinian corals	Marshall and Thom, 1976
	Inner Barrier sandrock	34000 +1200 - 1000 (GaK – 2320)	^{14}C, *Agathis robusta* log	Langford-Smith, 1971
	Inner Barrier sandrock	25900±1100 (GaK – 837)	^{14}C	Gill, 1967
Southern Queensland – North Stradbroke Island	Sand dunes – stratum name not established at time of publication	132000±5000 (QMF12385) 122000±4000 (QMF12400) 119000±3000 (QMF12041)	$^{230}Th/^{234}U$, Scleractinian corals	Pickett *et al.*, 1989

	Sand dunes	101000 +7000 - 8000 (QMF12385) 108000 +11000 - 10000 (QMF12400) 106000 +6000 - 8000 (QMF12041)	$^{230}Th/^{234}U$, Scleractinian corals (same samples as used for above determinations)	Pickett *et al.*, 1985
Southern Queensland – Gold Coast	(Freshwater?) peat, 26.8 m below MSL	10585±140 (SUA – 106)	^{14}C, peat	Thom and Chappell, 1975
Southern Queensland – Rainbow Beach	Inner Barrier sandrock	31000 +3200 - 2200 (GaK – 3013)	^{14}C , Driftwood embedded in inner barrier sandrock	Langford-Smith, 1972
Central NSW Coast – Forster/Myall Lakes	Reworked barrier dunes – Cape Hawk	76600±18700 (W1377)	TL, sand grains	Bryant *et al.*, 1994
Central NSW Coast – Newcastle Bight	Linear dune ridge/reworked barrier – Williamtown	17700±3700 (W1013) 20300±5600 (W1014) 30500±5700 (W015)	TL, sand grains	Bryant *et al.*, 1994; Thom *et al.*, 1994 (Same sample numbers and determinations appear in both papers)
	Sand dunes – Grahamstown. Stratum name not established at time of publication	142000±6000 (MMF27124) 155000±8000 (MMF27129)	$^{230}Th/^{234}U$, Scleractinian corals	Pickett *et al.*, 1989

6. BIOLOGICAL AND TAPHONOMIC ANALYSES

6.1 INTRODUCTION

In the absence of artifactual material it is necessary to study the biology and taphonomy of shells found in a deposit to determine whether or not it is likely to be an Aboriginal shell midden. In the presence of artifacts, taphonomic study provides vital information on site formation processes. Comparison of biological and taphonomic characteristics with other local Aboriginal shell midden deposits can also help determine whether a deposit is of anthropogenic origin. Study of the species composition of a shell midden deposit also provides information on resource use and availability at the time the deposit was formed and, in the case of sites representing multiple periods of occupation, changes in the availability and exploitation of these resources. The species present are also indicative of palaeoenvironmental conditions. Placing these shell deposits in a cultural and environmental context is an essential precursor to further studies of site formation processes and the development of erosion hazard models and assessment methods.

6.2 SPECIES COMPOSITION

6.2.1 **Woombah**

There are three species present in the site A sample and two in the site B sample, although both sites are essentially *Saccostrea glomerata* deposits with the same species composition. The site B sample consists of disarticulated *Saccostrea glomerata* valves and one *Pyrazus ebeninus* shell. It makes up only 0.005% of the sample by weight and as its presence is most likely incidental it has not been included in the species composition calculations for this sample. Thus, *S. glomerata* dominate the site B sample (Figure 6.1). Species present in the site A sample include disarticulated *S. glomerata* and *Anadara trapezia*, and negligible *P. ebeninus* (Figure 6.2, Plate 1). The weights of *A. trapezia* (one valve) and *P. ebeninus* (one individual) comprise 1.766% and 0.221% by weight respectively (Table 6.1). Thus, as at site B, it is fair to say that *S. glomerata* is the dominant species in this deposit.

Saccostrea glomerata, commonly known as the Sydney Rock Oyster, is an estuarine species which attaches to rocks or mangrove roots in mudflat areas. Its distribution ranges from southern Queensland south to Victoria (Northern Rivers Catchment Management Authority). During the Last Interglacial period *A. trapezia* extended as far south as coastal South Australia and Victoria, however it is now restricted to eastern Australia, where it is common in estuaries and mudflats (Ludbrook, 1984). *P. ebeninus* is a gregarious species abundant on estuarine mud flats which are exposed at low tide (Ludbrook, 1984). Both deposits contain species which inhabit similar environments indicating local resource use by the Aboriginal inhabitants of the area. Indeed, oysters are still prolific in the Clarence estuary and are commercially farmed (see Local Resources and Land Use section). No juveniles were present in samples collected from the WA and WB sites.

The deposit at Meehan's (1982) Wombah 1 excavation site is also dominated by *S. glomerata* and Department of Environment, Climate Change and Water (DECCW) records indicate sites WA and WB are also part of the Woombah midden complex (DECCW Aboriginal Heritage Information Management System). Although not excavated, these sites were noted and their location marked on a map produced as part of the Meehan study. The Yaegl Local Aboriginal Land Council has identified the Woombah midden complex as a significant local cultural site (Ferlin Laurie, personal communication) and signage has been placed at the site of the WB deposit, a product of collaboration between the Yaegl community and DECCW. Based on this evidence the shell deposits at sites WA and WB are considered to be anthropogenic in origin.

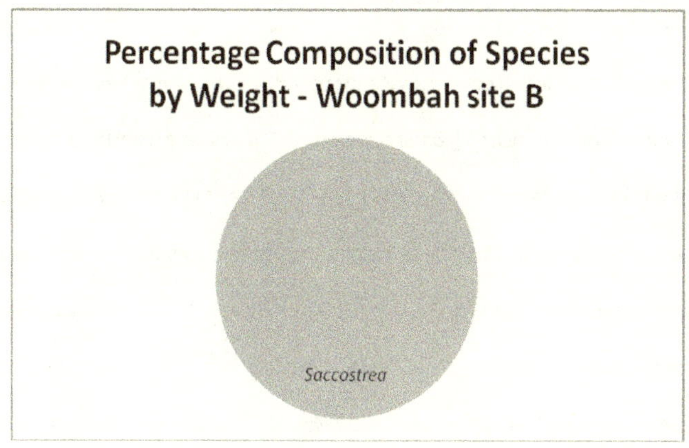

Figure 6.1: Percentage composition of species by weight – Woombah Site B.

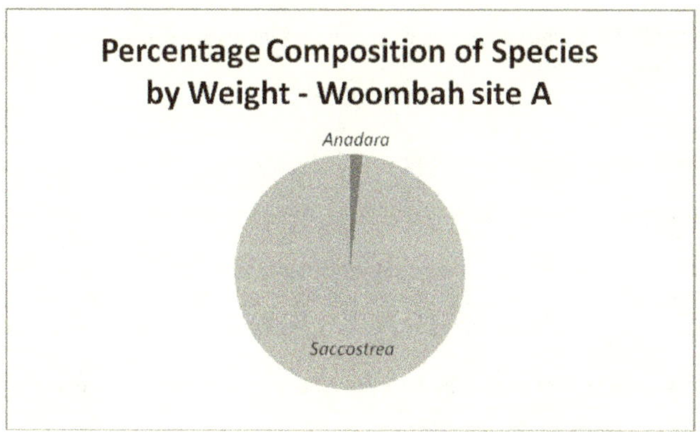

Figure 6.2: Percentage composition of species by weight – Woombah Site A.

Table 6.1: Woombah Site A – percentage composition of species by weight. Size Range (U) = size range of upper valves. Size Range (L) = size range of lower valves.

WOOMBAH SITE A PERCENTAGE COMPOSITION OF SPECIES BY WEIGHT				
SPECIES	*Pyrazus ebeninus*	*Anadara trapezia*	*Saccostrea glomerata*	TOTAL WT. (g)
WEIGHT (g)	1	8	444	453
% COMPOSITION	0.221	1.766	98.013	
SIZE RANGE (U)	n/a	n/a	4.5-9.9 cm	339
SIZE RANGE (L)	n/a	n/a	4.1-7.7 cm	105

6.2.2 **Sleeper Island**

The Sleeper Island midden comprises three species, all of which are edible (Ferlin Laurie, personal communication). *Saccostrea glomerata* is present in similar proportions by both weight (Figure 6.3) and minimum number of individuals (Table 6.2, Plate 1). *Anadara trapezia* is the dominant species, accounting for 71.692% by weight. Percentage composition was also calculated using individual counts in two ways (see Chapter 4, Methodology). No juveniles were present in samples collected from Sleeper Island. Valves both *in situ* and in the lag deposit are disarticulated so it is impossible to determine the exact number of individuals. The sample size is also relatively small and this may have had an influence on the results. Thus, percentage composition based on weight of shell material, as opposed to minimum number of individuals (MNI), appears to be the most appropriate method to use when assessing individual sites in this area, and also when comparing those sites.

The Sleeper Island midden shows a different pattern of resource utilisation to the deposits studied at Woombah. Other midden deposits at Woombah show a similar pattern of resource utilisation to sites A and B in the current research, with *S. glomerata* accounting for up to 95% by weight of shell material at sites studied by McBryde (1982). *Saccostrea glomerata* and *A. trapezia* occupy similar habitats however the species composition of the various midden deposits suggests local resource availability may have varied substantially from site to site. Exploitation of a wider variety of resources, coupled with the presence of stone artifacts, could indicate the Sleeper Island site fulfilled a different function to the oyster middens at Woombah. The position of the Sleeper Island site, present at the rapidly eroding western extremity of the island, may indicate this deposit was once much larger.

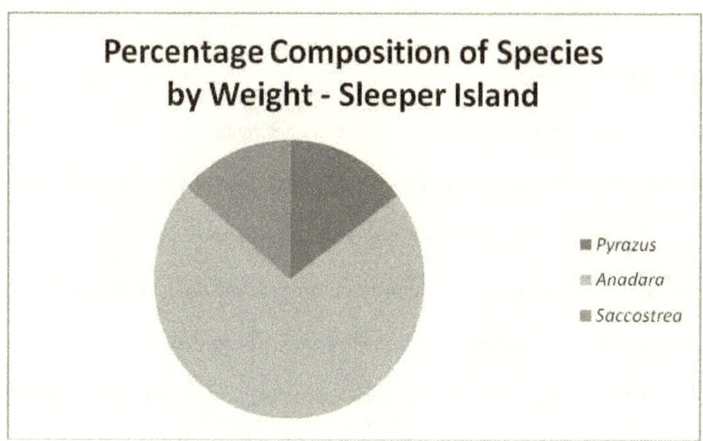

Figure 6.3: Percentage composition of species by weight – Sleeper Island.

Table 6.2: Sleeper Island – percentage composition of species by weight and minimum number of individuals.

SLEEPER ISLAND PERCENTAGE COMPOSITION OF SPECIES BY WEIGHT AND MINIMUM NUMBER OF INDIVIDUALS				
SPECIES	*Pyrazus ebeninus*	*Anadara trapezia*	*Saccostrea glomerata*	TOTALS
WEIGHT (g)	127	624	118	869
% COMPOSITION BY WEIGHT	14.729	71.692	13.579	100
MINIMUM NUMBER OF INDIVIDUALS (MNI)	10	22	6	38
% COMPOSITION BY MNI	25.974	57.143	16.883	100
in situ COUNTS	10	22	7	39
TOTAL MNI	20	44	13	77
AVERAGE WT. (g)	12.6	14.512	19.667	

6.2.3 Plover Island

Circumnavigation of the island and examination of its surface yielded no *in situ* shell remains. Soil exposures are easily seen around the entire island and contain Aboriginal stone artifacts. A large lag deposit of well-rounded shell fragments (see subsequent taphonomy discussion) is present at the base of the island on its north side. Identifiable fragments include shells of the genus *Turbo* and high spired gastropod shells likely belonging to several species of whelk (see Chapter 3 for pictures). As there is no evidence of an *in situ* source of these shells on Plover Island, only a brief discussion on their possible origin will be discussed in the Taphonomy section. The absence of any confirmed Aboriginal shell middens on Plover Island does not discount the site from this study. The presence of an extensive Aboriginal stone quarry on the island coupled with stabilised Aboriginal shell middens in the back dunes opposite Plover Island indicates this location was once important for the gathering and use of multiple resources.

6.2.4 **Minnie Water**

The Minnie Water site comprises *in situ* and lag shell deposits (see Chapter 3). Although the proportion of major edible species by MNI is slightly higher in the *in situ* deposit, there is no significant difference between the results when a 5% standard error calculation is applied. Values for edible and non-edible species present in the lag and *in situ* deposits on the other hand fall outside the assigned 5% error margin, indicating a statistically significant difference between the relative percentages of non-edible species present in the two deposits (Figure 6.4).

When the two major edible species, *Dicathais orbita* and *Turbo undulatus*, are considered separately further differences are apparent. While there is no significant difference between the weight of whole and fragmented *T. undulatus* in the *in situ* and lag deposit samples there is a significant difference between the weight of whole and fragmented *D. orbita* shells in both the deposits. Species composition of the two deposits is also variable (Figure 6.5).

The species composition of middens further north – South Beach, Evans Head and South Ballina Beach, Ballina – differs significantly from that of the midden at Minnie Water. Situated in a similar environmental setting and in the same region it is worth comparing these deposits. The South Beach midden is a monospecific assemblage containing Pipi shells present as a compact lens (Meehan, 1982). The South Ballina Beach Pipi midden also contains some oyster shells, although these are in the minority. The stratigraphic integrity of these two deposits appears much stronger than at the Minnie Water site although blowouts do occur at close by Schnapper Point (Meehan, 1982). The Schnapper Point archaeological site, however, only contains stone artifacts, so a direct comparison with the Minnie Water site is not possible. Coupled with the taphonomic evidence (see subsequent taphonomy discussion) the biological evidence presented here indicates the *in situ* deposit at Minnie Water has been reworked, most likely by the action of wind and waves.

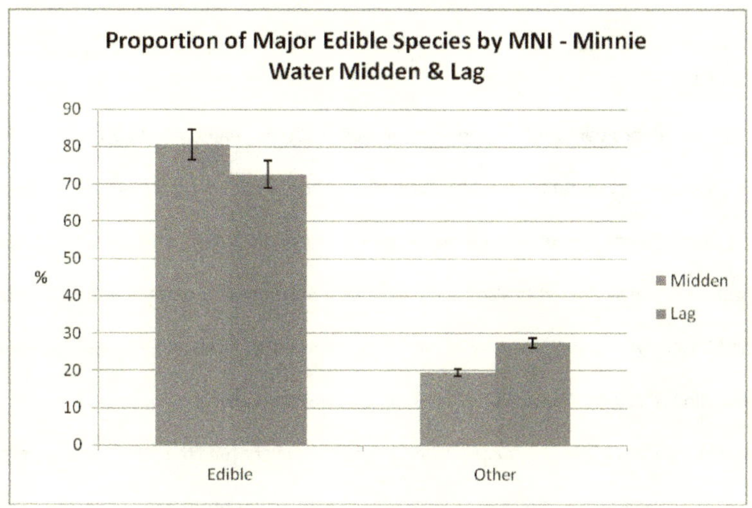

Figure 6.4: Proportion of major edible species by MNI – Minnie Water.

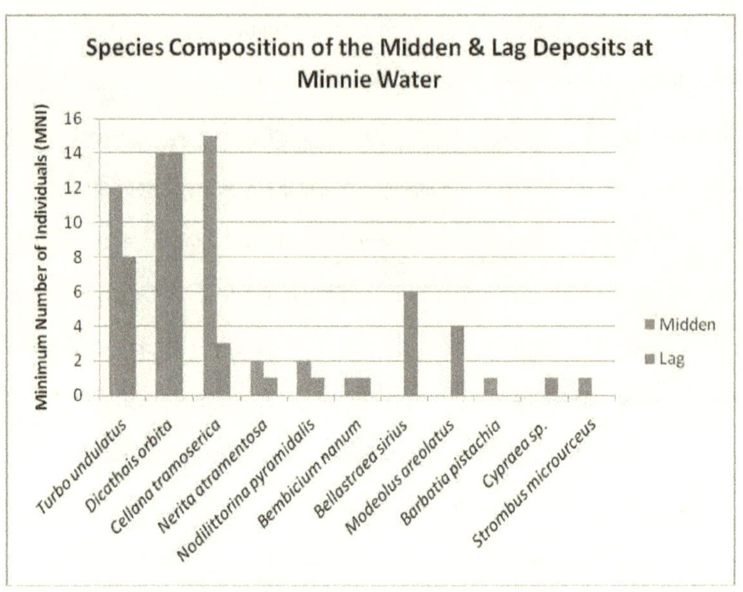

Figure 6.5: Species composition of the midden and lag deposits at Minnie Water.

6.2.5 **Wooli**

The shell deposit at Wooli comprises solely edible species, namely *Anadara trapezia, Pyrazus ebeninus, Saccostrea glomerata, Turbo undulatus and Velacumantis australis* (Table 6.3). *Anadara trapezia* is the dominant species, accounting for approximately half of the shell material by weight. *Pyrazus ebeninus* and *S. glomerata* also have a significant presence. Percentage composition by weight and MNI for *A. trapezia* and *P. ebeninus* is not significantly different when a 5% standard error calculation is applied (Figure 6.6). Values for *S. glomerata*, however, do differ significantly and this is most likely a result of the oyster shell being lighter in weight than the other two major species. Thus, there is an underestimation of up to 9% for the oyster shell contribution. *Anadara trapezia* shells remain in the majority, however, and percentage composition by weight calculations are used as the standard for comparison between deposits in this study.

Species composition of the Wooli deposit is most closely comparable to that of the Sleeper Island deposit. They are both estuarine riverbank deposits although one is present in a high energy, highly erodible environment (Sleeper Island) and the other a low energy depositional environment. Two deposits in locations with differing geomorphic dynamics having a similar species composition indicates shells may have been collected elsewhere up- or downstream and brought to a central location to be consumed. In addition, the distribution of the three major species varies throughout the Wooli deposit (Figure 6.7) and this likely reflects differential distribution by humans. The following taphonomic evidence also supports these conclusions.

Table 6.3: Species composition of the Wooli midden.

TOTALS BY SPECIES	WEIGHT (g)	MNI	% COMPOSITION BY WEIGHT	% COMPOSITION BY MNI
A. trapezia	825.43	60	48.68	41.96
P. ebeninus	607.94	46	35.85	32.17
S. glomerata	245.05	31	14.45	21.67
V. australis	5.5	4	0.32	2.8
T. undulatus	11.77	2	0.7	1.4
OVERALL TOTALS	1695.69	143	100	100

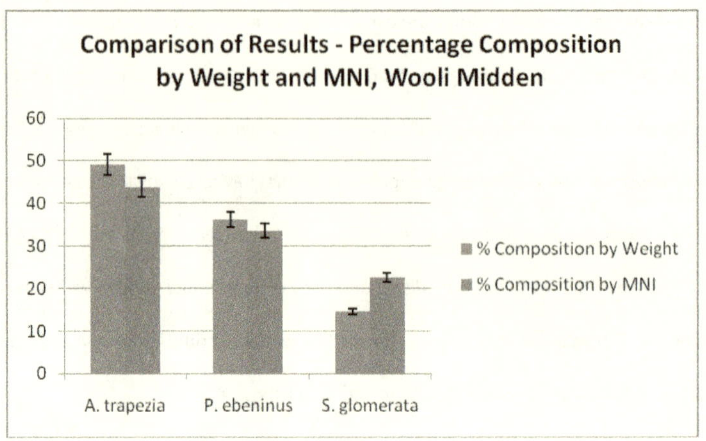

Figure 6.6: Comparison of results – percentage composition by weight and MNI, Wooli midden.

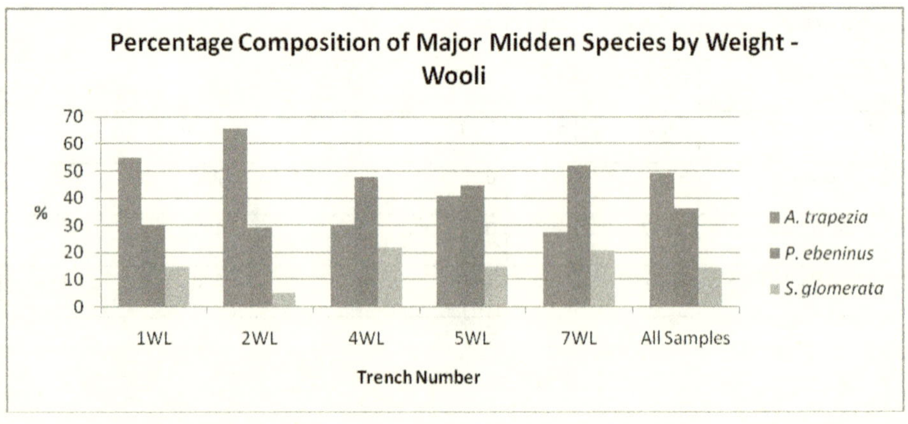

Figure 6.7: Percentage composition of major midden species by weight, Wooli midden.

6.3 TAPHONOMY

6.3.1 **Woombah**

The shells themselves are taphonomically similar at both Woombah site A riverbank oyster bed and site B creek bank midden exposure. Most upper and lower valves at both sites remain largely unbroken and shells do not appear very chalky, although some white material comes off onto the fingers when shells are handled. The nacreous layer is visible on many shells, although it is more commonly seen on the lower valves. Broken edges are angular to sub-angular, with some being sub-rounded, and surface features such as ridges and striae are clearly visible and have not been weathered away. This indicates burial or deposition in a low energy environment, in the absence of a continuous abrasive force.

Although there is a distinct lens in the creek bank exposure shells are randomly oriented within it. Shells at the site A riverbank exposure, however, have a more ordered orientation. Upper valves predominantly lie concave up, with some lying concave down and lower valves lie in a horizontal orientation. This also suggests burial or deposition in a low energy environment. Upper and lower valves are disarticulated at both sites and this indicates the shells did not die in their life position. Shells at the site A riverbank exposure may have been washed to their current position by tidal action post-mortem. Alternatively, they may have been deposited by humans although their burial position differs from the shells found at the site B creek bank midden exposure. Shells present in the creek bank exposure at Woombah site B appear *in situ* but may have been reworked. This is certainly the case for the shell surface scatter found in the A_p and A_o soil horizons at sites A and B. But these shells differ in appearance to those found at the site A and site B exposures, as they are highly fragmented and the depth of the scatter corresponds with the depth of the A_p and A_o soil horizons (see Chapter 5 and Appendix 1).

There appears to be no taphonomic bias towards the presence of upper or lower *Crassostrea* valves at site B. Upper valves in this sample account for 1.558 times more weight that lower valves but this may be attributed to the heavier weight of the upper valves of this species. At site A, however, upper valves account for 3.229 times more weight that lower valves –over double the weight difference at site B. If site A is an Aboriginal midden, this difference may represent a collection bias as the shells were prised off rocks. If site A is a natural shell accumulation this difference becomes harder to explain, as the shells were sampled *in situ*, rather than from their corresponding lag deposit, where a bias towards the retention of heavier shells is expected.

The condition of the shells themselves, as mentioned earlier, at a depth of 35-69 cm in the site B creek bank exposure does not indicate this part of the deposit is a reworked midden. The absence of pumice, gravel or large pieces of organic material such as twigs or branches also supports the idea these shells do not form part of a reworked midden at this depth. Comparison of radiocarbon dates between site A riverbank and site B creek bank shells may prove useful. The shell lenses sampled are present at approximately the same depth and if the apparently *in situ* site B midden material has been reworked we may see a random mixing of ages of shells. If the age determinations correspond between the two sites, site A may have been a food source and site B the discard location. Or site A may represent another midden in the Woombah complex. Taphonomically, the orientation of the shells, and weight ratios of upper and lower *Crassostrea* valves, are the only factors that differ between the site A and site B exposures. Differences between these factors do not provide conclusive evidence the deposits were formed by different agents.

Tables 6.4 and 6.5 (modified after Kidwell, 1991) summarise taphonomic, sedimentological and stratigraphic attributes of the Woombah site A and B deposits, from which shell material was taken for analysis. Features which differed between the two deposits are italicised and bold. From this table it can be clearly seen that the deposits at sites A and B differ negligibly when these broad-ranging factors are taken into account. The dimensions, relative abundance and orientation of shells differ between the two deposits. The dimensions of the two deposits are relatively similar and this feature alone is not diagnostic of site origin. Similarly, the relative abundance of shells in the two deposits does not differ dramatically, and the close-packing of shells is the same in both deposits, indicating they have a similar fabric. As mentioned above the orientation of the shells in both deposits is different. Considering there is no other evidence of a differing taphonomic history the taphonomic, sedimentological, stratigraphic and biological evidence strongly suggests the site A riverbank deposit has the same origin as the site B Aboriginal shell midden.

Analysis of the type of *Crassostrea* fragments present in the Woombah site A and B deposits (Table 6.6) provides further evidence in support of their similar origin. Results show approximately half the shell material present in both deposits is fragmented, and the fragmentation pattern is the same in shells from both deposits, with both upper and lower valves most commonly broken along the ventral margin.

Table 6.4: Attributes of shell concentrations – Woombah Site A.

Taphonomic features	
Articulation	Disarticulated and dissociated
Size sorting	Moderate
Shape sorting	Unsorted
Fragmentation	Some broken
Abrasion	Unabraded
Rounding	A-SA, some SR
Biological modification (bioerosion/encrustation)	Minor: shallow 0.2mm diameter pitting on shell surface
Orientation	***Mixed***
Sedimentological features	
Type of matrix	Clay/mud
Relative abundance (%) of shells	***15***
Close-packing of shells	Loosely packed (matrix-supported)
Associated sedimentary structures	Parallel to riverbank and present within a single, uniform stratum.
Stratigraphic features	
Thickness	0.19 m
Lateral extent	30 m
Geometry	Lens
Internal complexity	None, homogeneous

Table 6.5: Attributes of shell concentrations – Woombah Site B.

Taphonomic features	
Articulation	Disarticulated and dissociated
Size sorting	Moderate
Shape sorting	Unsorted
Fragmentation	Some broken
Abrasion	Unabraded
Rounding	A-SA, some SR
Biological modification (bioerosion/encrustation)	Minor: shallow 0.2mm diameter pitting on shell surface
Orientation	***All disturbed***
Sedimentological features	
Type of matrix	Clay/mud
Relative abundance (%) of shells	***25***
Close-packing of shells	Loosely packed (matrix-supported)
Associated sedimentary structures	Single, *in situ* creek bank shell lens overlain by shells disturbed and destroyed by farming machinery present in anthropogenic soils.
Stratigraphic features	
Thickness	0.24-1.13 m
Lateral extent	32 m
Geometry	Lens
Internal complexity	None, homogeneous

Table 6.6: Type of *Saccostrea glomerata* fragments present in the Woombah Site A and B deposit samples.

WOOMBAH SITE A	**WOOMBAH SITE B**
Lower valves: most commonly broken along ventral margin	**Lower valves**: most commonly broken along ventral margin
Intact shell weight= 52 g	Intact shell weight= 193 g
Fragmented shell weight= 53 g	Fragmented shell weight= 355 g
Total weight= 105 g	Total weight= 548 g
% Fragmented= 50.5	% Fragmented= 64.8
Upper valves: most commonly broken along ventral margin	**Upper valves**: most commonly broken along ventral margin
Intact shell weight= 191 g	Intact shell weight= 514 g
Fragmented shell weight= 148 g	Fragmented shell weight= 424 g
Total weight= 339 g	Total weight= 854 g
% Fragmented= 43.7	% Fragmented= 49.6
Total % Fragmented (upper and lower valves)= 45.3	**Total % Fragmented (upper and lower valves)= 55.6**

6.3.2 **Sleeper Island**

Shell material from the Sleeper Island lag deposit is similar taphonomically to the *in situ* material found at the site. Shells in both contexts appear chalky. Many *Anadara* have holes in their umbo. These holes are much larger than bore holes and the damage most likely appeared post-mortem as shells wouldn't have been collected as a food source if predation had removed the living animal. *Pyrazus ebeninus* shells all appear to have weathered in the same way. On many individuals the stronger columellar remains whilst the shell surrounding it has weathered away. This pattern is indicative of damage caused by an abrasive force such as wind or wave action in a sandy setting, or of acidic conditions. As the *in situ* material was found in soil and the matrix of the lag deposit consists of estuarine mud the former cause is unlikely.

Stone tools were also found in the lag deposit and they all consist of the same material (Plates 6 and 7). Meehan (1982) describes large stone artifacts from the excavated site Wombah 1 as being composed of greywacke. She notes the presence of bipolar pieces and unifacially flaked pebble tools, which is consistent with the artifacts found at Sleeper Island. The suite of stone artifacts found at Woombah and Sleeper Island corresponds with the general trend of technically and diagnostically undistinguished stone tools characteristic of recent levels from sites in eastern NSW described by White (1968). Meehan (1982) notes the greywacke used as a raw material for stone artifacts at Wombah 1 is likely derived from the eastern side of the Clarence Valley. The bedrock geology of the Clarence-Moreton Basin is consistent with this raw material, being composed of flat-lying soft Mesozoic sedimentary rocks (Troedson and Hashimoto, 2008).

Four cores and three flakes were collected in quadrat sampling of the lag deposit and this material constituted a representative proportion of the artifactual material present at the site. As the Sleeper Island midden site is clearly degraded it is impossible to know how much of the original cultural material remains, however Meehan (1982) also notes the Wombah 1 midden site is not rich in artifacts. Stone cores collected include one bipolar core and one retouched core tool (Plates 6 and 7). All flakes collected show bulbar points of percussion; flake scars are also present on one sample (Plate 7A). As minimal cultural material remains at the site it is impossible to gauge with any certainty whether or not the deposit was originally made up of a single, or multiple, occupation horizons.

Table 6.7 (modified after Kidwell, 1991) summarises taphonomic, sedimentological and stratigraphic attributes of the Sleeper Island lag and *in situ* deposits, from which shell material was taken for analysis. These features are typical of an Aboriginal shell midden deposit that is being eroded and reworked by tidal activity (Hughes and Sullivan, 1974; Claassen, 1998; Bonhomme, 1999). *In situ* shell material is present as a poorly sorted lens. Shell material present in the lag deposit is also poorly sorted with regards to size and shape; shells in both taphonomic contexts are disarticulated and dissociated. Minimal abrasion of *Crassostrea* and *Anadara* shells supports redeposition in a low-moderate energy environment subject to tidal action without perpetual high energy wave impact (Gill *et al.,* 1991) and this is consistent with the environmental context in which the midden is found. The pattern of abrasion seen on *Pyrazus ebeninus* shells may be a function of their shape. Experiments on conical shells (mean grain size -0.5ϕ, 1 700hrs) have produced a similar pattern of abrasion to that seen on *Pyrazus ebeninus* shells at Sleeper Island (Driscoll and Weltin, 1973).

Table 6.7: Attributes of shell concentrations – Sleeper Island.

Taphonomic features	
Articulation	Disarticulated and dissociated
Size sorting	Very poor (both *in situ* and lag deposits)
Shape sorting	Unsorted
Fragmentation	*Anadara* and *Crassostrea* all whole, some Whelk broken
Abrasion	*Crassostrea* unabraded, hole in umbonal region in many *Anadara*, Whelk abraded – columellar region remains intact
Rounding	SA-SR
Biological modification (bioerosion/encrustation)	Minor: shallow 0.2mm diameter pitting on *Crassostrea* surface
Orientation	All disturbed (both *in situ* and lag deposits)
Sedimentological features	
Type of matrix	Estuarine mud
Relative abundance (%) of shells	Shells concentrated as a lag deposit, little shell material remains *in situ* (<5%). Density of lag deposit reduced by ~90% on re-inspection 1 year after field work was carried out.
Close-packing of shells	Densely packed in lag deposit, dispersed (matrix-supported) *in situ*
Associated sedimentary structures	
Stratigraphic features	
Thickness	*In situ*: 0.10 m, lag: n/a (surface scatter)
Lateral extent	22.5 m (*in situ* and lag deposits)
Geometry	Lens
Internal complexity	None, homogeneous

6.3.3 Plover Island

A large lag deposit of well-rounded shell fragments is present at the base of the island on its north side. Identifiable fragments include shells of the genus *Turbo* and high spired gastropod shells likely belonging to several species of whelk (see Site Descriptions section for pictures). The source of this shell material is unclear. The shell fragments are mobile and there is no evidence of an *in situ* source for the shells on Plover Island. It may be they represent remnants of a once *in situ* Aboriginal shell midden located on Plover Island, have all weathered out and been reworked by wave action.

There are no identifiable artifacts present with the shells. The stones found in the lag deposit with the shells are also very well rounded and reworking by wave action may have obscured surface features pertaining to Aboriginal stone tools. The stones may have also been sourced naturally from the weathering of the rocky material constituting much of Plover Island, also quarried by Aboriginal people. The taphonomic, stratigraphic and sedimentological features presented in Table 6.8 (modified after Kidwell, 1991), coupled with the location of the deposit in the region where waves break at high tide, suggests exposure to high energy wave conditions. Whether or not the deposit is of anthropogenic origin is impossible to know. Even if it represented the remnants of an Aboriginal shell midden information loss has been profound and thus its scientific and anthropological value has been reduced. The presence of other valuable cultural deposits in close proximity to this deposit of unknown origin ensures the area retains its significance as an important Aboriginal cultural site.

Table 6.8: Attributes of shell concentrations – Plover Island lag deposit.

Taphonomic features	
Articulation	Disarticulated and dissociated
Size sorting	Very poor (both cobbles and shell material)
Shape sorting	Unsorted (both cobbles and shell material)
Fragmentation	All shells
Abrasion	Very worn (both cobbles and shell material)
Rounding	Very well-rounded (both cobbles and shell material)
Biological modification (bioerosion/encrustation)	None
Orientation	Random/all disturbed
Sedimentological features	
Type of matrix	Deposit of cobbles of same rock type comprising Plover Island. 0.01-0.3 m diameter, poorly sorted.
Relative abundance (%) of shells	30%
Close-packing of shells	Dispersed
Associated sedimentary structures	None
Stratigraphic features	
Thickness	<0.15 m
Lateral extent	30 m around north side of island

6.3.4 **Minnie Water**

Taphonomic evidence strongly suggests the Minnie Water midden has been reworked. The presence of pumice and complete lack of stratification coupled with the condition of the shells are characteristic of a deposit which has been reworked by the action of wind and waves. Gravel (well rounded and angular grains) is also present. Among the three main edible species, *Turbo undulatus, Dicathais orbita* and *Cellana tramoserica*, the amount of abrasion present on shells does not significantly differ between the *in situ* and lag deposits (Figure 6.8). Other species, however, do show a statistically significant difference between the deposits. This mixing of taphonomic characteristics is indicative of reworking (Claassen, 1998). The amount of biological modification also differs significantly between shells in the *in situ* and lag deposits and is consistently higher among *in situ* shells (Figure 6.9). This suggests a mixed origin of shells in the *in situ* and lag deposits.

Table 6.9 (modified after Kidwell, 1991) summarises taphonomic, sedimentological and stratigraphic attributes of the Minnie Water *in situ* deposit from which shell material was taken for analysis. All of the taphonomic features are indicative of a reworked deposit. The dispersed, matrix-supported packing of shells and lack of internal complexity are also characteristic of reworking (Bonhomme, 1999).

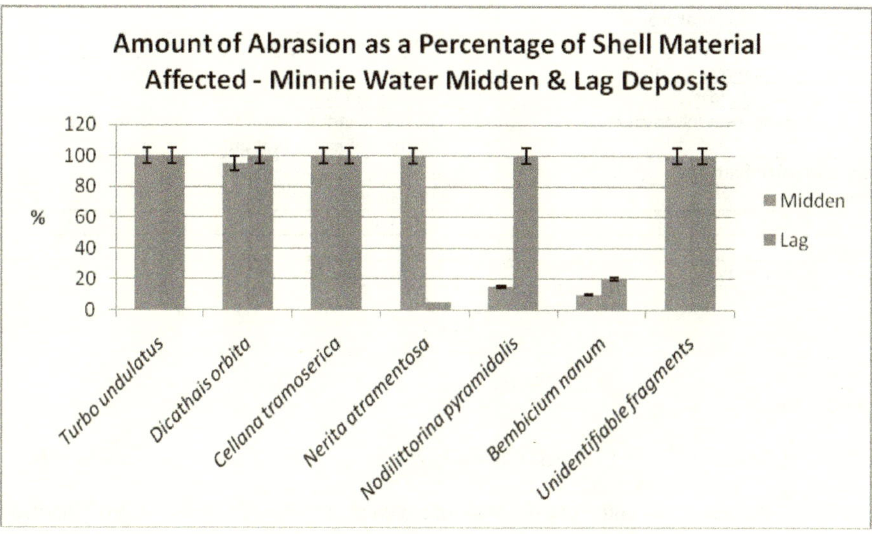

Figure 6.8: Amount of abrasion as a percentage of shell material affected – Minnie Water *in situ* and lag deposits.

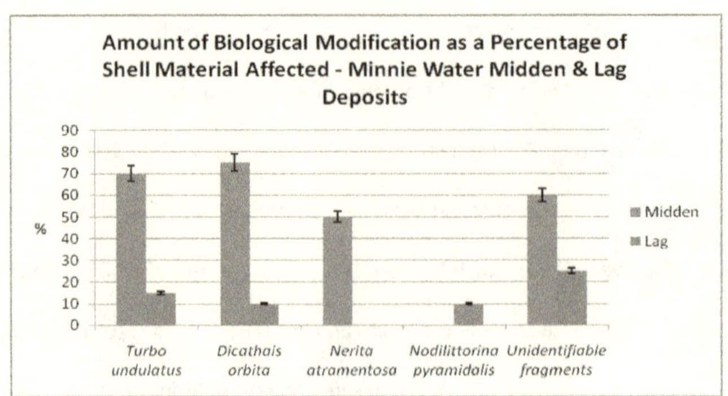

Figure 6.9: Amount of biological modification as a percentage of shell material affected – Minnie Water *in situ* and lag deposits.

Table 6.9: Attributes of shell concentrations – Minnie Water *in situ* deposit.

Taphonomic features	
Articulation	Disarticulated and dissociated
Size sorting	Very poor
Shape sorting	Unsorted
Fragmentation	80-90% shells broken
Abrasion	All shell material abraded. Abrasion present over 95-100% of shell surface in all but 2 minor species.
Rounding	SA-R
Biological modification (bioerosion/encrustation)	>50% coverage over major species and unidentifiable fragments, absent on minor species.
Orientation	All disturbed (both *in situ* and lag deposits)
Sedimentological features	
Type of matrix	Beach sand and gravel
Relative abundance (%) of shells	15%
Close-packing of shells	Dispersed (matrix-supported)
Associated sedimentary structures	Situated at the base of beach foredunes. Poor size-sorting of matrix in stratum containing shells.
Stratigraphic features	
Thickness	0.09-0.92 m
Lateral extent	85.3 m
Geometry	Lens
Internal complexity	None, homogeneous

6.3.5 **Wooli**

In the absence of artifacts biological and taphonomic evidence (Table 6.10; modified after Kidwell, 1991) supports an anthropogenic origin of the Wooli shell deposit. The shells are deposited in a lens of varying thickness, with no internal complexity and they are randomly orientated with poor size and shape sorting. The valves are disarticulated and dissociated. None of these characteristics support natural deposition in a low energy environment (Bonhomme, 1999).

Table 6.10: Attributes of shell concentrations – Wooli.

Taphonomic features	
Articulation	Most disarticulated and dissociated
Size sorting	Very poor
Shape sorting	Unsorted
Fragmentation	Fragmented and whole shells present
Abrasion	Unabraded
Rounding	A-SA, some SR
Biological modification (bioerosion/encrustation)	Very minor: shallow 0.1 mm diameter pitting affecting <2% of shells' surface.
Orientation	Random/all disturbed
Sedimentological features	
Type of matrix	River sand
Relative abundance (%) of shells	70%
Close-packing of shells	Densely packed (bioclast-supported)
Associated sedimentary structures	Parallel to riverbank and present within a uniform stratum of river sand
Stratigraphic features	
Thickness	0.04-0.16 m
Lateral extent	23.3 m (157m^2)
Geometry	Lens
Internal complexity	None, homogeneous

6.3.6 **Conclusions**

Biological and taphonomic study of shell deposits provides key information regarding site origin and site formation processes. This information is essential in the planning and preparation of appropriate erosion assessment techniques and conservation management strategies for Aboriginal shell midden sites. Biological and taphonomic studies of deposits at Woombah, Sleeper Island, Plover Island, Minnie Water and Wooli provide evidence of their anthropogenic origin, in addition to other characteristics of their depositional environment such as processes of reworking, erosion, deposition and the energy level of the environment. This provides a sound framework for the research presented in this Book.

7. GEOMORPHIC PROCESSES AND MAJOR IMPACTS

7.1 INTRODUCTION

This research focuses on geomorphological impacts affecting the accumulation, preservation and degradation of Aboriginal shell midden sites on the north coast of NSW, Australia. It is the interaction between these site formation processes which affects the degree of erosion or deposition at a site. The following chapter examines the role of major geomorphological impacts affecting the study sites at Woombah, Sleeper Island, Plover Island, Minnie Water and Wooli. Results of the three erosion hazard models presented in Chapter 4 are presented and discussed. Site-specific recommendations for conservation and management, based on the outcome of the models, are also presented.

Anthropogenic modifications to the main shipping channel of the Clarence River estuary from the late 1800's to the late 1900's have had a profound impact on the dynamics of sediment transport within the estuary. The structure of these changes, and accompanying alterations to the flow regime of the estuary, are examined. The scale of these modifications reflects the economic importance of facilitating commercial-scale transport of goods upriver to Grafton and other local ports. It also highlights the importance of adequate planning of such a large engineering project which has a multitude of environmental impacts.

Studying the impact of past sea level change provides valuable information on possible future impacts of such changes. It is important to consider susceptibility of sites to inundation caused by local sea level variation. Local, regional and global data on rates of sea level rise are used to calculate a possible time frame for inundation of low-lying sites. Factors driving local sea level variation are also examined.

In addition to studying the possible impacts of sea level rise, it is also important to understand the risk of inundation due to flooding and tidal activity. Predicted tide heights as well as tide and flood gauge data are used to predict the periodicity of inundation at the study sites, based on their elevation. The risk of, and robustness to, flooding and tidal inundation is a key indicator of erosion hazard.

Three methods for assessment of erosion hazard at Aboriginal shell midden sites have been developed as part of this research project (see Chapter 4). Each is formulated for use by a different stakeholder group and takes into consideration the purpose of data collection, scale at which data is required and levels and areas of expertise of those likely to be collecting the data and using the models. Similar key indicators of erosion are used across all methods however the models are structured differently for ease of use by the different stakeholder groups.

Using site-specific and regional data, the GIS model not only ranks erosion hazard on a site-by-site basis, it also illustrates regional trends and landscape-scale processes. Earth and environmental scientists would be most familiar with information in this format. The comprehensive method designed for use by archaeologists does include regional data however more site-specific data are included. Key indicators of erosion are matched with a site's geomorphic setting and a numerical ranking system is not used. The rapid assessment technique designed for use by the local Indigenous community focuses on collecting reliable data in a timely manner and format which is easy to interpret by both scientists and archaeologists. These simple methods of data collection and analysis yield very similar results to the more complex, scientific analyses used in the other two methods.

7.2 ANTHROPOGENIC MODIFICATIONS TO THE CLARENCE RIVER CHANNEL

There have been three stages in the modification of the Clarence River channel at its entrance to the Pacific Ocean (Figures 7.1 A to 7.1 H). These modifications have transformed the area from a shallow channel containing numerous sand spits and sand bars to a deep-sea port. When Matthew Flinders first landed on the shores of Yamba he was unimpressed by what he saw and, naming the place Shoal Bay, left it without further exploration upstream, as he was certain no major river would be found (Howland and Lee, 2006). In 1854 it became evident to the first white settlers that some modifications to the channel would need to be made if boats were to safely access the port on their way through to Grafton. Stage one focused on directing flows through the south side of the entrance and was named Moriarty's Scheme, after E. O. Moriarty, Engineer-in-Charge for Harbours and Rivers (Howland and Lee, 2006). When this scheme had little success a second, Coode's Scheme, was introduced by John Coode, an English consulting engineer (Howland and Lee, 2006). The third stage was a continuation of recommendations made by Coode. Table 7.1 summarises the channel modifications and their effect on the channel. Figures 7.2 to 7.5 show the current structure of the channel.

Table 7.1: Post-European Channel Modifications to the Clarence River mouth. Source: Howland and Lee (2006).

STAGE	MODIFICATION	EFFECT ON CHANNEL
Moriarty's Scheme (1860-1889)	*The Gantry Wall.* A river training wall extending along the Yamba shoreline (Fig. 7.1 C). Built in the 1860's. Building the wall created three bays between it and the original shoreline. These bays were later reclaimed by filling with sand dredged from the river channels and bar. *Moriarty's Wall.* Also built in the 1860's, along with other training walls, on the northern (Iluka) side of the channel.	By fixing the southern channel permanently open and directing flows south by building training walls on the north side of the channel, Moriarty hoped to create a permanent shipping channel on the south side. Instead this caused the shoals and channels on the north side to coalesce into a large spit (Fig. 7.1 B). This caused gradual silting up and widening of the entrance from ~450m in 1862 to ~800m in 1882.

Coode's Scheme (1885-1903)	*Middle Wall, Collis Wall* (off south east side of Goodwood Island) and the *north bank at Iluka* (creating Iluka Bay) (Figs. 7.1 D to F). The main channel was dredged in 1890 by the great flood of that year, assisting the man-made works. Coode also recommended construction of extended breakwaters projecting to sea from both north and south heads.	Coode proposed the reverse of Moriarty's Scheme. He argued flows naturally rushed out to sea via the shorter, northern route. Permanently opening the northern channel was also considered safer by mariners as it was easier to guide a vessel north rather than taking a sharp port side turn across the current to enter the southern channel. Coode's Scheme directed the flow of water and water craft through a stable channel north of the Middle Wall. As a result of these channel modifications sand shoals accreted on the south side of Middle Wall and today form Dart and Hickey Islands. The south entrance closed permanently in 1940 as sedimentation caused Hickey Island to join the mainland (Fig. 7.1 G).
North and south external breakwaters (1950-1971)	A continuation of Coode's recommendations. The southern breakwater was extended by 800m and a northern breakwater 1280m in length was created. The required channel depth of 5.5m was achieved by building the breakwaters 366m apart. A spur was also added along the southern end of Moriarty's Wall running upstream (Fig. 7.1 H).	The construction of extended breakwaters from the north and south heads created a funnel, the tide scouring the bar and thus removing sediment from it. The spur added to Moriarty's Wall created a one metre improvement in the width of the stable river channel.

It can be seen that alteration of the natural flow of the Clarence River estuary has had a profound impact on its dynamics and geomorphology. Whilst concentrating the flow has had the desired effect of creating a deep shipping channel, it has also caused sedimentation on the passive (south) side of Middle Wall. It is likely this change in flow regime has had an effect on the study sites at Sleeper Island and Woombah.

As a consequence of Coode's Scheme (Table 7.1), flow was directed to the north of Middle Wall, causing sedimentation to occur on the south side which resulted in the formation of Hickey and Dart Islands, and the broadening of Rabbit Island (Figures 7.1 D to H). These islands lie immediately east of Sleeper Island. Shallowing of the south channel due to sedimentation may have increased the susceptibility of Sleeper Island to erosion caused by boating wash generated by small recreational vessels with outboard motors. The southern and eastern sides of the island are directly exposed to this threat.

The implementation of Coode's Scheme may have also had an effect on the Woombah study sites, in particular site WA, located in the riverbank. The creation of Collis Wall, Middle Wall and Iluka Bay is likely to have reduced sedimentation on the southern and eastern sides of Goodwood Island, facilitating more effective flow from the North Arm of the Clarence River downstream into the main channel. Facilitation of flow along the North Arm will reduce the likelihood of sedimentation and may in fact cause erosion if riverbanks are not well protected by vegetation. These low-lying estuarine sites are also highly susceptible to erosion caused by flooding and tidal inundation, in particular if the local sea level was to rise. Possible effects of sea level variation are explored in the next section, followed by presentation of results and discussion of the effects of flooding and tidal inundation.

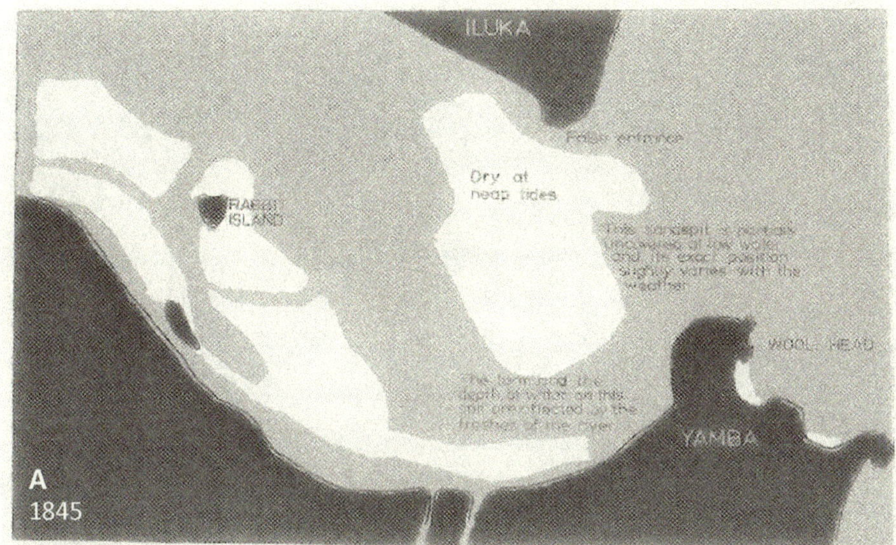

Figures 7.1 A-H: Diagrammatic representation of the anthropogenic modifications to the Clarence River estuary.

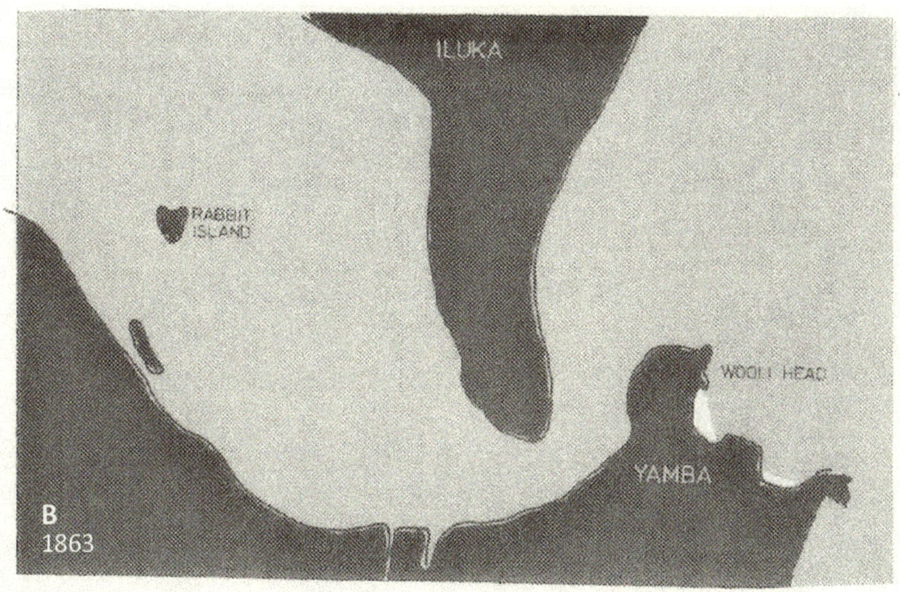

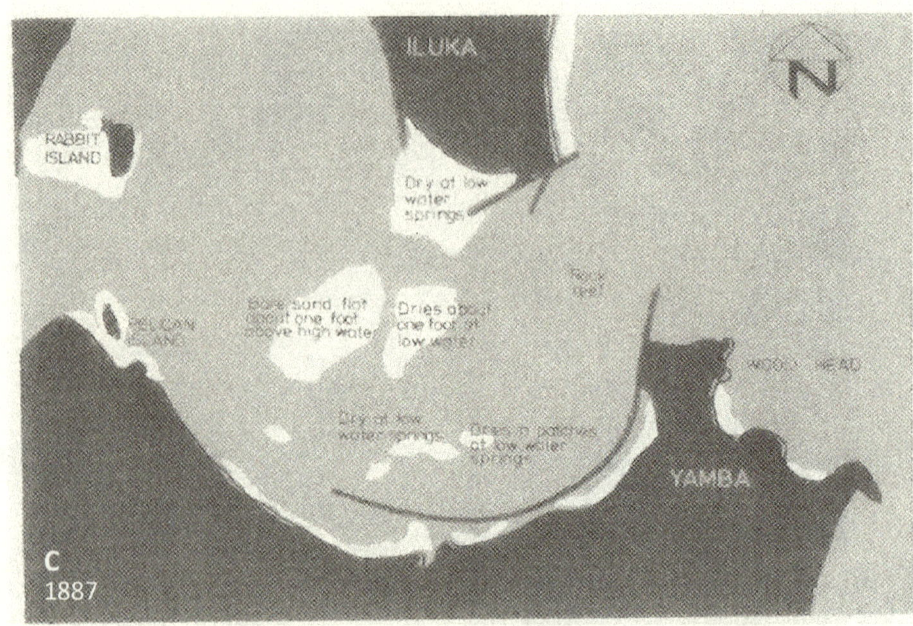
ILUKA
RABBIT ISLAND
Dry at low water springs
Rock reef
Bare sand flat about one foot above high water
Dries about one foot at low water
Dry at low water springs
Dries in patches at low water springs
YAMBA
C
1887

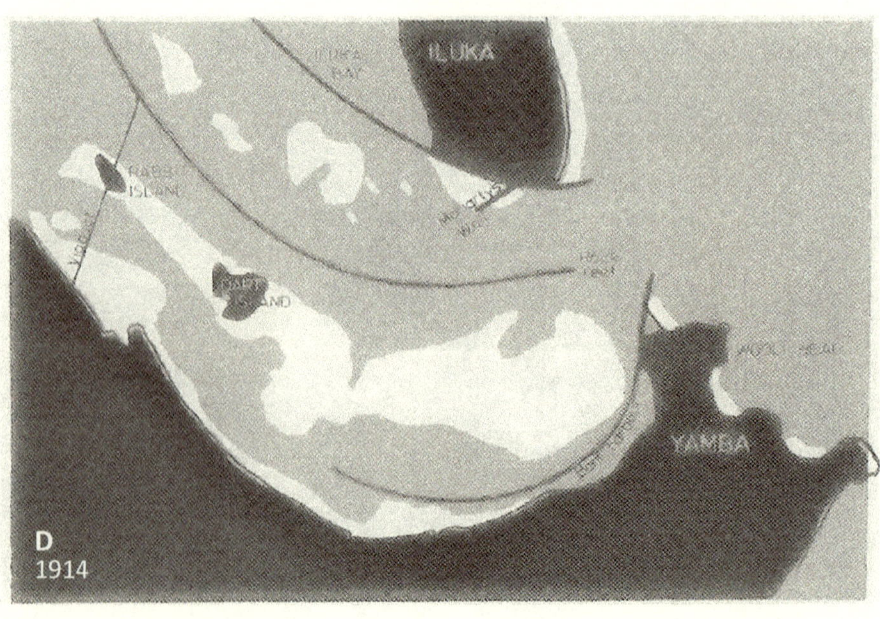
ILUKA
YAMBA
D
1914

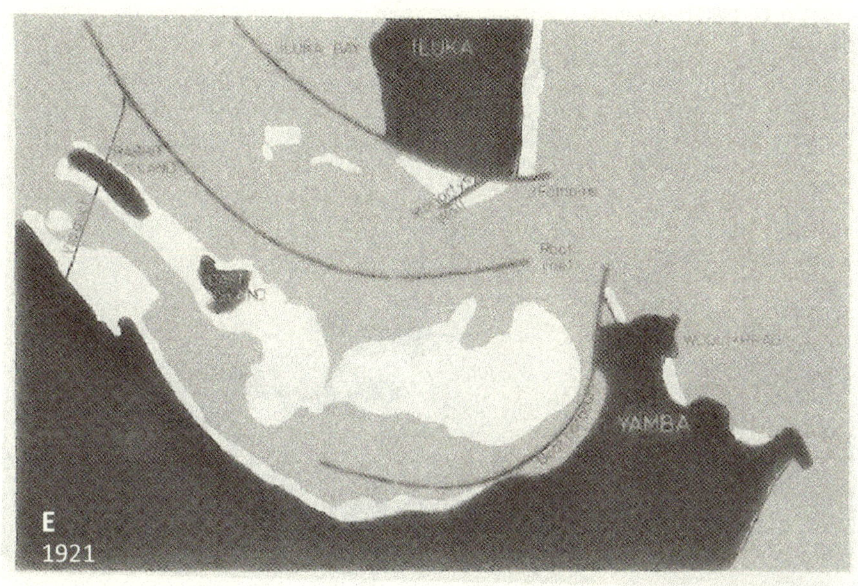
ILUKA BAY
ILUKA
YAMBA
E
1921

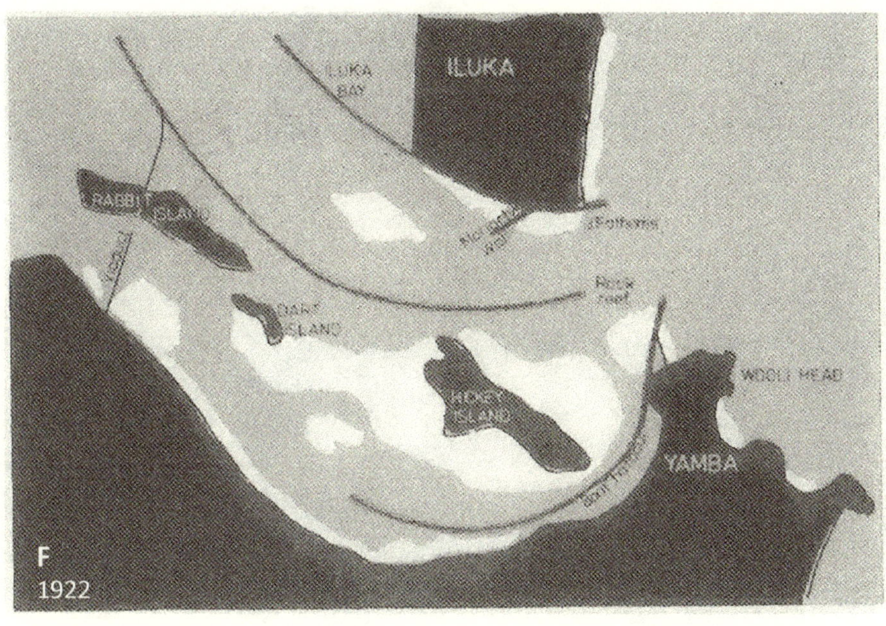
ILUKA
BAY
ILUKA
RABBIT
ISLAND
Rock
reef
WOOLI HEAD
YAMBA
F
1922

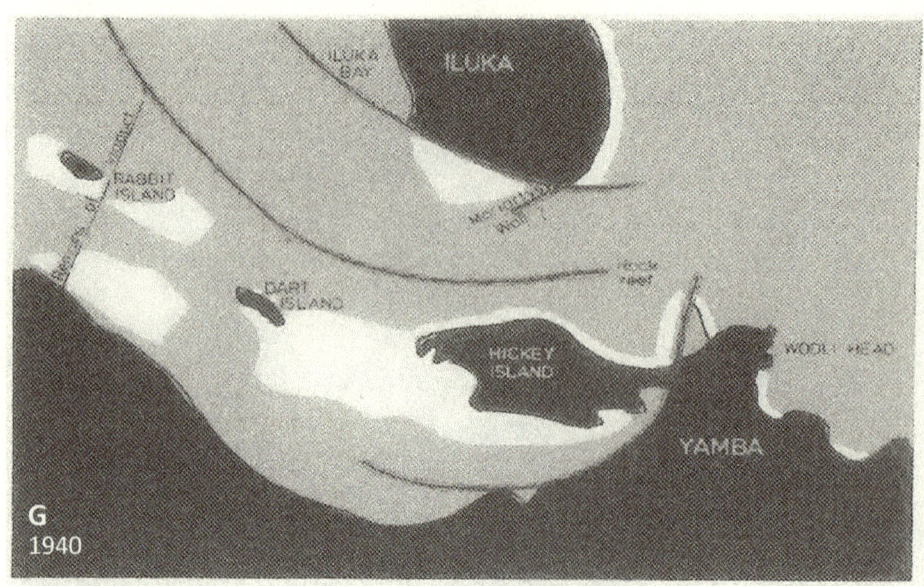
ILUKA
BAY
ILUKA
RABBIT
ISLAND
DART
ISLAND
Rock
reef
HICKEY
ISLAND
YAMBA
G
1940

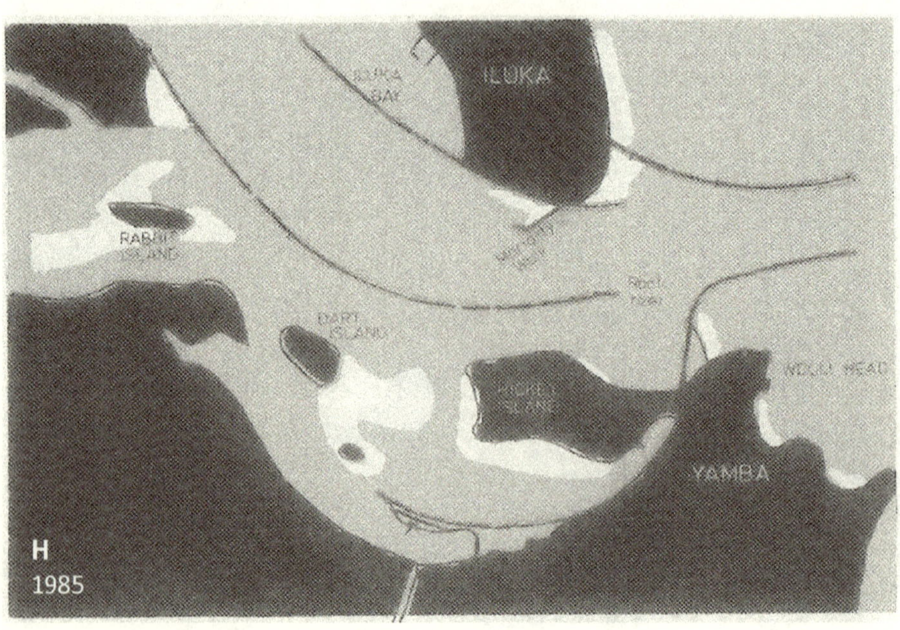
ILUKA
BAY
ILUKA
RABBIT
ISLAND
DART
ISLAND
YAMBA
H
1985

Figure 7.2: The south external breakwater at Yamba. The mouth of the Clarence River lies to the left of the wall.

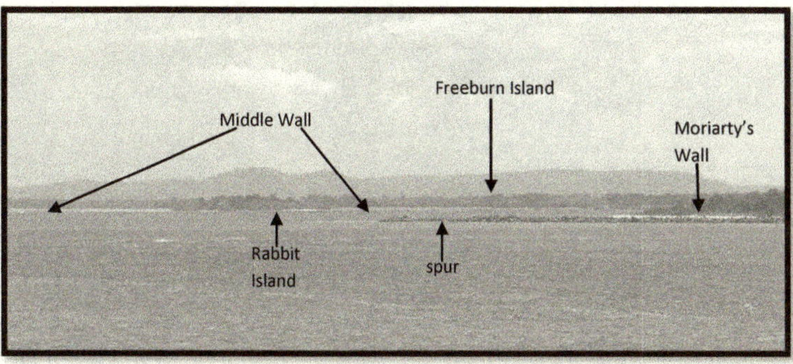

Figure 7.3: Moriarty's Wall, complete with spur directed upstream. Middle Wall can be seen in the background. Ilkua beach lies to the left.

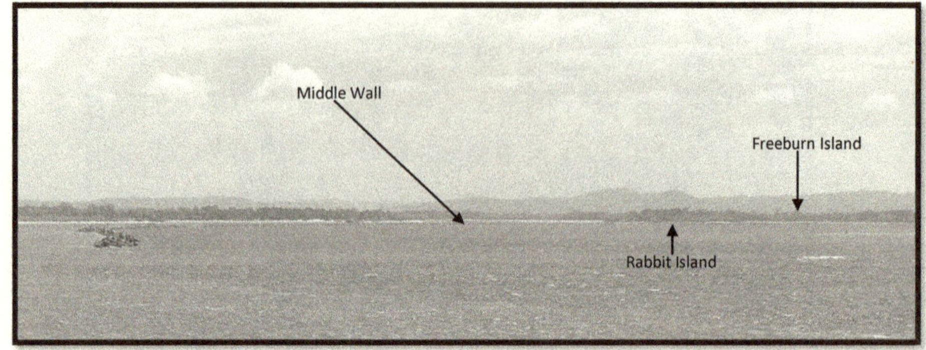

Figure 7.4: Middle Wall as seen from the south external breakwater.

Figure 7.5: Close up of the eastern end of Middle Wall, taken from the south external breakwater.

7.3 SEA LEVEL

It is important to consider the impact of future climate and sea level trends on study sites due to their proximity to the current coastline, and the fact that a number of them are located in low-lying areas (elevation <1 mAHD). The suitability of past global climate and sea level trends as analogues for current and future conditions is investigated, along with causes of sea level change. Holocene sea level proxy data and rates of sea level change for eastern Australia, as well as models of future rates of sea level change are reviewed. The risk of inundation by rising sea level to low-lying midden study sites is predicted based on local sea level data that have been reviewed.

7.3.1 **Sea level during interglacial stages**

The Holocene period (from 10000 years ago to the present) was characterized by warming climates and rising sea levels until around 6000 yrs ago when the current stable interglacial period was attained. Extensive coastal sediment deposits show that in preceding interglacial periods sea level also rose to around the same position as the Holocene (Thom and Murray-Wallace, 1988) and had a profound impact on the geomorphology of coastal estuaries, including the Clarence. The conditions leading to each of these interglacials and the evolution of the sea level and coastal response help to inform an understanding of the current Holocene interglacial, its future trajectory and recent past.

There is much agreement that interglacial Marine Isotopic Stage (MIS) 11 (410 000 to 340 000 years BP) is likely the closest Quaternary analogue to the Holocene (MIS 1) (Masson-Delmotte *et al.*, 2006; Raynaud *et al.*, 2005; Ruddiman, 2005; Berger and Loutre, 2003; Berger *et al.*, 2003; McManus *et al.*, 2003; Bender, 2002; Shackleton, 2000; Petit *et al.*, 1999; Bassinot *et al.*, 1994). Present and predicted future northern hemisphere summer insolation levels are comparable to those present during the MIS 11 interglacial (Ruddiman, 2005; Berger and Loutre, 2003; Milankovich,

1941; Figure 7.6) and atmospheric concentrations of carbon dioxide have a mean value of 278 p.p.m during the ~30 000 year duration of MIS 11, close to the pre-industrial level of 280 p.p.m (Pepin *et al.*, 2001). $\delta^{18}O$ records from both benthic and planktonic foraminifera contained within North Atlantic deep sea cores show values similar to those recorded in the Holocene (McManus *et al.*, 2003). Therefore MIS 11 can be considered a non-industrial analogue of the Holocene interglacial.

However, the way in which the chronologies of the two stages are aligned differs among groups of researchers. The NorthGRIP-community-members (2004) align MIS 11 and MIS 1 at their glacial terminations (Terminations I and V), whereas Ruddiman (2005), Bender (2002), Shackleton (2000), Petit *et al.* (1999) and Bassinot *et al.* (1994) align substage 11.24 (partly glacial) with the Late Holocene (Figure 7.6). Differing alignments of MIS 11 and MIS 1 lead to different interpretations of current and future climate trends.

If MIS 11 and MIS 1 are aligned at their glacial terminations the trend that occurred during MIS 11 suggests insolation in the Late Holocene will continue for another ~16 000 years (NorthGRIP-community-members, 2004). Keeping this alignment of obliquity signals Masson-Delmotte *et al.* (2006) and Raynaud *et al.* (2005) propose a much longer persistence of interglacial conditions. They argue that low orbital obliquity, coupled with minimal northern hemisphere summer insolation, conditions which led to glaciations at the termination of MIS 11, will not occur in the next tens of thousands of years, thus prolonging current interglacial conditions. Given that an interglacial is considered to be "an uninterrupted warm interval in which the global scale environment reached at least the present level of warmth" (Berger *et al.*, 2003, p. 117), Masson-Delmotte *et al.*'s (2006) and Raynaud *et al.*'s (2005) argument suggests temperatures will not fall in the immediate future. It follows that sea level will likely show a similar pattern.

Based on this interpretation of the alignment of MIS 11 and MIS 1 there are two likely risk outcomes at the study sites. Firstly, if sea level remains at its present level, risk of inundation of the study sites will remain consistent. Secondly, if a change in insolation or atmospheric concentration of carbon dioxide causes an increase in global temperatures and subsequent rise in sea level, risk of inundation of the study sites will increase.

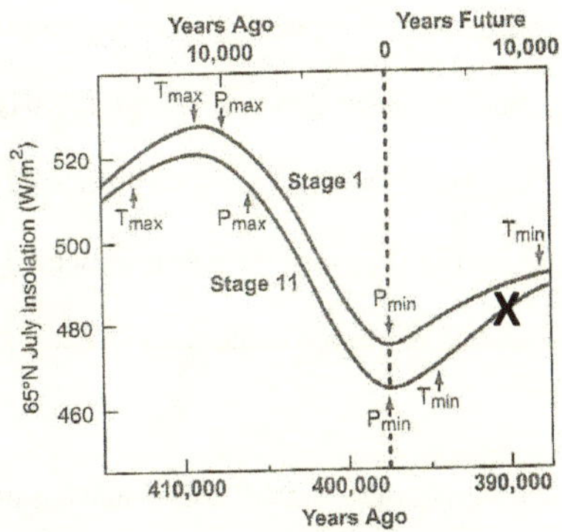

Figure 7.6: Alignment of MIS 11 and MIS 1 based on northern hemisphere summer insolation trends. Source: Ruddiman, 2005. X marks MIS substage 11.24.

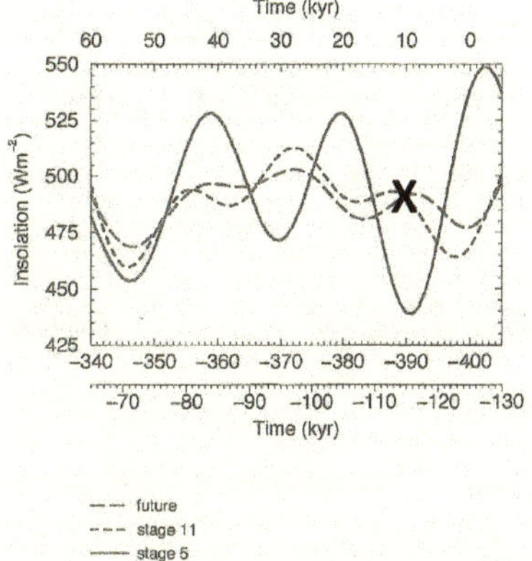

Figure 7.7: Northern hemisphere summer insolation levels during MIS 11 and MIS 5 and predicted future levels. Source: Berger & Loutre, 2003. X marks MIS substage 11.24.

Some researchers, including Bender (2002), Shackleton (2000), Petit *et al*, (1999) and Bassinot *et al.* (1994), align the Late Holocene insolation curve with MIS substage 11.24 (390 000 years BP) using climate proxy signals from the Antarctic Vostok ice core and northern hemisphere summer insolation trends (Figures 7.6 and 7.7). When aligned in this way it is evident that insolation levels are lower during MIS substage 11.24 than during the corresponding MIS 1 (Holocene) time period (Figure 7.6). In addition, instead of continuing to decrease, as happened during MIS substage 11.24, Holocene atmospheric concentrations of carbon dioxide and methane begin similar decreases but then start to increase again from around ~8 000 to 5 000 years BP (Figure 7.8). An increase in the atmospheric concentration of these gases, coupled with a postulated increase in insolation levels, is likely to lead to a rise in sea level based on the trends presented in Figures 7.6 and 7.8. A rise in sea level will increase the risk of inundation to the study sites.

Figure 7.7 shows predicted levels of insolation. Based on these predictions insolation is expected to increase over the next 10 000 years, at which time the level is postulated to mirror the MIS substage 11.24 level (Berger and Loutre, 2003). Although the MIS substage 11.24 insolation level varies between Figures 7.6 and 7.7, predicted insolation levels at +10 000 years are consistent. The predicted 65°N July insolation level of 490 W/m^2 is higher than the current level. A raised insolation level is consistent with the persistence of interglacial conditions, and thus, a similar or elevated risk of inundation of the study sites.

In contrast to both the Holocene and MIS 11, insolation levels during the Eemian interglacial (MIS 5e, Last Interglacial) were much more variable (Berger & Loutre, 2003; Figure 7.7). Greenland ice cores NGRIP, GRIP, GISP2, Camp Century and Renland all contain maximum $\delta^{18}O$ isotopic values 3‰ higher than the present value during the Eemian, indicating temperatures were ~5°C warmer than present for a period during the Last Interglacial (Figure 7.8), the isotopic 'maximum' occurring

~123 000 years BP (NorthGRIP-community-members, 2004). δD (stable deuterium isotope) values obtained from the Antarctic Vostok ice core also support these temperature conditions, with an isotopic 'maximum' occurring ~125 000 – 130 000 years BP (EPICA-community-members, 2004). Despite this evidence which that temperature and level of atmospheric carbon dioxide present during Stages 1 and 5 are not analogous to MIS 11 records, a similar trend in ice volume can be seen to occur through Stages 11 and 5, although the resolution of the records for Stage 1 are not ideal for comparison (Figure 7.8).

Comparison of MIS 11 and MIS 5 shows that the relationship between ice volume, insolation, temperature and atmospheric concentration of carbon dioxide is not straightforward. As the relationship between these variables changes through time it is essential to understand the effects of a variety of potential future sea level scenarios. Relatively minor alterations to the elevation of low lying sites can have a profound impact on their vulnerability to sea level rise, as well as to flooding and tidal inundation. The remainder of this section examines further causes of sea level rise as well as the risk of inundation of the study sites based on regional and local Holocene sea level proxy data and existing models of future sea level change.

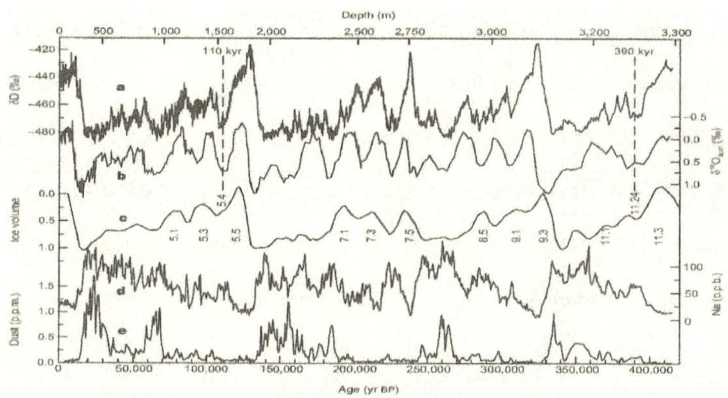

Figure 7.8: Vostok time series and ice volume. Source: Petit *et al.*, 1999.

7.3.2 **Causes of Sea Level Rise**

Factors influencing sea level rise can be non-climatic (geodynamic), climatological or oceanographic. Non-geodynamic changes in ocean volume can be either eustatic or steric. Eustatic sea level change is defined as "the result of water being added to or subtracted from the oceans, mainly through an exchange with ice held in the polar ice caps" (Lambeck, 1990, p. 206). Eustatic sea level change can also have a geodynamic component, being affected by changes in the shape of ocean basins (Lambeck, 1990). Steric changes in sea level result from changes in water density (Patullo *et al.*, 1955). Climatological and oceanographic factors influencing Eustatic and steric sea level include (Goodwin, 2003; Lambeck, 2002):

- **Ocean temperature and salinity**, which affect thermohaline circulation and sea water volume.
- **Ocean currents**, which cause tidal variation in sea level.
- **Surface wind stress** can cause monthly, bi-annual and decadal variability in steric sea level and is linked to the El Nino Southern Oscillation (ENSO) in the Pacific. Fluctuations in wind stress due to ENSO drive equatorial sea level ranges of up to ±0.40 m at Pacific eastern and western basin boundaries (Figure 7.9).
- **Increased ice ablation and meltwater contributions from glacier and ice sheet melting.**
- **Ice accumulation**. Increased precipitation occurs over the Antarctic ice sheets during interglacial periods due to the increased moisture carrying capacity of the warmer air mass, decreased extent of sea ice and increased ocean evaporation (Budd and Simmonds, 1991). These conditions may lead to a lowering of sea level through an increase in snow accumulation across the Arctic (Goodwin, 1998), North America and Europe.
- **Anthropogenic surface water impoundment and groundwater extraction**.

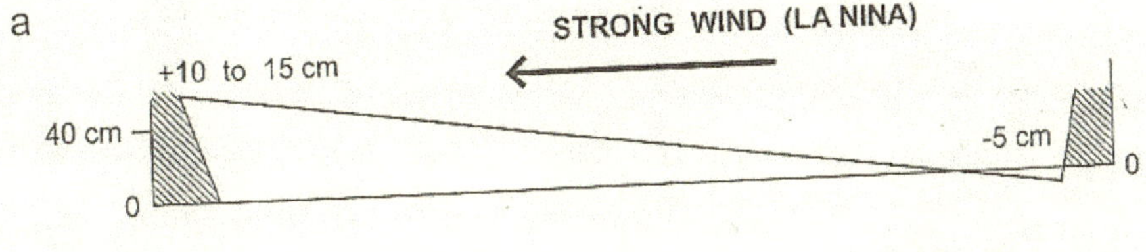

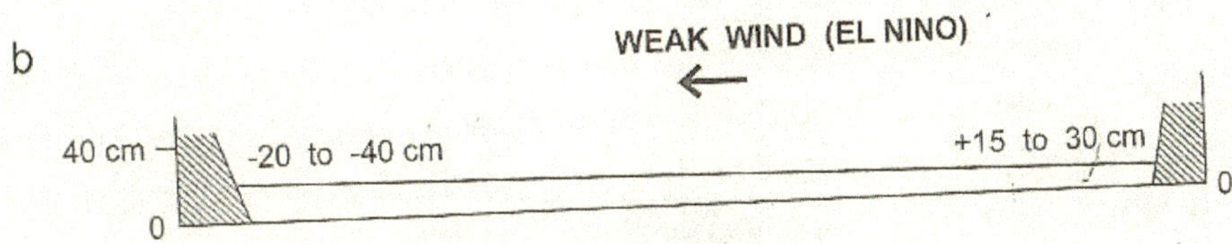

Figure 7.9: The effects of surface wind stress at the east and west Pacific basin boundaries. Source: Goodwin, 2003.

Geodynamic factors include:

- **Glacio-hydro-isostasy**, defined as "the loading of the sea floor by the rising sea during [a] postglacial marine transgression" (Lambeck and Nakada, 1990, p. 145), is illustrated in Figure 7.10. It can be seen that the sea level forms a high stand as a result of added meltwater. The increased ocean volume causes deformation of the crust along the continental margin which responds to the pressure of the water above it. A thin lithosphere and low viscosity upper mantle typically leads to enhanced high stand amplitudes, whilst thick lithospheres and high viscosity upper mantles show high stands with a reduced amplitude (Lambeck, 2002). The upper mantle viscosity appears to be lower for the Australian region than Europe, however lithospheric thickness is comparable (Lambeck, 2002); this may lead to higher amplitude Holocene high stands in Australia. Holocene high stand amplitudes can also be affected by the geometry of the coastline as this affects the distribution of added ocean water (Lambeck, 1990). Figure 7.11 shows higher amplitudes at bays and gulfs and lower amplitudes at open coastline locations; retreat of ocean water from upwarped areas causes flexing of the earth's crust.

- **Tectonism**, which can cause uplift in tectonically unstable locations and yield misleading palaeo-sea level information (Murray-Wallace, 2002).
- **Coastal and inner-shelf bathymetric changes**, which can cause changes in the tidal range at a particular location (Goodwin, 2003).
- **Tsunamis** (Goodwin, 2003).

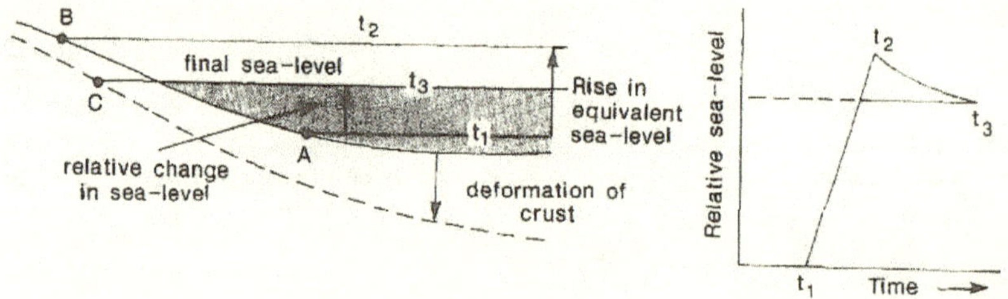

Figure 7.10: The mechanism of hydro-isostasy and its influence on sea level. Source: Lambeck & Nakada, 1990.

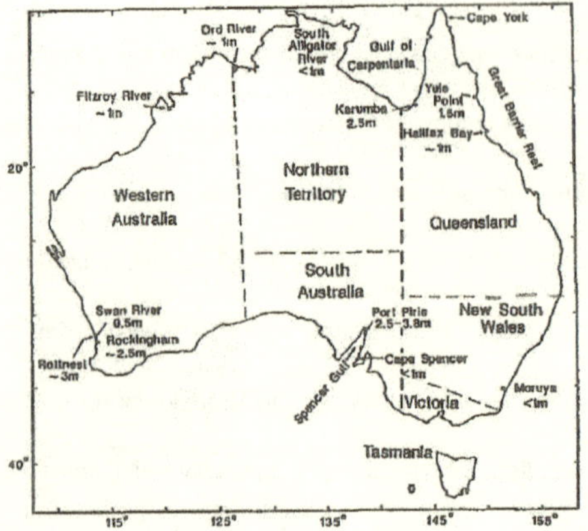

Figure 7.11: Summary of observed Holocene sea level highstands along the Australian coastline, showing higher amplitudes at bays and gulfs and lower amplitudes at open coastline locations. Source: Lambeck, 1990.

To interpret Late Pleistocene and Holocene sea level data it is easiest to study tectonically stable regions (Murray-Wallace, 2002; Goodwin, 1998; Lambeck and Nakada, 1990). However some of the most comprehensive sea level records come from the Huon Peninsula and Barbados but these areas are tectonically active. In such cases the tectonic uplift is so rapid it can be assumed to be constant and, once independently determined, subtracted from the apparent sea level heights. The Australian mainland margin is a passive continental margin situated in a tectonically stable intraplate setting (Brooke *et al.*, 2008; Lambeck, 2002; Murray-Wallace, 2002). The continental margin of Australia is considered a far-field site, meaning it is not in close proximity to the location of former ice sheets (present during glacial maxima) (Murray-Wallace, 2002). Sea level change in far-field sites is generally glacio-eustatic in origin and is modulated largely by local hydro-isostatic effects (Nakada and Lambeck, 1989). A minimal hydro-isostatic contribution of <0.50 m per 5000 years has been calculated by Lambeck (2002) for the Australian mainland margin, reinforcing the stability of the region.

7.3.3 **MIS 5e and Holocene sea levels along the east coast of Australia**

Included in Figure 7.15 is a global sea level reconstruction (Waelbroeck *et al.*, 2002, red line) and a curve for the Huon Peninsula, Papua New Guinea (Lambeck and Chappell, 2001, solid black lines). The global reconstruction is derived from benthic foraminiferal isotopic records and the Huon Peninsula curve is inferred from the height-age relationships of raised reefs and submerged fossil corals. There is general agreement in the trends of the two curves, although the peaks of the Waelbroeck *et al.* (2002) reconstruction are lower than those measured at the Huon Peninsula. Peak levels during MIS (OIS) 4 and 3 are also lower in the Waelbroeck *et al.* (2002) reconstruction. This may be due to tectonic uplift in the Huon Peninsula region or unrecognised sea water chemistry effects on the benthic record. The two sea level curves in Figure 7.15 show maximum MIS 5e sea levels of -5.0 m to +5.0 m. The post-LGM curve of Lambeck and Chappell (2001) shows a +2.5 m highstand at ~8000 years BP; data for this section of the curve were collected from Bonaparte Gulf, northwestern Australia. The global sea level curve of Waelbroeck *et al.* (2002) does not reflect this highstand. When considering past sea level it is best to use local data from a variety of sea level proxies and check this data against global models, taking into account tectonic setting, glacio-hydro-isostasy and other factors which can affect sea level at local and regional scales.

A variety of sea level proxies along the passive continental margin of Australia have been identified and dated using different methods. Proxies located along the central and northern NSW coastline and in southern Queensland include fossilised fixed biological indicators such as tube worms and barnacles (Lewis *et al.*, 2008; Baker *et al.*, 2001; Baker and Haworth, 2000; Flood and Frankel, 1989), fossilised corals (Marshall and Thom, 1976; Pickett *et al.*, 1989), organic material, such as estuarine shell, *in situ* wood and organic mud (Thom and Roy, 1983), marine shells (Murray-Wallace *et al.*, 1996; Thom and Murray-Wallace, 1988) and relict beach sediments (Roy and Boyd, 1996). Agreement of the ages and elevations (and implications of these elevations) between different sea level proxies would add credibility to them.

Fixed biological indicators (FBIs) are "sessile organisms confined to the intertidal zone that upon death become palaeo-sea level indicators" (Lewis *et al.*, 2008, p. 75). Species which inhabit a relatively narrow environmental range, such as the tube worm *Galeolaria caespitosa* and a variety of oyster and barnacle species, provide the most reliable palaeo-sea level data for use with the FBI methodology, which takes into consideration the relative height difference between the upper boundaries of relict and current species and assemblages (Baker *et al.*, 2001). It is argued that the resultant palaeo-sea level has only a small margin for error, relative to the habitat of the single species or assemblage present (Lewis *et al.*, 2008; Baker *et al.*, 2001). However it is important to note that fixed biological indicators are a proxy for palaeo-sea level. Verification of a variety of indicator species over a broad area is necessary to confirm the biological indicators are *in situ* (within their known habitation zone) and to ensure accuracy of results.

Age determinations can be made from *in situ* fossilised scleractinian corals using radiometric $^{230}Th/^{234}U$ analysis. If multiple determinations are made from common and abundant species this proxy can add valuable information to the sea level record (Marshall and Thom, 1976) in tectonically stable regions. Radiometric ^{14}C analysis of organic material located within relict marginal marine environments can also provide useful sea level data (Thom and Roy, 1983), provided the context of the *in situ* material is accurately gauged, and the environment to which it belongs is narrowly restricted (Sloss *et al.*, 2007). Amino acid racemisation (AAR) techniques provide information on relative ages of marine shells (Murray-Wallace *et al.*, 1996) and thermoluminescence (TL) dating of quartz grains yields age determinations from relict beach sediments (Roy and Boyd, 1996).

Table 7.2 contains palaeo-sea level information for the central and northern NSW and southern Queensland coastline. Radiocarbon (^{14}C) age determinations of fixed biological indicators show the sea level to be between 1.0 and 1.7 m above present sea level (APSL) for the period between 5500 and 1890 years BP, with small error margins of up to 0.25 m, with one exception of 0.5 m. Constant sea levels through time are not evident, rather sea level appears to fluctuate slightly. An age determination of 3810 years BP from *Galeolaria caespitosa* at Valla Cave was recorded in two separate studies (Baker *et al.*, 2001; Flood and Frankel, 1989) although inferred sea levels differ slightly in each study. Verification of a variety of indicator species over a broad area is necessary to confirm the biological indicators are *in situ* (within their known habitation zone) and to ensure accuracy of results.

Data obtained by Thom and Roy (1983) from relict marginal marine environments show a general trend in sea level rise immediately following the Last Glacial Maximum. The radiocarbon age determinations have large errors (analyses were performed over 25 years ago) and there is a sea level discrepancy of 0.8 m between the Port Stephens age determination and one of the Palm Beach determinations. Increasing the sample size and using a contemporary ^{14}C dating method would likely resolve these issues.

In situ fossilised corals at North Stradbroke Island and Evans Head were dated using the $^{230}Th/^{234}U$ method and found to be Last Interglacial in age (Marshall and Thom, 1976; Pickett *et al.*, 1989; Table 7.2). Original age determinations (Pickett *et al.*, 1985) placed the age of the corals at North Stradbroke Island at 108 000 – 101 000 years BP, providing evidence of a sea level highstand during MIS 5c. The same samples were re-dated (Pickett *et al.*, 1989) and found to be of Last Interglacial (MIS 5e) age (Table 7.2). Results from North Stradbroke Island indicate sea level was 1-3 m higher during MIS 5e and those from Evans Head indicate a sea level of 4-6 m higher than present at this time. However sea levels obtained from these corals have a high error margin and more accurate resolution would be beneficial to palaeo-sea level studies.

Anadara valves from the Largs shell bed in the Lower Hunter Valley (Thom and Murray-Wallace, 1988) have a valine D/L ratio of 0.30 (Table 7.2), showing time-equivalence with other Last Interglacial marine strata in southern Australia (Murray-Wallace, 2002). Although a relative dating method, AAR analyses provide a means of corroborating absolute ages obtained using other methods, and are a way of linking relict marine strata throughout Australia. It is important to note, however, that temperature is the primary factor exerting control over racemisation rate; the higher the temperature, the faster L-amino acids will convert to their D-forms (Miller & Bringham-Grette, 1989). Therefore, *Anadara* of the same age exposed to different water temperatures can yield different D/L ratios. Thus, the diagenetic temperature history of the species used for analysis must be able to be estimated with confidence (Miller & Bringham-Grette, 1989).

The elevation of the Largs deposit suggests a Last Interglacial sea level of 4.0 m above present sea level (Thom and Murray-Wallace, 1988). The elevation of the shell bed is above present sea level, indicative of a higher sea level in MIS 5e than the present, however, once again the error range of postulated palaeo-sea level is large (±1.0 m) and a more accurate resolution would be beneficial.

Quartz sand from the Nabiac barrier west of Tuncurry yielded TL ages between 94 400±11 500 and 79 600±680 years BP (Roy and Boyd, 1996; Table 7.2). Based on these ages the barrier could be correlated with either MIS 5c or 5a (sea level regression after the Last Interglacial). Roy and Boyd (1996) have assigned it to MIS 5c, likely based on the elevation of the barrier (Murray-Wallace, 2002). Palaeo-sea level proxies such as those discussed above are absent, however facies architecture suggests deposition at a time when the sea level was at least 10.0 m below its present level (Murray-Wallace, 2002).

Table 7.2: Late Quaternary sea level measurements along the east coast of Australia.

LOCATION	SEA LEVEL (m APSL)	SAMPLE NUMBER	DATING METHOD	CALIBRATED YEARS BP	MATERIAL	REFERENCE
Nambucca Heads (Valla Cave)	1.0±0.1	Beta-30959	^{14}C	3810	Fossil tube worm *Galeolaria caespitosa* as a fixed biological indicator	Flood and Frankel, 1989
	1.7±0.1	VALC1 Waik-8459	^{14}C	3810	As above	Baker *et al.*, 2001
	1.7±0.25	Val C7B Waik-8491	^{14}C	3730	As above	Baker *et al.*, 2001
	1.0±0.1	Val C6 Waik-8492	^{14}C	3460	As above	Baker *et al.*, 2001
Patonga, Broken Bay	1.1±0.25	PAT1 Waik-8495	^{14}C	3650	As above	Baker *et al.*, 2001
Caves Beach	1.2±0.1	CaveB1A Waik-8375	^{14}C	2610	As above	Baker *et al.*, 2001
	1.3±0.1	CaveB2 Waik-8236	^{14}C	2250	As above	Baker *et al.*, 2001
Vaulcluse, Sydney	1.1±0.25	Waik-8234	^{14}C	3250	As above	Baker *et al.*, 2001
	1.4±0.5	Beta-132994	^{14}C	5500	Surf barnacle *Catophragmus* as a fixed biological indicator	Baker *et al.*, 2001
Port Hacking	1.0±0.1	PortHSite 2A Beta-111205	^{14}C	2230	Fossil tube worm *Galeolaria caespitosa* as a fixed biological indicator	Baker and Haworth, 2000
	1.0±0.25	PortHSite 4A	^{14}C	1890	As above	Baker and Haworth,

		Beta-111204				2000
	1.3±0.1	PortHSite 4B Beta-111206	^{14}C	1980	As above	Baker and Haworth, 2000
	0.8±0.25	PortHSite3 Beta-116620	^{14}C	1350	As above	Baker and Haworth, 2000
	1.4±0.1	PortHSite5 Beta-111203	^{14}C	1920	As above	Baker and Haworth, 2000
Newcastle Bight	-20.4	ANU-1678	^{14}C	10640±400*	Estuarine shell fragments	Thom and Roy, 1983
	-10.7	ANU-1481	^{14}C	9130±400*	Woody peat	Thom and Roy, 1983
	-12.4	ANU-1334	^{14}C	8760±770*	Estuarine shells	Thom and Roy, 1983
Port Stephens	-4.9	ANU-1674	^{14}C	8400±190*	Fibrous peat-reed swamp	Thom and Roy, 1983
Palm Beach, Sydney	-5.7	SUA-1353	^{14}C	8450±270*	Organic mud	Thom and Roy, 1983
	-3.8	SUA-1352	^{14}C	7230±760*	Estuarine shell fragments	Thom and Roy, 1983
North Stradbroke Island	1.0 to 3.0	QMF12385	$^{230}Th/^{234}U$	132000±5000	Coral - *Porites* sp.	Pickett *et al.*, 1985; Pickett *et al.*, 1989
	1.0 to 3.0	QMF12400	$^{230}Th/^{234}U$	122000±4000	Coral – *Symphyllia* cf. *recta*	Pickett *et al.*, 1985; Pickett *et al.*, 1989

	1.0 to 3.0	QMF12401	$^{230}Th/^{234}U$	119000±3000	Coral – *Goniastrea aspera*	Pickett *et al.*, 1985; Pickett *et al.*, 1989
Evans Head	4.0 to 6.0	MMF20572	$^{230}Th/^{234}U$	119000±4000	Coral – *Montipora* sp.	Pickett *et al.*, 1989; Marshall and Thom, 1976
	4.0 to 6.0	MMF20602	$^{230}Th/^{234}U$	119000±4000	Coral – *Acropora* sp.	Pickett *et al.*, 1989; Marshall and Thom, 1976
Nabiac barrier	-10.0		TL	94400±11500 to 79600±6800	Relict beach sediments (quartz sand)	Roy and Boyd, 1996
Largs, Hunter Valley	4.0±1.0		AAR	Valine D/L ratio = 0.3 (LIG)	*Anadara trapezia*	Murray-Wallace *et al.*, 1996

Models have been used by Lambeck (2002) and Lambeck and Nakada (1990) to predict Late Holocene sea levels around Australia. Figure 7.12 shows predicted levels for four locations in NSW, including Nambucca Heads, for the period from 7000 years BP to the present. At Nambucca Heads a maximum sea level of ~0.5-0.9 m APSL occurs 5000 years BP. Sea level predictions are based on the rheological model E14(50), which includes a hydro-isostatic component (Lambeck and Nakada, 1990). Figure 7.13 shows predicted sea levels around Australia at 6000 years BP. Two models incorporating different upper mantle viscosities were used for these predictions and both models incorporate Antarctic melting, including ongoing melting of ~2.5 m equivalent sea level rise, during the past 6000 years. The predicted level for northern NSW, based on an upper mantle viscosity of 10^{20} Pa and a lower mantle viscosity of 1022 Pa, is 0.9 m; a doubling of the upper mantle viscosity yields a predicted sea level of 1.3 m APSL (Lambeck, 2002). The predicted levels for southernmost Queensland are 1.5 m APSL (upper mantle viscosity of 10^{20} Pa) and 2.1 m APSL (upper mantle viscosity of 2 X 10^{20} Pa) (Figure 7.13). The variation among predicted levels from southern Queensland is likely a product of the locations for which the predictions are being made. As mentioned earlier, Holocene high stand amplitudes can be affected by the geometry of the coastline (Lambeck, 1990).

Geographically, the Clarence River estuary is located between the two locations mentioned above, so based on the predictions of Lambeck (2002) and Lambeck and Nakada (1990) it is likely the sea level at 6000 years BP would have been between 0.9 and 1.5 m APSL. Model E14(50) (Lambeck and Nakada, 1990) predicts the sea level at Nambucca Heads 4000-3500 years BP to be ~0.5 m APSL. This differs from sea levels of 1.0 m and 1.7 m APSL during this time, based on data from FBIs at the same location (Baker *et al.*, 2001; Flood and Frankel, 1989).

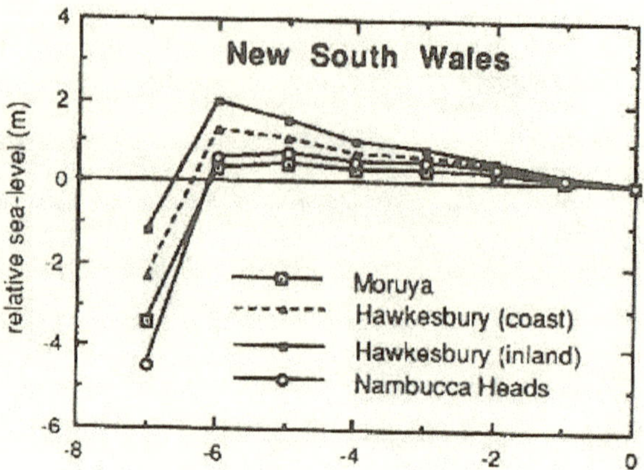

Figure 7.12: Predicted Holocene sea levels for NSW, based on rheological model E14(50). Source: Lambeck & Nakada, 1990.

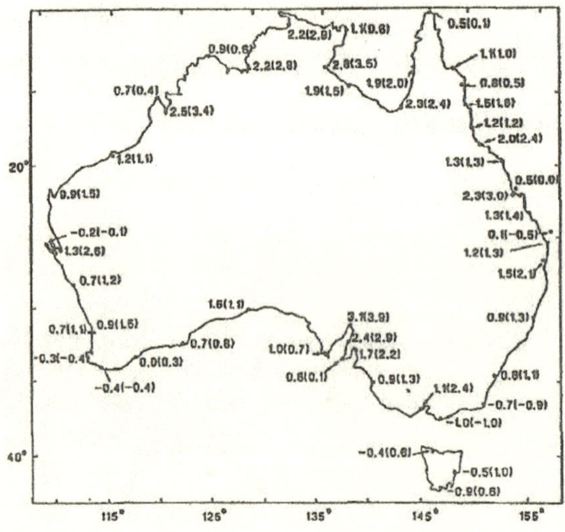

Figure 7.13: Predicted sea levels for the Australian coastline at 6000 years BP, based on based on an upper mantle viscosity of 10^{20} Pa and lower mantle viscosity of 1022 Pa, and an upper mantle viscosity of 2 X 10^{20} Pa and lower mantle viscosity of 1022 Pa (values in brackets); both models incorporate Antarctic melting, including ongoing melting of ~2.5 m equivalent sea level rise, during the past 6000 years. Source: Lambeck, 1990).

Many researchers believe Holocene sea levels in eastern Australia reached their maximum between 7000 and 6000 years BP and started to fall to current levels between 3000 and 2000 years BP (Lewis *et al.*, 2008; Baker *et al.*, 2005; Lambeck, 2002; Larcombe *et al.*, 1995). Figure 7.14 shows a revised Holocene sea level envelope for eastern Australia using extensive data from fixed biological indicators, as well as sea level curves of Baker *et al.* (2005), Larcombe *et al.* (1995) and Chappell *et al.* (1983) for the same region. The curves of Larcombe *et al.* (1995) and Chappell *et al.* (1983) indicate a steady decrease in sea level whereas the curves of Baker *et al.* (2005) and Lewis *et al.* (2008) show some oscillation in sea level. Although the curves all show a peak sea level 7000-6000 years BP followed by a fall to the present level, timing and duration of possible stillstands and postulated sea levels varies, indicating the need for greater resolution of sea level data from many different sources. Evidence and modeling of a raised Late Holocene sea level in eastern Australia has implications for the chronology of Aboriginal shell midden formation. Evidence from sea level studies suggests Late Holocene shell middens occurring at elevations below ~1 m APSL would need to have been formed after about 2000 years BP. Re-evaluation of sea level evidence and modeling, taking into account archaeological evidence, is required to resolve the apparent disparity between fossil and archaeological records.

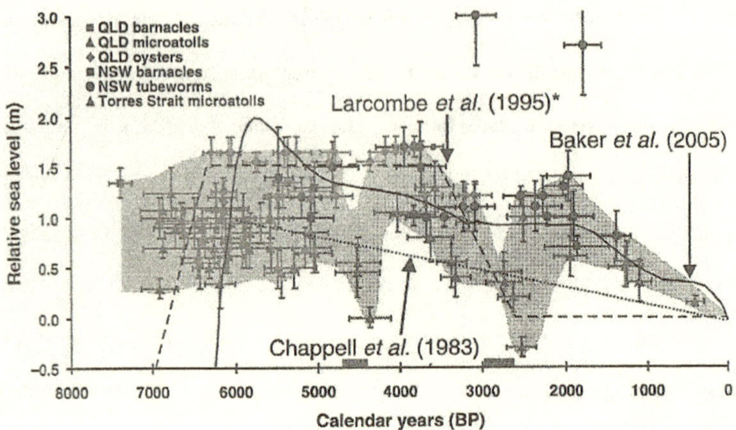

Figure 7.14: Sea level data from fixed biological indicators, forming a postulated sea level envelope for the east coast of Australia. Sea level curves of Baker *et al.* (2005), Larcombe *et al.* (1995) and Chappell *et al.* (1983) for this region are also shown. The Larcombe *et al.* (1995) curve has been recalibrated by Lewis *et al.* (2008).

Source: Lewis *et al.*, 2008.

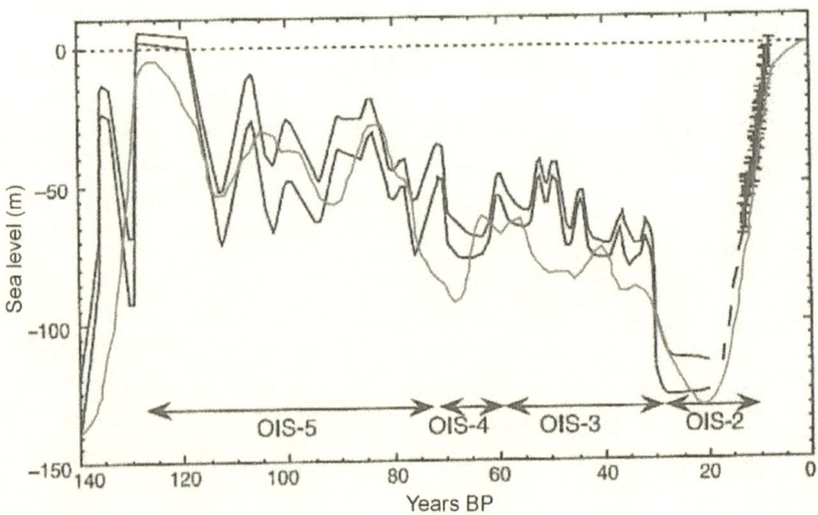

Figure 7.15: Sea level curves of Lambeck and Chappell (2001, solid black lines) and Waelbroeck *et al.* (2002, red line).

7.3.4 **Past, present and projected rates of sea level change in eastern Australia**

Research and review of sea level data obtained from fixed biological indicators suggests an Early Holocene rate of sea level rise of 1.0-2.0 mm/year for the east coast of Australia (Lewis *et al.*, 2008). This rate is in agreement with a current global sea level rise of 1.0-2.0 mm/year (Church *et al.*, 2001). Records from the Fort Denison tide gauge in Sydney, New South Wales, suggest a sea level rise of 1.16 mm/year based on 81.8 years of recorded measurements (Lambeck, 2002). Lambeck (2002) argues for the reliability of these data, as the tide gauge is situated on rocks remote from harbour installations, is situated in relatively deep water and is unaffected by fresh water riverine input. Measurements at the Newcastle (III) tide gauge have been recorded for 31.6 years and indicate a rate of sea level rise of 1.48 mm/year; considered less reliable than Fort Denison records, the period of data capture is much shorter, the harbour is located on floodplain sediments and is susceptible to perturbation by river discharge (Lambeck, 2002). Bryant (1992) performed an Australia-wide analysis of spatial trends in tide gauge measurements and found a likely current rate of sea level rise of 1.25 mm/year in northern NSW.

Yamba tide gauge records are available from 1987-2007 (from the NSW Department of Commerce, Manly Hydraulics Laboratory) and show a 0.85 mm/yr drop in mean sea level over this time. Lambeck (2002) proposed isostatic corrections of -0.30 mm/yr for Fort Denison and Newcastle (III) tide gauges and -0.33 mm/yr for the Bundaberg tide gauge in Queensland. Application of these correction values to the Yamba data gives an isostatically corrected rate of sea level lowering between 0.52 and 0.55 mm/yr. Data from surrounding tide gauges at Fort Denison, Newcastle (III) and Bundaberg all show an increase in mean sea level between 0.30 and 1.48 mm/yr over a 30-80 year period to 2002 (Lambeck, 2002), contrary to the lowering seen at the Yamba gauge. Adjacent gauges at Ballina (to the north) and Coffs Harbour (to the south) have also recorded a lowering of mean sea level during the period from 1987-2007, however gauges at Brunswick Heads, Tweed

Heads (further north), Port Macquarie and Crowdy Head (further south) recorded a rise in mean sea level during this time (NSW Department of Commerce, Manly Hydraulics Laboratory). These data suggest localised factors are likely to contribute to mean sea level variance.

Possible local effects causing variation in the measurement of sea level data may be related to the position of the Yamba tide gauge. It is situated in the mouth of the Clarence River where peak flood discharges are likely to influence sea level measurements. Also, it is located on sediment. An increase in water volume resulting from peak flood discharges may carry enough weight to cause subsidence of sediment, which has the capacity to alter tide gauge readings.

The usefulness of the Yamba data for assessing long term trends is somewhat limited, as the records currently only extend back 20 years. Despite an overall trend towards lower mean sea level at Yamba, records show oscillations in mean sea level at intervals between one and four years, with a maximum range of 0.168 m over the 20 years from 1987-2007. The duration of the ENSO cycle is typically 3-5 years and historical records show this interval can vary from 2-7 years with El Nino conditions lasting 9-12 months up to 2-4 years and La Nina conditions typically lasting 1-3 years (Queensland Department of Primary Industries, 2009). The 1-4 year oscillations in mean sea level recorded at Yamba between 1987 and 2007 may be a reflection of the ENSO cycle however this appears unlikely in a regional context, given the variability in the measurements at surrounding gauges (both the overall sea level trend and the sea level oscillation patterns) as discussed in the previous paragraph, with some showing a rise in sea level between 1987 and 2007 and others such as Yamba recording an overall fall in sea level.

Postulated future rates of sea level rise vary. Gregory *et al.* (2004) suggest a rate of 7.0 mm/year, based on a 3°C warming in Greenland and melting of the Greenland ice sheet. Most other estimates fall within the range of 1.5-2.0 mm/year (Miller & Douglas, 2004), including a 0.5 mm/year rise as a result of ocean volume change due to atmospheric warming, as derived from ocean temperature and salinity data (Levitus *et al.*, 2000). With a transition to La Nina conditions, mean sea level along the east coast of Australia, including Yamba, is expected to rise. In the future, tide gauge records extending through multiple ENSO cycles will provide valuable data on long term sea level trends.

7.3.5 **Effects of current and future rates of sea level rise on study sites in northern NSW**

Table 7.3 shows the number of years until total inundation of Aboriginal shell middens at Sleeper Island, Woombah, Wooli, Minnie Water and Plover Island based on rates of sea level rise discussed above. As data from Yamba show a local trend in falling sea level over the 20 years from 1987 to 2007 they cannot be used to calculate the risk to sites of sea level rise. This trend towards a slight lowering of sea level over a recent 20 year period indicates that, currently, the study sites are likely at minimal risk from rising sea level and factors having a more immediate impact on their destruction can be seen in the erosion hazard table of results (Appendix 5). With other gauges along the east coast of Australia recording a rise in sea level over the past 30-80 years, however, the threat of sea level rise and its possible impacts must be considered. Stable, buried deposits with very low susceptibility to erosion, such as the midden site at Wooli, are in a far better position to remain intact post-sea level rise than sites with a high erosion hazard that are susceptible to riverine and estuarine tides and flooding, such as Sleeper Island. The artifact deposits at Plover Island are considered to be at much lower risk of destruction as a result of rising sea levels due to their elevation on the rocky island. Combined with other factors which are affecting archaeological information loss at low-lying Aboriginal shell midden sites highly susceptible to erosion (Appendix 5), inundation as a result of rising sea level will most likely contribute to further destruction. As the study sites would be increasingly susceptible to storm, flood and wave damage as sea level rose, these dates are considered absolute maxima.

Table 7.3: Number of years until total inundation of Aboriginal shell middens at study sites in northern NSW based on various rates of sea level rise discussed in the text.

Site	Elevation (mLAT)	Years to total inundation at Sydney rate of rise (1.16mm/yr)	Years to total inundation at Newcastle rate of rise (1.48mm/yr)	Years to total inundation at postulated rate of rise for northern Australia (1.25mm/yr)
Sleeper Island	1.92	1655	1297	1536
Woombah Site A	1.93	1664	1304	1544
Woombah Site B	2.25	1940	1520	1800
Wooli	1.86	1603	1257	1488
Minnie Water	1.10	948	743	880
Plover Island	6.21	5353	4196	4968

7.4 FLOODING AND TIDAL INUNDATION HAZARD AT ESTUARINE AND RIVERINE STUDY SITES

As Aboriginal shell midden sites within the study areas at Woombah, Sleeper Island and Wooli are located on the floodplain in close proximity to river channels the impact of flooding and tidal inundation on these sites must be considered. The method formulated for assessing flood risk in this study can be applied to floodplain midden sites if their elevation (m AHD) and flood return period (ARI) for the area are known or can be calculated; risk of tidal inundation can also be calculated using the elevation of sites calculated from a known high or low tide height (see Chapter 4 for a full explanation of these calculations).

7.4.1 **Flooding**

Results indicate the Woombah site A river bank deposit is more susceptible to flooding than the site B creek bank deposit (Table 7.5). Although both sites are situated on the floodplain, the elevation gently increases across the floodplain to the first levee rise. At an elevation of 2.825 m AHD (Table 7.5) the site A deposit is susceptible to flood levels caused by floods with a return frequency of 6.5-9.7 years based on data from the Maclean flood gauge (NSW Department of Commerce, Manly Hydraulics Laboratory) whilst the site B *in situ* deposit has a maximum elevation of 3.145 m AHD (Table 7.5), making it susceptible to floods with a return frequency of 9.7-19.5 years based on data from the Maclean flood gauge (NSW Department of Commerce, Manly Hydraulics Laboratory).

Results were also generated using data from the Palmers Channel flood gauge (Table 7.5; NSW Department of Commerce, Manly Hydraulics Laboratory) and they different significantly from those generated using the Maclean flood gauge data. As the elevations of both Woombah Aboriginal shell midden sites are above the highest recorded flood level at the Palmers Channel gauge for the period from 10/8/1990 – 3/7/2008 the flood magnitude required to inundate these deposits cannot adequately be gauged from the Palmers Channel data. Floods measured at the Maclean gauge show more shorter return periods associated with lower flood heights (Appendix 4, data from NSW Department of Commerce, Manly Hydraulics Laboratory). This difference in height and return period between the gauges at Palmers Channel and Maclean is likely a function of local topography, elevation and historic flood frequency. The flood threshold at the Palmers Channel gauge is 2.00 m AHD, whilst the threshold at the Maclean gauge is 0.60 m AHD (NSW Department of Commerce, Manly Hydraulics Laboratory).

Given the position of Woombah in the Clarence River estuary, calculating susceptibility to flooding of the study sites at this location is best achieved using data from the Maclean flood gauge. The midden sites sit on and close to the riverbank which is situated in the comparatively narrow North Arm of the Clarence River. Similarly, a narrowing of the channel occurs on the western side of Palmers Island. The Woombah midden sites are situated on the floodplain. The maximum elevation of these sites is higher than the highest recorded flood level at the Palmers Channel gauge for the period from 10/8/1990 – 3/7/2008 but within the elevation of floods measured at the Maclean flood gauge during this period.

According to the Manly Hydraulics flood data for 1990-2008 from the Maclean gauge there is no correlation between the maximum rate at which flood water levels rise (cm/hr) and flood ARI. Less severe floods can have the capacity to rise faster or equally as fast as those with a greater ARI. Thus, flood levels considered alongside ARI alone can quantify flood risk and susceptibility of low-lying estuarine and riverine Aboriginal shell midden sites.

The *in situ* midden deposit at Sleeper Island has a maximum elevation of 2.815 m AHD (Table 7.5). At this elevation the deposit is above the highest recorded flood level at the Palmers Channel gauge for the period from 10/8/1990 – 3/7/2008, and thus susceptible to total inundation by flood events with a return period of >18.9 yr based on these data (NSW Department of Commerce, Manly Hydraulics Laboratory). Clarence Valley Council Floodplain Services records for the Palmers Channel gauge indicate flood levels of 2.44 m AHD have a return period of 20 years while a flood reaching 2.86 m AHD has a return period of 100 years. Therefore the in situ midden deposit on Sleeper Island is susceptible to total inundation by floods with a return period between 20 and 100 years.

Data from the Maclean flood gauge for the period from January 1990 to July 2008 show floods with an ARI of between 6.5 and 9.7 years have a corresponding elevation to the *in situ* midden deposit on Sleeper Island. The Palmers Channel gauge has the closer proximity to the Sleeper Island midden and is also located in a similar geomorphological setting to Sleeper Island, indicating its data are more suitable for use in flood risk calculations at Sleeper Island.

Historic flood data obtained from Manly Hydraulics Laboratory and the Clarence Valley Council (Appendix 4) shows flood levels greater than 2.82 m AHD have only been recorded once at Palmers Channel, in 1890. Records at this gauge are incomplete and include the years 1890, 1945-1980 (Clarence Valley Council Floodplain Services) and 1990-2008 (NSW Department of Commerce,

Manly Hydraulics Laboratory). The majority of the cultural material associated with the Sleeper Island midden (shells and stone artifacts) is present as a lag deposit at the base of the *in situ* deposit. This material is situated in a tidal channel and is regularly subjected to tidal flows (see tidal inundation discussion below).

The Wooli Aboriginal shell midden has a maximum elevation of 2.755 m AHD (Table 7.5). At this elevation the deposit is above the highest recorded flood level at the Wooli River Entrance flood gauge for the period from 1/5/1991 – 20/10/2009, and thus susceptible to total inundation by flood events with a return period of >19.5 yr based on these data (NSW Department of Commerce, Manly Hydraulics Laboratory). Clarence Valley Council Floodplain Services records for Harold Lloyd Park, site of the Wooli Aboriginal shell midden forming part of this research study, indicate flood levels of 1.80 m AHD have a return period of 20 years while a flood reaching 2.30 m AHD has a return period of 100 years (Wooli River Floodplain Management Plan, 1999). Both these levels are well below the measured site elevation of 2.755 m AHD. The Wooli River Floodplain Management Plan (1999) also estimates a flood level of 4.22 m AHD is the probable maximum flood (PMF) level at the southern caravan park, located ~1.4 km to the north of Harold Lloyd Park. Based on these calculations the Wooli Aboriginal shell midden deposit is susceptible to inundation only by a theoretical extreme flood event.

During mid-2009 a significant flood event occurred in the Northern Rivers region of NSW and road access to many coastal towns in the Grafton-Wooli area was cut off. The damage caused by this flood was witnessed in the field by the researcher. Widespread flooding caused inundation of farmland in and around Pillar Valley, Tucabia and Tyndale and on the Clarence estuary islands. Although floodwaters covered much of the low-lying farmland in the region flood peak levels did not reach the elevation required to inundate the Aboriginal shell midden deposits at Woombah, Sleeper

Island or Wooli. Peak levels of 2.61 m occurred at the Palmers Channel gauge on 23/5/2009 at 2030 and 1.35 m at the Wooli River entrance gauge on 22/5/2009 at 0330 (NSW Department of Commerce, Manly Hydraulics Laboratory).

7.4.2 **Tidal inundation**

When assessing the impact of tidal inundation on the Aboriginal shell midden sites at Woombah, Sleeper Island and Wooli two sets of results were generated (Table 7.6). The first set of calculations was based on the 2009-2010 tide predictions for the Yamba and Wooli gauges. The second set was based on the actual occurrence of tides over an 18-20 year period (Appendix 4, data from NSW Department of Commerce, Manly Hydraulics Laboratory). Results generated from each of these datasets differ considerably; those generated using historic tide level data are considered more reliable. They are based on actual data which have been collected over an 18-20 year period at the Yamba and Wooli River entrance gauges and are more appropriate for gauging longer-term susceptibility to tidal inundation as the period of data capture encompasses perturbations which may be caused by factors such as ENSO. Statistical analyses performed by the Manly Hydraulics Laboratory have allowed for the formulation of tidal inundation classes, based on the frequency of occurrence of measured tide heights (Tables 7.4 and 7.5, Appendix 4) and these can be used to measure and compare the susceptibility of midden sites to tidal inundation. For a discussion of how tidal inundation classes have been applied to midden sites in this study, refer to Chapter 4.

Table 7.4: Tidal range and corresponding inundation class. Source: Manly Hydraulics Laboratory.

TIDAL RANGE (depth mLAT)	INUNDATION CLASS
2.300-2.101	4
2.100-2.001	3
2.000-1.801	2
1.800-0.101	1
0.100-0.001	2
0.000- -0.199	3
-0.200- -0.399	4
-0.400- -0.499	5

LAT=Lowest Astronomical Tide.

Based on their elevation, Woombah site A and Sleeper Island fall into tidal inundation class 2, which includes the second most frequently occurring range of tide heights measured at the Yamba tide gauge for the period from 1/7/1987-30/6/2007, as calculated from the tide height frequency data (Appendix 4, data from NSW Department of Commerce, Manly Hydraulics Laboratory). Woombah site B falls into tidal inundation class 4, as high tides occur much less often at this elevation. The elevation of the Wooli Aboriginal shell midden site is above the tidal range recorded at the Wooli River entrance gauge and thus out of the limits of the tidal inundation classes (Table 7.6). The higher tidal inundation class number prescribed to Woombah site B indicates it is less susceptible to tidal inundation than the midden sites at Woombah site A and Sleeper Island and this is confirmed by the tide data discussed below.

Based on data from the Yamba tide gauge the Woombah site A and Sleeper Island midden deposits have been completely tidally inundated 276 times over the 20 year period from 1/7/1987-30/6/2007, approximately 14 times per year (Table 7.6). When taking into account other risk factors contributing to erosion (Appendix 5 and Erosion discussion) the level of erosion hazard differs at these sites so it is likely other factors are also influencing erosion at these two sites. In contrast, the Woombah site B midden deposit has only been completely inundated 4 times over the same 20 year period (Table 7.6), or once every 5 years. Having a higher elevation than the Woombah site A and Sleeper Island deposits considerably reduces the susceptibility of the Woombah site B midden deposit to tidal inundation and therefore reduces its susceptibility to erosion. The elevation of the Wooli Aboriginal shell midden places it above the tidal range as measured at the Wooli River entrance tide gauge. Tidal inundation is therefore not an erosion risk factor associated with this site.

Separating the effects of tidal inundation and flooding is a taphonomic issue. The rising water levels caused by both these processes can result in erosion. In the case of tidal inundation wave action is the main erosive agent, thus fetch and weather conditions are also important. These are considered in the first erosion hazard model (see Erosion section in this chapter for a discussion of the model; Appendix 5). At Woombah sites A and B and Sleeper Island flooding occurs less often than tidal inundation. Taphonomic evidence (Chapter 6) at the Woombah site A deposit including characteristics of shell material and absence of foreign material such as gravel, pebbles and wood within the matrix of the deposit suggests that bank erosion at Woombah site A and Sleeper Island may be a result of a regular process of stripping, such as that caused by tidal inundation. The presence of lag deposits at the base of the Woombah site A and Sleeper Island midden deposits also supports this conclusion, as flooding causing bank erosion is likely to wash away or re-deposit the shell material at the level reached by the flood waters.

Tidal inundation is considered to be a major factor affecting the lag deposit of cultural material at Sleeper Island (Appendix 5). According to the 2009-2010 Yamba tide predictions (www.bom.gov.au/oceanography/tides/MAPS/yamba.shtml) there are most often two high tides per day. The lag deposit at the base of the *in situ* material is inundated by all high tides, as it is located in a tidal channel. As the majority of the cultural material at the site was present as a lag deposit on first inspection in 2007, and it is this material which is susceptible to daily tidal inundation, tidal activity is currently an important process contributing to site degradation. Evidence of this could be seen on a return visit to the site a year after field work was first carried out; less than 10% of the cultural material first observed in the lag deposit remained at the site.

Results show the majority of estuarine sites studied in this research project are susceptible to flooding and tidal inundation. As such, it is postulated that the occurrence of a relatively minor rise in sea level would greatly increase the frequency of flooding and tidal inundation in the study area. The 0.32 m difference in elevation between Woombah site A and B has a marked influence on relative frequency of flooding and tidal inundation. At lower elevations this difference is even more pronounced (Appendix 4). There is great potential for further study in using flood and tide gauge data to model the effects of sea level rise on flood and tide frequencies at different elevations.

Printed in the USA
CPSIA information can be obtained
at www.ICGtesting.com
LVHW040725130424
777212LV00019B/45

9 798869 003942